THE PUBLISHER GRATEFULLY ACKNOWLEDGES THE GENEROUS
SUPPORT OF THE SIMPSON HUMANITIES ENDOWMENT FUND OF
THE UNIVERSITY OF CALIFORNIA PRESS FOUNDATION.

Field Days

Field Days

A YEAR OF FARMING, EATING, AND DRINKING WINE IN CALIFORNIA

JONAH RASKIN

PHOTOGRAPHS BY PAIGE GREEN

UNIVERSITY OF CALIFORNIA PRESS

BERKELEY   LOS ANGELES   LONDON

University of California Press, one of the most distinguished university presses in the United States, enriches lives around the world by advancing scholarship in the humanities, social sciences, and natural sciences. Its activities are supported by the UC Press Foundation and by philanthropic contributions from individuals and institutions. For more information, visit www.ucpress.edu.

University of California Press
Berkeley and Los Angeles, California

University of California Press, Ltd.
London, England

Library of Congress Cataloging-in-Publication Data
Raskin, Jonah.
    Field days : a year of farming, eating, and drinking wine in California / Jonah Raskin ; photographs by Paige Green.
        p.   cm.
    Includes bibliographical references and index.
    ISBN 978-0-520-25902-7 (cloth : alk. paper)
    1. Farm life—California—Sonoma—Anecdotes.   2. Organic farming—California—Sonoma—Anecdotes.   3. Farmers—California—Sonoma—Biography.   I. Green, Paige.
II. Title.   III. Title: Year of farming, eating, and drinking wine in California.
S521.5.C2R37   2009
630.9794'18—dc22   2008031261

Manufactured in the United States of America

18   17   16   15   14   13   12   11   10   09
10   9   8   7   6   5   4   3   2   1

The paper used in this publication meets the minimum requirements of ANSI/NISO Z39.48–1992 (R 1997) (Permanence of Paper).

For Otto Teller (1908–1998)
environmentalist extraordinary

CONTENTS

ILLUSTRATIONS

INTRODUCTION

THE RENAISSANCE IN FARMING

Call it local pride, a love of region, or an eagerness to welcome the world to my part of it. In any case, I like to believe that sooner or later, nearly everyone who cares about wine and food comes to Sonoma and spreads the word of its spectacular food and wine around the world. Carlo Petrini, the founder of the Slow Food movement, came thousands of miles from his home in Italy and was amazed at the variety of crops and the earthiness of the farmers. Alice Waters made the journey from Chez Panisse, her restaurant in Berkeley, an hour away, and walked farmers' fields that provide produce for her award-winning kitchen. Wine connoisseurs arrive and put their palates to work, and cutting-edge chefs come, too, with their knives and their dreams of delicious meals. World leaders, such as Felipe Calderón of Mexico, arrive with their bodyguards, while immigrants who have slipped across the border illegally show up in town without papers. U.S. ambassadors such as Ted Eliot, who once served in Afghanistan, make Sonoma a destination and end up living here. Tourists from Europe climb Sonoma Mountain, eat the food, and drink the wine and take some of it home in bottles with memorable labels. The old come to retire and for the fine weather, and the young come to play in the wild outdoors.

The world has been coming to Sonoma for hundreds of years, in fact, and while the paradise that the original settlers found and explored has been damaged, the feeling of paradise lingers. There's the smell of it in springtime and fall, the taste of it at autumn harvest, and the sounds of it in the plaza at the town center that is Sonoma's own Times Square and Piccadilly Circus. How much longer this feeling of paradise will last is a matter of heated debate. Some of my friends say these are its last glorious days, and that it had better be seen and experienced today before it vanishes forever. If that's the case, then this is a book about a way of life that is fast disappearing. But *Field Days* might also be regarded as a glimpse into the future. That's how I'd like to see it.

Sonoma might have been one of the American towns that inspired Rachel Carson—our prescient and prophetic twentieth-century nature writer—to create the nameless, fictional town in her *Silent Spring* (1962), the paradigm-shifting book that awakened readers around the world to the fact that human beings were poisoning the environment with chemicals such as DDT, killing plants and animals, and condemning themselves to cancer and early deaths. Carson describes a town where, once upon a time, "all life seemed to live in harmony with its surroundings," and where "the first settlers raised their houses, sank their wells and built their barns." All that and more happened in Sonoma, too, in the nineteenth century, and life seemed good.

But then things in Carson's nameless town began to change for the worse. A blight spread across the town and the surrounding valley. Water, land, sky, plants, animals, insects, and human beings were poisoned by chemicals. "The ecology of the world within our bodies" became contaminated, Carson wrote. Moreover, because of environmental degradation, food contained deadly poisons, too. "To find a diet free from DDT and related chemicals, it seems we must go to remote and primitive lands, still lacking the amenities of civilization," she noted.

No longer is that true. We do not have to go to Alaska for organic lettuce, radishes, beets, and peaches, and that's due in large measure to Carson's timely warning. In Sonoma, and in towns and cities like it, citizens heard her and began to act responsibly. They took the road away from DDT and other toxic chemicals. They began organic farms such as the ones that appear in this book. They respected nature, fed the soil healthy nutrients, protected forests and streams, and grew food that was wholesome and not harmful to human beings.

This is a book about some of those environmentally conscious people—farmers, eaters, chefs, winemakers, farmworkers, and environmentalists themselves—who live and work in Sonoma: the town, the valley, and the county that share one name and together form one of America's heartlands of organic produce.

But I want to begin elsewhere, albeit not far away, because history, tradition, and longevity matter. Organic farming in California has an honorable past, and it's important to honor its founders. So I shall start with stories of Warren Weber, one of the fathers of organic farming in California, and of his Star

Route Farm in Marin County, close to the Pacific Ocean, the oldest certified organic farm in the state. Perhaps by learning about him, readers will get beyond stereotypes of farmers. Like many of us who read *Silent Spring* when it first appeared, Weber became an eater who longed for healthy food. Unlike most of us, though, he left the city, settled in the country, and began to plant fruit trees and vegetables on a farm with rich soil, good drainage, and a mild microclimate made for growing fruits and vegetables from April to November. For almost four decades— more than half his lifetime—he has grown tomatoes, carrots, and peas on the outskirts of the town of Bolinas, and in the process he has also enjoyed the advantages of a rural life.

Born in St. Louis in 1941, Weber worked on farms as a boy, and later he attended Cornell University's School of Agriculture and the University of California at Berkeley, where he studied Shakespeare and received his PhD. He can still speak eloquently about the Forest of Arden and the pastoral ideal in *All's Well That Ends Well*. It was farming, however, that became his passion and the one constant in his life that outlasted friendships, transcontinental moves, and radical changes in lifestyle. Weber doesn't claim to be one of the leaders of the twenty-first century's renaissance in farming, but Britain's Prince Charles, an avid organic gardener, made it a point to visit Star Route when he came to California. He'd heard about Weber's organic produce and his commitment to protecting natural habitat and the environment. "He came because he wanted to know what we were doing," Weber said. "And we wanted to know what he was doing in England." The prince wasn't disappointed by either the place itself or its diversity and ingenuity. On most farms, for example, workers get around in pickup trucks. At Star Route

Warren Weber (right) talks with the author about small farms, local farms, and sustainable agricultural practices.

they ride bicycles. It's a relatively simple change that's inexpensive, and it means less pollution, less harm to the land, and less dependence on foreign oil.

Weber didn't broadcast Prince Charles's visit. It wasn't mentioned on his web site, and you cannot find Weber himself in most of the contemporary books about organic farming, among them Michael Abelman's *Fields of Plenty* and Michael Pollan's *Omnivore's Dilemma,* both of them excellent books. Still, Weber is a role model for California farmers. He has been able to translate eaters' dreams into farming realities. From his point of view, farming is a business. He also sees it from two other, related perspectives, as he explained one spring morning when we stood in the middle of his forty-acre farm on the Bolinas–Olema Road while the sun burned off the fog.

"Farming is a human activity that's about personal relationships to the soil," he said. "It's also about service to the community." Weber has also been savvy about the market and its fluctuation. He survived hard times in farming, reinvented himself, and stuck to his dream. He was part of Berkeley's counterculture in the 1960s, and he saw organic agriculture as its mainstay. The farther the 1960s recede, the truer that point of view has become. Critics of the 1960s, as well as many of today's food writers who examine the roots of the organic food movement, have often ridiculed counterculturalists. And, indeed, the rebels were far from perfect. As Weber himself admits, "A lot of hippies were busy smoking stuff." But hippies high on marijuana weren't the only representatives of the counterculture. There were also Shakespearean scholars and graduates of the Cornell School of Agriculture such as Weber, people who ate brown rice, tofu, and bok choy not because they thought these foods were cool or groovy but because of their nutritional value.

When he was a student in Berkeley, Weber shopped as often as possible for fresh, organic produce at "health food" and "natural food" stores, as they were called. In 1969 he visited a small farming collective in Fresno, California, worked by Mexicans who raised just one crop—cherry tomatoes. He was struck by the simplicity and efficiency of their operation. Other pioneering organic farmers influenced him as well, among them Russell Walter. Though they are now all but forgotten, these farmers helped him to see that farming was an admirable, even a noble, profession and could be a promising career alternative to Shakespearean studies. He was also encouraged by memories of the Missouri farmers of his boyhood who grew black-eyed peas and raised chickens and sheep.

After studying the work of Robert Rodale, the avatar of organic farming and gardening in the United States, Weber began in 1974 to farm, and he did so with a horse-drawn plow because he wanted to do it the old-fashioned way. He picked Bolinas for his venture, a town that has often been ridiculed as a home of the elite and the eccentric. At the same time the town has also been fertile ground for innovative enterprises, including the contemporary renaissance in farming that Weber helped launch. And because of its geographical isolation, as well as its relative proximity to San Francisco and Berkeley, West Marin probably will continue to be a good place to farm. Indeed, when I visited him, four other organic farms were within shouting distance of Weber's Star Route. Marin aims to become the first all-organic county in the country, and it has a good chance of achieving its goal. It has feisty citizens and representatives in local government willing to fight for organic farms and food.

"The renaissance in farming in Marin and all around the country has happened in large part because people want to know where their food is actually coming from," Weber said. "People are thinking about their health, about watersheds, housing developments, and their communities. They realize that everything is connected and that farms and farmers are essential if we're to survive. They see, too, that we can reclaim our agricultural heritage and take it to a higher level. Local is important, and small is important, too. Small is beautiful, as E. F. Schumacher recognized. But we can't forget sustainability and sound farming practices. It has to be organic."

Like Marin, Sonoma is rich in agricultural heritage and pioneering farmers. In 1906 the best-selling author Jack London bought 129 acres of prime real estate on Sonoma Mountain and became one of the grandfathers of the back-to-the-land movement that spread across California and the country. Jack and his wife, Charmian, wanted to get away from the world: away from San Francisco, where he was born and had first achieved renown, and away from Oakland, with its urban strife, crowding, and pollution. Jack had a way of going against the grain. Even as America catapulted itself pell-mell into the factory age, he chose to return to an agrarian ideal that harkened back to the days of Thomas Jefferson.

Jack and Charmian were among the ancestors of today's organic farmers and ranchers. Though they weren't purists—a bartender in Oakland pre-mixed their martinis and shipped them by railroad to Sonoma County—they aimed to be self-sufficient and to grow everything they needed. And they aimed to use the natural resources around them—the redwoods and the boulders—in what today would be called green construction. They planted trees, made grape juice, and raised horses and pigs in a pen that struck journalists as so refined as to deserve the description "a pig palace." That didn't deter London. He treated his animals as humanely as possible, and he created a life for himself on Sonoma Mountain that gave him a great deal of satisfaction. Thanks to environmentalists, his estate today is nearly as wild as it was one hundred years ago.

London loved the wilds of Sonoma County, and he described them to friends and fans around the world as one of the most beautiful places in the world. But by the time he arrived, the land had already been cultivated intensely by European immigrants for nearly one hundred years, and products and produce were already being shipped overseas. Sonoma went global long before "globalism" became a watchword. Before that, for thousands of years before the advent of the Europeans, indigenous peoples— the "aborigines," as London called them—tended the land and lived quite comfortably on its bounty. They ate acorns and salmon, and they wove wild grasses into beautiful baskets that could hold water and carry and store anything and everything imaginable. Moreover, they had a wealth of stories about the earth and a rich oral tradition. "Sonoma" was their name for the place; according to anthropologists it means "village of the earth" or "earth village," which seems appropriate. Sonoma is still an earthy place, and it still has the feel of a large village, albeit one that, like many agricultural valleys in California, is in danger of losing its identity.

Jack London preferred to call Sonoma Valley the "Valley of the Moon," and although he was not the first to apply that nomenclature, he was the first to make it stick. Poetic license has a way of making phrases memorable, and "Valley of the Moon" took hold of the popular imagination. Even today, wineries, environmental groups, and businesses use the name "Valley of the Moon" to advertise themselves. Shortly before he died, London wrote a glorious novel entitled *The Valley of the Moon* about two Californians not unlike himself and his wife who search for paradise and find it in Sonoma Valley. The novel, which serves as an advertisement for rural life, is still in print, still read, and still readable, and it continues to add to the mystique of the place.

Sonoma is a remarkably small valley. It's about forty square miles, or about twice the size of Manhattan. In forty-five minutes you can drive from its southern edge at San Pablo Bay, which connects to San Francisco Bay, to its northern edge in the town of Kenwood, on the outskirts of the county seat, Santa Rosa, which the botanist Luther Burbank called "the chosen spot of all the earth." Citizens of Sonoma like to say that the entire valley—not just the city of Santa Rosa—is the "chosen spot," and they have good reasons for saying so. The climate is Mediterranean, even semitropical, and farmers cultivate avocados, oranges, pomegranates, pineapples, grapes, olives, peaches, apples, and much more. Almost everything that one would want to grow can be grown in rich, beautiful soil on farms that are satisfying to look at. It is as beautiful a valley as any I have ever seen. For beauty, too, was a part of the farming renaissance.

Sonoma Valley, which I have come to love as my own native ground, is the focus of this book. I have written *Field Days* as part field report and part memoir: it is the story of my odyssey in search of health, harmony, and a sense of place—and nourishment, too. In the course of researching and writing I have become a locavore, though I am not a purist or a fanatic. That means I aim to eat food that is grown organically, with minimum damage to the environment, and close to home. I remain aware, and I am willing to take small steps that may make a difference to me and the world around me.

I believe that the hands on the hoes in the fields are connected to the hands on the knives and the forks at the dinner table. In turn those hands are connected to the trees in the forests and the fish in the streams. In writing this book I aim to trace the connections among ourselves, the earth, and the species that live here with us. Small local farms such as Star Route in Marin and Oak Hill in the Valley of the Moon—a farm profiled in the pages that follow—can help to save the planet. Moreover, families sitting down together and eating fresh, nutritious produce from those same farms are helping to save their own lives. They are also sustaining community. For the most part the renaissance in farming is taking place not at the heart of agribusiness but at the edges of farming, on relatively small plots of land in places like Bolinas and the Valley of the Moon that have become models of the way we might grow and market our fruits and vegetables.

I did not intend this book to be about politics or economics. Originally I saw it as a picture book in which the images would speak for themselves. But while I was researching and writing, food and farming became front-page stories. The 2008 Farm Bill was debated in Congress, the price of organic food rose sharply, and there were food shortages around the world. Increasingly, the small organic farm has come to look like a solution to many of the economic, environmental, and health crises facing the world.

Soon after I finished this book I heard Alice Waters, the founder of the fabled Berkeley restaurant Chez Panisse and an advocate for small organic farms, speak at Copperfield's Books in Petaluma about "the delicious revolution" she saw unfolding before her eyes. Waters has known the landscapes, farmers, seasons, and crops of the Valley of the Moon intimately for decades. She buys produce from small, local farmers there, as well as from farmers throughout California. "Chez Panisse would not still be in business if it were not for local farmers," she said.

"They nourish me, and the agreement to buy from them, come rain or shine, is what ensures the supply." She added, "We're just now at the start of the delicious revolution that aims to bring people back to their senses, back to the land, back to farmers and farmers' markets."

I also want to tell readers that this book follows faithfully my experiences over the course of a year. It is as close to the real-life chronology as I could make it. I have not imposed an artificial order on the events, and I have not cleaned up or beautified the furrows of my story. I suppose I could have weeded the narrative, fenced it in discretely, and marked it more clearly than it is at present. But like some of the organic farmers I portray in this book, I don't mind weeds, and I don't mind digressions here and there to explore other, related fields of interest close by. I have invented nothing and no one in these pages; everyone's real name is used, and no one is disguised. If my book therefore has some of the messiness of real life, so be it. I have even violated the lessons I give in the classes I teach on memoir writing, in which I demand that the students invent the truth and create a narrative structure. I insist that they cannot do what I have done here. But I also tell students they can break the rules, if they know what they are and why they're important. And in the process of putting this book together, I have learned as much about writing as I have learned about farming. Indeed, farming has taught me as much about writing as any text, teacher, or seminar I have attended. So in my own defense I can add that I had a good reason for breaking the rules—it was the best way to reflect accurately the life I led and observed.

1

FIRST FORAYS

CLOSE TO HOME

In 2006, when I began my odyssey across the landscape of California's organic farms, I was nearly sixty-five years old and beginning to feel that I had a finite amount of time on earth. I was living in Santa Rosa in an old barn that had been converted into a small house with electricity, plumbing, and windows. It sat on a road dotted with barns filled with melons, hay, wool, and animals. The fall semester at the college where I taught writing was drawing to a close. I had time, energy, and curiosity. I wanted to get out and explore. Before it was too late, before life passed me by. I wanted to be in touch with the earth again. I wanted to regain something I felt I had lost, and to work alongside men and women who were cultivating the earth. I wanted to eat as though for the first time, with a sense of newness.

What I had lost was not a mystery to me. I had lost the world of my childhood in the 1940s and 1950s, when Long Island was agricultural and I had played in barns and gone to school with the sons and daughters of farmers with names like Romanowsky and Schobel that I have not forgotten. I lost that rural life when suburbia rose up around me. My own father, too, had lost the rural environment of his youth. He had grown up in the 1920s and 1930s, living on a farm. Then, as a lawyer in real estate after the war, he helped to pave the way for tract houses and highways, shopping centers and unending development. He had helped to transform the rural world he knew and loved. When he retired, he moved to California in search of land to farm, hoping to regain his old life. He and my mother became pioneers on a remote plot of land with redwoods, two streams, and rich soil. But suburbia grew around them once again, and in watching the disappearance of their farming community I experienced the loss of a kind of childhood innocence. To those of my generation and that of my parents, the fundamental social and cultural shift from agrarian to suburban life happened not once, but twice. By contrast, the political upheavals of the 1960s felt less dislocating. The coming of suburbia altered the landscape beyond recognition, and I experienced a sense of profound displacement.

I began my quest for the old rural life by going to nearby farms in Sonoma that were on my own road, those that advertised themselves and that I could find without the aid of a map. I went to farms owned by friends, or friends of friends, and there I immediately noticed new directions in agriculture. In the 1970s, when I first arrived in California, farms were often sadly inaccessible, and I had only rarely been able to satisfy my curiosity about crops and barns. Back then all the signs read "Keep Out" and "No Trespassing." Barbed-wire fences and

The author takes field notes at the end of a year when he also planted crops, culti-
vated, weeded, and harvested side by side with farmworkers, most of them from
Zacatecas, Mexico.

locked gates sent the same message. "Trespassers Will Be Shot" deterred even outlaws in a county known for such outlaws as Joaquin Murrieta, the legendary nineteenth-century folk hero who robbed from the rich and became a symbol of opposition to Anglo rule. Even farmers I knew, such as my parents' close friend Benedict Sobler—a veteran apple grower who taught me the art of pruning trees—were often reluctant to let outsiders onto their property.

In the 1970s Benedict owned a beautiful old barn that I coveted, in which he stored his Gravenstein apples, a variety that was once the pride of Sebastopol. The barn also served as a garage for his beloved blue Mercedes-Benz. Soon after I arrived in Sonoma I went to work pruning his apple trees so that sunlight and air might penetrate to their innermost boughs, and now they looked beautiful. And with a Husquarna chainsaw I cut down his old, diseased cherry trees, which were entwined with poison oak, and carted the wood away to split, burn, and heat my house. In contrast to Benedict's farm, there were others that I avoided out of fears for my health and safety. Across the street from my parents' acres, for instance, there was the farm of a man whose face I rarely saw. Several times each year he used to cover himself from head to toe in protective gear and drive his tractor around his farm, spewing chemicals on the trees and the ground and into the air. Rachel Carson would have been appalled. Afterward he posted a sign with a skull and crossbones that read "Danger. Keep Out." Of course I kept out! Neither he nor anyone else seemed to consider the fact that the wind blew those toxic chemicals across Morelli Lane and into the fruit trees my father had planted, which neither he nor I wanted to be sprayed. We didn't want the chemicals on us, either.

That cranky apple farmer, with whom I exchanged heated words on the telephone, felt that he had the right to spray whatever and whenever he chose to, neighbors be damned, and he felt no compunction about chopping down all the stately redwood trees on land he owned. That was the attitude of many old farmers—it was their property, and they could do anything they wanted with and to it. This attitude is slowly changing, thanks to the work of environmentalists, whose hard-fought victories benefit everyone. The county of Sonoma still insists in official proclamations—mailed with annual tax bills—that citizens have the "Right to Farm," and that citizens who live near farms must expect to "be subject to inconvenience or discomfort arising from agricultural operations." But farmers no longer have the right to spray toxic chemicals on crops and into the air, and citizens are protected from exposure to poisons such as DDT.

MIMI GOES LOCAL

After moving away from the family farm in 2004, I needed to find another place where I could feel close to the earth. I knew I would be welcome at Windrush Farm. Mimi Luebbermann, a farmer in Chellano Valley and the sister of my dear friend and colleague J. J. Wilson, invited me to visit anytime. She is a good example of the new farmers who are far more transparent than were the farmers of old. As often as farm operations allow, she opens her Windrush Farm to the public. Every summer, swarms of kids arrive to learn what it means to be a farmer and discover the smell of barns and pastures. She has also hosted events for adults. I attended one such event, when Mimi made dozens of delicious pizzas in her outdoor brick oven and Molly Katzen, the author of *The Moosewood Cookbook,* told stories about her legendary hippie restaurant in upstate New York and her own kitchen in Berkeley. I did not notice a gate at the entrance to the long, shaded driveway that led to the farmhouse, or any barriers to the barns, sheds, and pasture. "Welcome" was the watchword, generosity the style.

Mimi had come from Oakland, where she raised rabbits and chickens and grew vegetables. For years she wanted more open space, more land, and friendly neighbors who were farmers, too, to whom she could turn for wisdom about crops and animals. In 1995 she made her big move from an urban to a rural existence, and the change ignited her creativity. In the past decade or so she has written how-to books with titles such as *Pay Dirt: How to Raise and Sell Herbs and Produce for Serious Cash,* which offer "simple secrets" for farmers and gardeners on how to make money and find happiness by growing orchids, herbs, heirloom tomatoes, cactus, daffodils, quince, and kumquats. In these books, which I heard about as she wrote them, she provides valuable information that is not always accessible but is all the more important to anyone who wants to farm successfully. How much "serious cash" Mimi makes from her books and her farm I do not know, and I did not feel it would have been polite to ask. After all, she is from Virginia and has Southern manners, and I did not wish to encroach on her privacy. I could observe, though, that Mimi keeps her farm going with a combination of old ways and reinvented new ones. In addition to selling eggs, rabbits, lamb, and wool at farmers' markets, she gives classes in the skills she has taught herself and learned from neighboring ranchers. She's always on the go—up at sunrise most days—and everyone who knows her comments on her seemingly inexhaustible energy. One of her sons calls her "a whirlwind mom." Her vehicles are usually old, often battered, and rarely attractive, but they get her and her goods where they need to go, which is to say that she's practical and efficient and doesn't care about mere appearances.

Mimi was the first person I got to know who talked vigorously—years before it became popular to do so—about the importance of buying local produce and supporting local farmers. She was a long way ahead of the curve. Even some of her own family laughed at her ideas and thought she was silly and provincial. They pointed out that almost year-round you could get attractive fruits, vegetables, and meat from Argentina, Mexico, New Zealand, and elsewhere. It took her family and friends—and me, too—a while to understand that local produce is likely to be safer and fresher and to have more nutrients than produce grown and shipped from far away. Only after outbreaks of contaminated meats, tomatoes, spinach, and other fruits and vegetables have many shoppers learned to search out produce grown by responsible farms close to home.

The author I found most helpful on the vast, complex idea of "the local" was Lucy Lippard. In her groundbreaking *The Lure of the Local: Senses of Place in a Multicentered Society,* she wrote about land, landscapes, art, and the balance between urban and rural, public spaces and private ones. There wasn't a single major area of contemporary American life that she didn't touch on, and her provocative book helped me when I went to farms like Mimi's. Lippard insists that it's important to remember that each individual has a *point of view.* Indeed, I learned that everyone on a farm—from the owner to the Mexican fieldworker, tractor driver, and truck driver—sees that farm in a slightly different way depending on a variety of factors, including age, ethnicity, gender, and class. Moreover, before you can even see a farm you have to believe in it. Otherwise it will remain invisible to you. This is why tourists from urban places who are unaccustomed to farms often do not see them or notice their beauty. If you associate carrots, peas, and potatoes with frozen packages in a supermarket, you may not be prepared to see them actually growing in a field.

Understandably, as she wrote the book at a time *before* there was a general understanding and appreciation of "the local,"

Lippard sometimes sounds defensive, as when she notes, "Local does not have to mean isolated, self-indulgent, or inbred." Clearly everything and everywhere is local, whether it's New York, Calcutta, Dublin, Shanghai, or Sonoma. Although some places are dismissed as being peripheral or provincial and rarely become world capitals or global centers, no place can escape its own locus. I resonated to Lippard's observation that "understanding the local history, economics, and politics is a complex, fascinating, and contradictory business everywhere." Certainly my part of California seems to me to be as rich, complex, and contradictory as any place I have ever known. Sonoma has farms and vineyards, a long coastline along the Pacific, majestic mountains and fertile valleys, Indian tribes, settlers, outlaws, writers, movie producers, and gourmet restaurants listed in the Michelin guide.

What is produced in this specific locality—wine, cheese, wool, and olive oil—is sent around the world, and workers and tourists come here from afar. It is connected to the whole world and is an integral part of it. I remember my exhilaration when in the midst of my farm odyssey I met the men who belong to the international circuit of sheep shearers. Mike Donovan, who was born and raised in New Zealand, traveled to California and from there to Utah, Idaho, and Wyoming to shear sheep, and then he went on to Spain, Scotland, and Germany. He was paid $2.65 a head, and he could shear nearly 250 sheep in a day. "Wherever there are sheep I go," Donovan told me one afternoon, when he took a break from shearing sheep on a farm close to my own home. "Last year I sheared more than fifty thousand sheep."

From Mike and Mimi I learned to respect physical labor and to pay attention to the tasks at hand and the tools in my hands. On days I did not teach at the college I worked at Mimi's Windrush Farm, which is in Marin, just over the border from Sonoma. I did the simplest of chores. For a couple of months, on cool afternoons in autumn, I dismantled the raised beds just behind the farmhouse: after that I carted countless wheelbarrow loads of soil to another corner on the property. I wasn't paid a cent—that was agreed—but Mimi always provided thick homemade soups that were meals in themselves, steaming hot after simmering on a back burner of the old-fashioned stove all day long. Sitting in her warm kitchen, I also tasted the cheeses she experimented with from milk from her own cow. You can't get more local than that.

When I asked about her farming neighbors, she introduced me to Mike and Sally Gales. They had retired after long professional careers and now grow apples and raise beef for fun (and some profit) at Chileno Valley Ranch, which has been in Sally's family ever since 1862. "We bring in money," Mike explained in the stately living room of their renovated farmhouse. "But I wouldn't say that ranching is profitable." Sally added, "We must be crazy to do this. We're grandparents, and we do all the work ourselves, including all the sales and marketing, and we sell every single apple we grow. It has been sad to see ranchers taking out apple trees, but we're putting them in. There's nothing as beautiful as an apple tree in bloom, and we've derived immense pleasure from our orchard."

I met their animals, who were obviously well treated in the pasture, and Sally explained that they were "harvested," not slaughtered. After Mike sent me home with a package of ground beef, from which I made delicious, juicy burgers, I got to thinking that he and Sally were probably right: grass-fed cows, raised in a largely stress-free environment by ranchers who love them, make for tastier beef than the assembly-line variety from animals that have been abused and exposed to disease and contamination. "I have a couple of animals that should have gone to market a long time ago," Mike told me. "But I have an attachment to them. I have one cow that is invaluable. She'll follow me anywhere, and if she moves, all the other cows will move with her. They're not as dumb as you think." Tongue in cheek, he added, "Some are smarter than me."

WALKING INTO THE PAINTING

A young photographer named Paige Green lived in a converted barn on Mimi's farm together with Mimi's youngest son, Arann, a singer and songwriter, who helps his mother during the day and performs at night in clubs and cafés with his band, the Bluebellies. Arann's repertoire includes humorous songs about farms and farming; one song in particular, about milking cows, is a favorite with audiences. I first saw Paige's dramatic black-and-white photos of old Marin farmers when she exhibited them in a barn on Mimi's property that serves as art gallery and auditorium. Right away I recognized that Paige knows how to bring out the character and personality of her subjects; their deeply furrowed faces seemed to mirror the furrows in their fields. I was so taken with her work that I decided to invite her to accompany me on my farm odyssey and take photos of the places I would visit. Then I would have permanent images of them and wouldn't have to rely on memory.

Odd as it may sound—it seems odd to me now—I wanted my journey to provide an aesthetic experience. Alice Walker entitled

a book of her poetry *Horses Make a Landscape Look More Beauti-*
ful, borrowing the expression from Lame Deer, a Sioux Indian
writer. I, too, feel that landscape is beautified by horses, and especially by farms and farmers. During my drives to Sonoma State
University, where I teach, the landscape never failed to move me
to awe and wonder. I was inspired by the sight of farmers on their
tractors, plowing the land; I assumed they had to be in a meditative state, and I envied them. The look of freshly furrowed, dark,
rich soil was beautiful to my eyes, and I enjoyed the dozen or so
barns that line Petaluma Hill Road, including two painted bright
red that looked as new as the day they were built. One farm
struck me as a particularly beautiful tableau. I first became aware
of it in the summer, when I stopped at a farm stand near the side
of the road and bought juicy red tomatoes and colorful squashes
from a large person who seemed part boy, part grown man. From
the road, the farm looked like a canvas painted in vibrant color by
a French landscape artist of the nineteenth century—say, Camille
Corot, whose work I had admired at the Louvre in Paris and at
the Metropolitan Museum of Art in New York. This farm, called
Valley End, stretches along Petaluma Hill Road between my barn
and the university.

I passed it every day on my way to and from my office and
classrooms, and I enjoyed gazing at the fields and at the unknown people moving slowly in those fields. Valley End
looked picture perfect. From a distance, I could not tell for
certain whether the workers—they were little more than stick
figures that moved now and again—were men or women, old
or young. From the evidence of the brightly colored scarves, hats,
and sweaters that some of them wore, I suspected that men and
women labored together. And for a time, not knowing suited

me better than knowing. I was content to gaze at the scene from a distance, as though standing in a museum before a framed work of art by Monsieur Corot, who I wished had set up his easel on Petaluma Hill Road and painted the scene before me.

For weeks Paige and I talked about getting together to work on a book of farm photos, and one Saturday we finally met early in the morning to start our project. On the side of the road, with the traffic roaring by, I asked Paige to take photos. She insisted that we get permission first. I didn't like the idea. I'd had too many unpleasant interactions with surly old farmers. I didn't want another one, but I agreed to Paige's suggestion. She was right. So, in the fog and cold, we headed toward the farmhouse in the distance, and toward a big, sprawling oak tree and the usual assortment of farm vehicles—various trucks and tractors, big and small, old and new. I felt as if I had stepped into the painting, as if I were part of it now. I could imagine myself growing smaller and smaller as I moved from foreground to background, and as I approached the farmhouse, it grew ever larger, and the hills that had been in the far distance crept up as well, filling more and more of the canvas. Once we had reached the house, we felt a little uncomfortable; up close the farm that now surrounded us on all sides didn't look as beautiful as it had looked from a distance. The yard clearly needed a gardener; the spent flowers along the walkway needed clipping; and there was debris outside the shed that should have been taken to the dump. A sticker on the bumper of the newest-looking vehicle—a white Chevy SUV—read "Support Organic Farmers"; another one read "CCOF—California Certified Organic Farmer." Clearly, whoever owned and operated the farm had

In California, certified organic farming took off at the start of the twenty-first century, but it has been in existence since the 1970s. Farmers advertise their commitment not to use harmful pesticides and herbicides, as in this bumper sticker from California Certified Organic Farmers.

gone to the trouble of paying a California state agency for the certification and was willing to allow inspectors onto the property to test the soil and assess the operations. Clearly, too, the owner wasn't using chemical herbicides and pesticides.

I knocked on the door, and Paige and I waited in the fog under the overcast sky. After what felt like a long time, someone opened the door a crack. It was the large young man from the farm stand. He had short hair and was wearing glasses, a white T-shirt, white socks, and no shoes, and he asked what we wanted. "To take pictures and talk," I said. "Just a minute. I'll ask my mom," he replied. The door closed, and we waited. I was sure we'd be turned away, but the door opened again, wider than before, and we were invited inside and motioned into the living room, where we sat and waited some more. Finally, Sharon Grossi appeared, wearing baggy sweatshirt and sweatpants.

Aside from Mimi, who had one foot in the pasture and one at her writing desk, Sharon was the first real full-time female farmer I'd met, and I was surprised by her informality and colloquial speech. Women on farms have often been the farmers' wives, sisters, and daughters. They have played essential parts; sometimes they were even more indispensable than their husbands, brothers, and fathers. They worked hard, took chances, and broke new ground with new crops while men were cautious. Traditionally, however, the farmer has been thought of as a man. The mass media has popularized that view in movies such as *The Real Dirt on Farmer John* and novels such as Jim Harrison's *Farmer*. Say the word "farmer" and people tend to imagine a man in overalls riding on a tractor. But that is quickly changing; it had already changed at Valley End. Here now was a woman on a farm who had a leading role and no husband. She was strong and outspoken and wasn't about to be pushed around by anyone. With encouragement from me, and under the influence of Paige's genuine smile and natural graciousness, Sharon talked about herself, her son, Clint—-the part man, part boy in white socks—and Valley End Farm. Sharon displayed a self-deprecating sense of humor, and she had a way of exaggerating to make a point. It was always blazing hot or freezing cold. Market prices for beans or peas were always outrageously low. Moreover, in her view everything could go wrong disastrously. "I plow ahead," she said, putting her head down and plowing ahead with words. "I went through a divorce, raised kids on my own, borrowed money, dug a well, installed a septic system. Friends joked that I'd gone to the 'funny farm,' and sometimes I thought maybe I had. I can tell you I've been through hell a couple of times, but I'm still here. I'm a survivor."

She had named the farm, she said, for the obvious reason: the valley ended here. East of her property, behind it, lay rolling hills, too steep to farm and without the rich soil of the flat bottomland. West of it—clear across the county—lay the rugged coast and the Pacific Ocean, source of the fog and the cool temperatures that provide natural air conditioning and mitigate the effects of the hot sun that beats down on the land mercilessly in summer, baking it sometimes as hard as rock.

The more Sharon talked about her seventy-acre farm—it is the largest certified organic farm in Sonoma County—the more I felt that the name "Valley End" was metaphorical, that it seemed to symbolize the end of a way of life. This rich valley is one of many, each with its own distinctive microclimate, that have, for more than a century, made Sonoma suitable for growing crops almost all year round. But how much longer can this kind of farming go on?

That question was certainly on Sharon's mind, and it was what had prompted Ed Grossi, her handsome ex-husband—he lived just down the road—to give up growing vegetables to raise rare trees and exotic shrubs to sell to the multimillion-dollar estates in the hills. According to Sharon and other farmers I met, he said that he made more money in a month as a landscape gardener than he used to earn in a whole year as a truck farmer. Sharon knew that she could do as well if she were to turn to landscaping, but she wasn't ready to abandon Valley End. Keeping the farm meant living a life on the edge, where she never knew what the future might bring. But she seemed to relish that state. Life on the edge apparently motivated her, and she told me that she was continually coming up with new ideas for crops to grow and ways to market them. She told me that if she could figure out a way to sell her produce to the seven thousand or so students, professors, and staff at the university across the road, most of her financial problems would be solved. "I'm freaked," she told Paige and me on that day we met her. "Everyone says they love the farmer. Everyone says they love agriculture. But everyone, it seems, wants to move here and live here, and that means more houses, more people, diminishing water, and less farmland. I want to go on living and farming here, but I'm not sure how I'm going to do it."

I could see what she meant. Directly across the road from her farm there lay a large open area where a developer wanted to build more than a thousand houses. Not far away the county had embarked on a massive project to restore Hinebaugh Creek, which meandered through the valley. That meant that men on huge machines were scooping out dirt, making big mounds of earth, and radically altering the contours of the land—all in the name of preserving the land. On the face of it, the county seemed to be destroying the environment in the name of saving it. If there was a method to their madness, it wasn't apparent. Only later, after the rainy season had arrived, did I understand. The men on the dozers had carved out a dozen or so shallow ponds. They had created a wetland. Soon egrets gathered there, and they were pleasing to see. So were the ponds. The landscape came to life. Environmentalists and men on big machines had saved an endangered ecosystem.

Down the road from Valley End, Sonoma State University had built an intricate complex of buildings to the tune of one hundred million dollars. Named the Green Music Center, the complex was to house the Santa Rosa Symphony, an upscale restaurant, and state-of-the-art classrooms for music majors studying syncopation, hip-hop, and George and Ira Gershwin's legacy to American culture. It was hard to argue against the civic contributions of the Green Music Center, but Sharon wondered how the increased traffic and pollution would affect her farm. And how would all those toilets, flushing human waste products all day long, affect the groundwater she used to irrigate her crops?

With so much earth in upheaval all around her, Sharon wasn't putting all her eggs in a single basket, to borrow a farm metaphor. By the time I met her she had already bought a spectacular ranch in the fertile Capay Valley in Yolo County, near Sacramento, about two hours by car from Valley End, and she was growing vegetables there, too. In Capay, she had riparian rights, which meant that she could pump as much water as she wanted from Cache Creek, which runs along the back of the farm. Cache Creek flows rapidly, even in the dry season, and provides seemingly unlimited amounts of water—more than she could use even if she were to run the pump twenty-four hours a day, seven days a week. Farmers the world over would envy her for that water supply.

Whole Foods Market, as part of its program to rely less on distant suppliers and generate more produce from local farmers, had agreed to lend Sharon fifty thousand dollars, which she spent on an elaborate underground irrigation system that provides water to every corner of the Capay Valley farm. She wasn't using chemical fertilizers and pesticides there, either, but because the previous owner had, she would have to wait for two years before she could sell that produce as organic. In the meantime, she could sell her Capay Valley produce under the "conventional" rubric. The price per pound for conventionally grown produce is about half the price for organic, she told me, but on the Capay Valley land she could grow twice what she produced at Valley End, so she would make the same amount of money in the two places. Or so the figures showed on paper. But Sharon can find the dark lining to any cloud, and she found one here, too. "Organic is mainstream now," she said. "It's not a niche product anymore, and the change is driving the price way down. If the trend continues, it might put small and medium-sized growers, like me, out of business! Or else I'll have to reinvent the wheel."

Warren Weber had nearly lost his farm in the mid-1990s, and he had been forced to reinvent himself and his whole operation. In 1996–1997 Grimmway Farms, the giant corporation, began to grow and sell organic produce, and prices went down dramatically. Weber simply could not compete. He had to scale back his operations, and when Grimmway came to him for certified organic farmland, he leased his fields to them. For a time he wasn't sure if he'd survive. It was only by a radical shift in marketing and sales that he stayed in business: today 75 percent of his produce goes to restaurants in the San Francisco Bay Area.

With so many uncertainties, and so many risks involved, it is a wonder that Sharon continues to farm. Of course, it is what she knows best. Raised by her mother and father on a California ranch, she came of age mending fences, milking cows, and pulling heifers out of ditches. "Dad worked me like a man," she told Paige and me. "I did boy stuff all through my teen years." After high school she attended California Polytechnic State University, studied agriculture, and received a certificate to teach home economics. This training gave foundation to her skills. She knows what to tell her friends and customers about nutritious foods and how to cook them.

When she and Ed Grossi were married, she ran the business end of the farm. She had a head for figures and kept the books. She also raised their two children. Renee, her daughter, ended up not wanting to have much to do with farming, but Clint became her right-hand man; he learned to sell produce at their roadside stand, delivered it, and kept in touch by cell phone with the stores they supplied. Clint and his mother make a good team.

Still, I could not stop wondering why Sharon stuck to farming. Did she perhaps want to show her ex-husband that she could succeed without him? She also seemed to want to prove that she could make it in a man's world. "Some distributors seem to think that women are dumb, and that they can cheat me," she said. "I have to stay on my toes." But perhaps, I speculated, she may also have wanted to leave the farm intact to Clint and, as a former home-economics teacher, teach Renee a lesson or two about the value of having a home and running a successful business from your home.

Ed Grossi wasn't growing vegetables for sale, but he was enjoying his work as a gardener and landscaper. He told me he worked seventy-five hours a week, and that his father at ninety-five had just started to slow down. On a tour of his property he showed me the rare raspberries he grows—they were bright and shiny as gold—and an even rarer deciduous redwood tree, thought to be extinct, that he had nurtured from a cutting taken from an ancient grove in China. Ed was stoked about growing things, anything from such ordinary produce as pumpkins to his prized Asian pears. And although he wasn't selling produce anymore, he still grows enough of it to feed himself, his wife (he had remarried), and the workers at his nursery and their families. He was making effective use of his land. He was generous and good-hearted, and while he didn't give his stamp of approval to agribusiness, he didn't launch into tirades against it as some organic farmers did.

"After World War II, manufacturers had to find a market for all those chemicals they'd developed for war, so they sold them to farmers instead," he explained. Once he started to talk about this and related topics, there was no stopping him. He had the gift of gab. "DDT can work wonders, but it has downsides, as most of us know from Rachel Carson," he said. "In hindsight we can see the damage from reliance on all those chemicals and on technology. We probably also lost a lot in terms of old-fashioned farmer know-how. Have we caused irreparable harm to the earth and ourselves? Maybe we have. But now we are going back to the future. We're developing alternatives. On my farm we don't use pesticides or herbicides—not in the garden, the nursery, or the vineyards where we grow Sauvignon Blanc grapes. We have cut back on the use of machinery, and we use much less fuel than we used to. Everything is labor-intensive around here. All in all, I'd say that we do a better job of farming and protecting the environment, here in California, than almost anyone does anywhere else in the world."

Where Sharon sees obstacles and problems, Ed tends to see opportunities and challenges. He likes to philosophize, too, and offer words of wisdom based on his experiences. "I must be getting old," he said, smiling broadly. "I have homilies I trot out. What I learned from my dad was hard work and that if you take care of the business, the business will take care of you. Be frugal. That's essential. Farming is wonderful because you can walk to work. On the other hand, it's a very long walk to get away from it." As though to make his point, he gazed off into the distance at the cars on the road.

Having farmed for decades, Ed finds that homilies about it come easily to mind. In fact, I've noticed that human beings, after thousands of years of planting and harvesting, seem to find it difficult, if not impossible, to talk about farming without homilies and clichés. In the fields, the literal can be elusive, and it's hard to coin new, fresh language to express the ways of ancient agriculture. "If you want to understand metaphor, go to a farm," someone told me. It's true. Metaphors lurk everywhere on farms, and students of literature would indeed benefit from visiting them.

Farming is literally a tough row to hoe. You have to cultivate from the ground up. You reap what you sow, and of course it pays off to separate the wheat from the chaff. Nearly everything about farming has a metaphorical as well as a literal meaning, and the very farm itself could be a metaphor. That's part of its charm. Moreover, the word "farm" can be used both as a noun and as a verb, which suggests the versatility of the practice. So it makes sense that Ed Grossi wasn't "farmed out," to borrow an expression I often heard. Neither was Sharon, and if circumstances dictated, she very well might reinvent the wheel, as she had suggested she might do if she had to.

When Paige and I first stumbled into her farmhouse that cold, foggy autumn day, she gave voice to dire predictions, but at the same time she was upbeat. Nothing could stop her. The previous summer had been a financial success, and she'd received accolades from San Francisco's wholesale produce distributors, most of them men eager to make good deals and put money in the bank. At Valley End, Sharon had grown four different kinds of beautiful beans—yellow, green, purple, and French filet; the last-named had become popular with cutting-edge chefs in the city. As a result, she'd been named "The Bean Queen." It was a title she was eager to retain. Perhaps she was also eager to garner new accolades. Certainly Sharon Grossi was driven to succeed, and I knew she'd triumph over adversity.

Her ability to make a life in farming depends heavily on her seasonal field laborers, who are paid by the hour, minimum wage, a paycheck every two weeks. Sharon's Mexican field-workers were not speedy, but they worked steadily. Whether the job was planting, weeding, or fixing the irrigation system that got clogged with adobe and twigs, they got the job done. Leno, the foreman of the crew, came from Oaxaca—"They have big troubles there now," he mentioned, and I could tell that he was informed about the latest social upheavals in Mexico. He had been in the United States for seventeen years. He and his wife, Malu, had worked on farms since childhood. Leno spoke excellent English. He was smart and also stubborn and did not like to be told what to do or how to do it, which sometimes landed him in trouble. Malu seemed to be of the earth itself. She was no more than five feet tall. Her skin was as brown as the earth, and she was about as round as a globe. She might have served as a model of the earth mother, and she assumed a maternal role with me. Married in a Catholic church in a small village in Oaxaca, Malu and Leno carried on Mexican traditions. On their own they grew chile peppers from seeds brought from home, ate rice, beans, and tortillas, and worked on cutting red meat, sugar, and fats from their diet because they were *malo*— bad for Leno's diabetes. They were as well-informed about health as any middle-class couple in the suburban neighborhood across the street, but they had no health plans and little money to spend on health care. Malu told me that she did not have papers, and I suspected that Leno might not have any either. But neither of them seemed worried about the law. They didn't look nervously over their shoulders. They had bank accounts in the United States—all the Mexican workers at Valley End did— and they were hopeful about their ability to make a comfortable life for themselves.

OUTSIDERS IN EL NORTE

Over the past century, the plight of migrant Mexican farm laborers in California has been documented, photographed, studied, and analyzed as thoroughly as that of any other group of workers in the Americas. "What about the farmworkers?" people ask, even if they have never actually known a real farmworker. "Who are they?" "Why do they come here, and what do they want?" These are fair questions. Some of the answers to these questions are available in popular movies such as *El Norte, A Day Without a Mexican,* and *Under the Same Moon.* Steven Street's monumental and moving *Beasts of the Field: A Narrative History of California Farm Workers, 1769–1913* covers the subject magnificently. TV documentaries that expose atrocious living and working conditions provoke shock, outrage, and condemnation. Yet worker exploitation and oppression have often remained largely unchanged for decades, especially in California's Great Central Valley. Refugees from the so-called underdeveloped world who live and labor in the shadow of immense wealth and power, farmworkers are indispensable to the political economy of two nations. Again and again they have been pushed back and forth across borders and forced to work in mechanized agriculture and toxic environments. Perhaps this will sound melodramatic and even grotesque, but they strike me as living skeletons haunting the American dream. Jorge Posada, the Mexican artist who saw skeletons everywhere, would certainly view them this way and depict skeletons holding hoes and planting crops. Indeed, farmwork has exposed migrants to deadly poisons.

That's the big picture. Now, what about the lives Mexican farmworkers lead today? Could we perhaps learn something about the subject by looking at one life? I think so. Let me, therefore, introduce you to Uriel, who was born in the 1960s in the village of Chamacuaro, in the state of Guanajuato, and who now lives in Santa Rosa, California, in a multiracial working-class neighborhood. His house looks like every other house on the street, though the Obama sign on the front lawn makes it stand out. It's the only sign in the whole neighborhood. Uriel's story is dramatic and reflects much beyond the arc of his own immediate experience.

I've known Uriel and his wife, Molly, a native-born Californian, for more than a decade. I attended their wedding, and I'm an unofficial uncle to their daughter, Maya, who is bilingual and perhaps a sign of things to come in our multicultural future. Uriel and Molly exemplify the ways in which the Anglo and Latino worlds have come together to create something new and exciting. But the two worlds continue to be deeply divided. I've attended celebrations, for example, where Latinos, at once proud and subservient, praised their Anglo bosses, after which the same bosses, sometimes paternalistic but usually genuinely caring, praised the Latinos. And then the Anglos and the Latinos sat at opposite ends of the fiesta without any further contact. Speeches are one thing, behavior another. I've also been to fiestas with Uriel where one group spoke English, the other Spanish, and no one from either group reached out to the other.

It takes real effort to bridge the gulf between the two cultures, and I've worked at it for decades in the United States and Mexico. I've watched Uriel work as a mason and a tile setter, and I've seen him make woodcuts of César Chávez, one of which hangs on the wall above my computer. He taught me to make salsa and use words like *tejolote* and *molcajete*. Uriel is a good storyteller, too. I especially like his story about the time he tried to walk across the border on a crowded street by pretending to be a paperboy but gave himself away by forgetting to collect the money owed him. On another occasion, he and an ex-girlfriend pretended to be *cachondos,* two people lusting for each other. The police wouldn't notice them, they thought, if they were kissing passionately. But they weren't good enough at faking lust, and two California police officers sent them back across the border. Uriel made it across by climbing a chain-link fence that separates Mexico from the United States.

I've heard Uriel talk about his life: poverty and unemployment; hunger and loneliness; deadly rattlesnakes in vineyards where he picked grapes. But was he complaining? Maybe he was simply describing what he had experienced. In fact, Mexicans—and especially farmworkers who are illegal—rarely complain, and it can be a fault. They collude with the system that exploits them. Uriel is unique. He expresses himself and complains loudly. What I find most vivid are his accounts of his own feelings, which can be as significant and revealing as actual facts. "From the moment I arrived in El Norte, I felt like an outsider," he told me. "I still feel that way. For years, I lived in fear of arrest and deportation. I knew that everything about me gave me away—the way I walked and talked, the clothes I wore, the expression on my face." More than anyone else I know, Uriel helped me to understand that Mexicans often feel—and are made to feel, too—like aliens in the United States. They are the proverbial strangers in a strange land.

One warm spring afternoon I sat with him behind the house that he didn't yet own. Possibly he never would own it, for his mortgage payment is $2,200 a month, and he hadn't had a decent-paying job in months. But he wasn't panicking. As always he seemed cool and self-confident; having come this far in life, he wasn't about to accept a return to poverty and homelessness, especially with another child on the way. "I feel as if I've struggled my whole life," he said. "I'm struggling right now. The reason I came here—the reason every single one of us has come to El Norte—is because we have to come here to survive. We don't want to starve to death. It's all about work, work, work. Before I came here I was naive. I thought you could pick up mounds of money with a shovel on a street. I was rudely awakened. I jumped from job to job, and from trade to trade, to get out of the hole I was in. For years I had no steady job or work, no home, no car, no support system, and no legal status. In the eyes of America I was a nobody. Almost everyone I know has been in the same place."

Uriel saw a lot of injustices, and he also saw that Mexicans often seemed to contribute to perpetuating the inequality between them and the Anglo establishment. They live and work largely outside the American dream, but at the same time they are living advertisements for that dream. It is ingrained in them not to dwell on their exploitation, alienation, and homesickness but instead to be positive and upbeat. "People in my village would always talk about the wonders of El Norte," Uriel said. "They came home and boasted about the car, the TV, and the cell phone they bought. I never heard anyone say, 'I'm killing myself in the fields' or 'I'm dying every day I'm at work in California.' This was after I'd been in the United States. I had gone back to my village to visit. I would ask, 'What about the time you were cut and bleeding from the knife you were using to harvest grapes? What about the fact that the bank owns the car you drove?'"

Uriel came to the United States for the first time in the late 1970s and became an American citizen in 1996. While he has made something of himself here and adapted well, he doesn't want to end his days here, where time and money seem to drive everyone. He wants to go back to Chamacuaro in Guanajuato, where, as he put it, "I never have to wear a watch or use a cell phone. I can sit and look at the church on the hill, visit with my mother, and drink a beer without having to rush off." That Sunday, when we spoke in his backyard, I heard the longing in his voice. But of course he won't be going home for a while. He has to find work and pay his mortgage or be out on the street. The closest we could get to Mexico that day was a taqueria, that ubiquitous Mexican institution that can be found from Texas to Maine, California to New York. I like to think that Uriel finds solace in eating genuine Mexican food at El Patio, just a few minutes from his Santa Rosa home, but perhaps it only makes the distance from Chamacuaro feel all the greater. Eating our tacos at a table surrounded by murals of traditional Mexican scenes, Uriel remembered that as a teenager he was hungry, alone, and without a car. "I had to go miles on foot to a fast food restaurant to eat, then walk back to the apartment in the darkness," he said. "That was a lonely time."

ADDICTED TO THE RURAL LIFESTYLE

Before I left Valley End on that first visit, I told Sharon Grossi that I would like to see her fields again. "You're always welcome here," she had responded warmly. But I also wanted to explore other farms. And I soon recognized that no two farms are identical, no two farmers the same, and, indeed, that farmers take on the personalities of their farms. In the way a farm is laid out and run, you can see a reflection of the farmer's personality, and, conversely, just by looking at a farmer you can get a pretty good idea of the kind of farm he or she might have. There were farmers as messy in person as their fields, and others as neat and orderly as the furrows they plowed.

Sadly I had to continue my odyssey without Paige, who was headed for London to study photography. Before she left she sent me her digital color pictures of Valley End. While I knew that they would inspire me and frame everything else I saw, I also felt that I had lost a companion and natural-born artist. In a way I knew I would have to develop eyes of my own and see more deeply and precisely than before. Later, when I returned to Valley End and walked the fields with Sharon, I realized that as owner and farmer she did not see them as I now did. For her the farm was not an aesthetic experience. When she looked at the crops she saw profit, loss, and the hard work that had to be done. "This cabbage needs to be weeded," she'd say. "And look at this fennel that's bolted, and bugs have gotten into the bok choy. Boy oh boy, it doesn't look pretty. This whole field is a wreck."

The next farm I visited belonged to Joseph Minocchi, who hailed from Canton, Ohio, and was raised in a blue-collar Italian family. Joseph had carved out several small plots of land—White Crane Springs Farm, he called his enterprise—in a steep and forbidding canyon in a remote corner of Sonoma County. Joseph stood at the opposite end of the agricultural spectrum from Sharon. On his farm he grows tulips and twenty or so ingredients for his salad mix, which he sells for thirty-eight dollars a pound at the upscale Saturday farmers' market at the Ferry Building in San Francisco. My youngest brother, Adam, who had met him there, connected us. Joseph also ships his salad mix to exclusive restaurants in Napa, Las Vegas, and

Berkeley. "Alice Waters loves my watercress," he said, thus adding himself to the impressive list of farmers who grow, or claim to grow, for Alice Waters's Berkeley restaurant Chez Panisse. Waters is of course generally acknowledged as *the* Bay Area chef who has single-handedly persuaded large segments of the Bay Area to eat fresh, local organic fruits and vegetables. Nearly every Northern California farmer wants to sell to her and be a part of her network of suppliers.

If I had to describe Joseph Minocchi, I'd call him the quintessential hermit herbalist. I'd say he is a wise businessman, too, and dedicated to his craft. "I'm way beyond organic," he explained. "I use no machines or machinery of any kind, and no chemicals. I'm biodynamic. I've learned almost everything I know about farming from Rudolf Steiner." The name sounded familiar, but I wasn't sure where to place it. "I believe in double digging," Joseph went on. "This farm is a self-contained organism. Nothing comes from outside. The water is from a pure spring, and White Crane Springs Farm takes its nourishment from the forest that surrounds it." And then, rather ominously, he added, "They're destroying the forest," which I took to mean that he believes that his self-contained, forest-fed farm—which seemed almost as much a thing of the wild as the wild itself— might not survive. The only part of the wild that he tries to keep out are the feral pigs, for they would dig up the earth with their tusks if left to themselves. So, reluctantly, he had built a fence. Something wild always has to be kept out—or kept at bay—if human beings are to farm, I reflected, as I listened to the sound of the wind in the trees and felt the cold knife of winter in my bones. The farmer with a fence, whether made of stone or wood, goes back thousands of years.

The day I met him, Joseph surprised me by giving me a list of what I took to be all of the ingredients for his salad mix: arugula, beet tops, burnet, chickweed, curly cress, frisée, red Russian and Toscano kale, mallow, mâche, minutina, mizuna, parsley, orache, sorrel, spinach, Swiss chard, trefoil, watercress, and miner's lettuce, or purslane. Of course, I didn't know the proportions that he used. Some of the names I heard for the first time that winter afternoon when the ground was covered in frost and the temperature hovered just above freezing. Kale I knew. And Swiss chard, too. But orache and burnet? Where would I find them? Someone else might use the same ingredients as Joseph, but the mix would never taste exactly the same. The forest *terroir* would give all the ingredients a unique quality.

The sun did not shine on Joseph's house, or on his garden, all that December day near the start of winter. The steep hills kept out the light, and, with the solstice coming, there wasn't much sun at all in the sky anywhere in Sonoma that day. Still, Joseph was happy. He enjoyed telling stories about his Italian grandfather, who had made ricotta cheese from goat's milk, and about the happy faces of the men and women who buy his salad mix in San Francisco. The greens that he grows, and those he gathers from the forest floor, are medicinal, he explained. They make those who eat them healthier human beings. And before I returned to civilization, he handed me a pound of his "wild and herbal" mix.

Shortly before Christmas, as part of my odyssey, I attended a panel in Santa Rosa on the subject of farming. The event was moderated by David Katz, a longtime environmentalist, organic farmer, and political activist. A new farm bill was taking shape in Washington, DC, and local farmers and organizations were hoping that it would cut the hefty federal subsidies to a small group of wealthy farmers across America who grow soy beans, wheat, and corn and would instead promote small organic farming and public education about organic produce. The panel was meant to bring local attention to national issues and inform the public about local farmers and their plight. There were entertaining and informative talks. Stan Denner, an eighty-six-year-old fourth-generation Sonoma County farmer, told stories about Luther Burbank, whom he had met as a seven-year-old boy. Burbank was a patron saint of the place, and someone was bound to bring him up; it made sense that that someone was Denner, the oldest person in the room.

Burbank had arrived in California in 1875; by that time the state already had a reputation in the country and Europe for grapes, dairy, and fruit. General Mariano Vallejo, the early-nineteenth-century lord of Alta California, had made a fortune growing and selling crops. So had others. It's no wonder that when the young Luther set foot in Sonoma, he regarded it as a cornucopia. Just days after unpacking his bags, he wrote to his mother back east, "I firmly believe from what I have seen that this is the *chosen* spot of *all* the Earth so far as *Nature* is concerned." He asked her not to repeat his comments "to *anybody* outside the house," because he was afraid that "if it is generally known what a place this is all the scuffs would come here, get drunk, and curse the whole country." Burbank built a greenhouse and started a nursery; before long the "wizard," as he came to be known, had developed a spineless cactus, a white blackberry, and the russet potato that, decades later, McDonald's chose for its French fries.

I could also see that Stan Denner likes to wear Burbank's mantle and boast about his knowledge of agriculture. Wearing a cowboy hat and boots, he explained that his farm was now fourteen feet higher than when he was a boy, and that in his lifetime the mountains had grown lower and the valleys higher. He seemed to be spinning legends for our amusement, as well as boasting about his own expertise. "Hops were once a big crop, then prunes, pears, and now grapes," Stan said. "When there's a crop that pays well, farmers will jump on it. You have to make a crop pay or you won't be a farmer."

Winemaker Lou Preston told the audience that he was "a dreamer, not a farmer," and he complained that not enough people were growing food. Rick Kay, a former Peace Corps volunteer who had worked in Panama, now sat in an office much of the time as an employee for the resource conservation district. "I'm a wanna-be farmer," he proclaimed, and proceeded to give the audience a brief introduction to California's resources. Some of his information clearly made the audience feel good, but he also brought people down to earth with sobering facts: "California is the ninth largest economy in the world, and California provides the country with much of its food," he reminded them. "But all across the U.S.A. we lose two acres of farmland every two minutes." Someone at the back of the room noted that the price of land in Sonoma County made farming prohibitively expensive, and that if you wanted to farm, you almost had to have inherited land from parents, or marry into a farming family.

Kevin McEnnis, another panelist, offered his experiences on this topic. He couldn't afford to buy land, and hadn't married into a farming family. He could, however, afford to lease land from the city of Santa Rosa. The arrangement worked well for him, as it does for other young men like himself who aim to become "master farmers." Later that week I met with McEnnis at

Quetzal, his ten-acre farm, and walked across the fields where he grows certified organic tomatoes. He dry-farms them, which means growing them all summer without water, and he cultivates all kinds of peppers—poblano, jalapeño, Round of Hungary, Italia, and gypsy—for restaurants in Berkeley, including Chez Panisse. "At farmers' markets in Sonoma County, Quetzal is usually taken for granted," Kevin said. "In Berkeley, my partner Keith and I are regarded as great green giants. To get any respect, we've had to transport our produce away from here."

The son of college professors, and a graduate of the University of California at Santa Cruz, Kevin had worked with a human rights organization that repatriated Guatemalans who were forced to leave their own land to settle in Mexico during the civil war of the 1980s. He watched peasants burn the forest so that they might plant crops, and he urged less destructive methods for clearing land and making it suitable for agriculture. He also concluded that, although overtly political goals like peace and justice are admirable, people, if they are to survive, need above all to be able to grow their own food. They would also need to learn to respect the environment, and so he turned from repatriation to education about land and food and to "ecological agriculture," which he practiced and taught to students at New College in Santa Rosa.

In 2004 Keith Abeles had taken over the marketing end of the business because Kevin had burned out and was in danger of going bankrupt. Now the two men share responsibilities, and their partnership makes Quetzal economically as well as environmentally sustainable. Standing in an open field on a winter day, Keith offered a helpful definition of the word "sustainable," which I had begun to hear everywhere. "Sustainable means that you farm and farm and farm, and because you grow cover crops and don't deplete the soil, the land will be as good or better a hundred years later." Kevin and Keith are young and have a kind of seductive male energy. They exude cool. From the start I thought of them as Butch Cassidy and the Sundance Kid, but unlike the movie outlaws played by Paul Newman and Robert Redford, they aren't self-destructive, and they know how to survive.

"It's all about relationships," Kevin said, standing in the shed where he houses a new New Holland tractor, his pride and joy. "Relationships with consumers, with the state bureaucracy that certifies us organic, and with the soil itself." He took off his gloves and hat and scratched his head. "Farming is a weird profession to be in," he said. "People tend to have stereotypes. If you tell folks you're a farmer, they expect you to be wearing overalls and have a pitchfork. When you don't, they look at you in a funny way. It's a challenge to get out of the box."

He and Keith had broken the mold, and of course farmers come in all shapes and sizes. They wear all kinds of hats, and they certainly don't look like the dour couple in Grant Wood's 1930 painting *American Gothic,* in which the man holds a pitchfork and the woman looks like the original Puritan. Most of the young farmers I met are, like Kevin, college graduates. They are diligent students and serious readers. Some are also college teachers, and their farms are schools where students can learn the science and the economics of agriculture.

What about money? Was Quetzal financially stable? "Of course we have cash flow problems," Kevin said. "We borrow tens of thousands of dollars a year in much the same way that

American farmers have always borrowed money in the spring, but we make money, and we pay back our loans after harvest. I'd say we're a success story. Consumers like the way our tomatoes and our peppers taste and look. We're selling beauty as well as flavor, and that beauty helps to make Quetzal a profitable business."

If there is one farmer in Sonoma County who has solved the cash flow problem, it is Scott Mathiesen of Laguna Farm on the outskirts of Sebastopol, the town that once thrived on the Gravenstein apple and that reinvented itself when Gravensteins couldn't compete with apples from Washington State and elsewhere. But don't write off the Gravenstein. Even as I write this, the Russian River Convivium of the Slow Food movement is rallying to resurrect the apple that made Sebastopol famous, and Alice Waters has joined the campaign. Mathiesen inherited the land from his parents, who had, in turn, inherited it from Scott's dairy farmer grandparents. Over the years, Mathiesen has built up a large, loyal group of sustainers who rely on him for their produce, and he also sells to Whole Foods in Sebastopol, a mile or so away, which means he doesn't have to haul his produce long distances.

After graduating from Sacramento State University with a degree in environmental studies, Scott wanted to work as a park ranger, but he soon decided that working for the government wasn't for him. To this day he doesn't care much for government, which is a partial explanation for the fact that Laguna Farm is not certified organic. Mathiesen insists that "local is more important than organic"—a point of view I heard from others, too. To me that seems like an unfortunate dichotomy. Why not both? Couldn't one have local *and* organic?

Scott is intensely political in a New Age way. He has spiritual values that inform his farming practices. He has adopted seminal ideas from Wendell Berry, the Kentucky-born environmentalist, sage of rural life and living, and author of dozens of books, including *The Unsettling of America* (1981), *Standing on Earth* (1991), and *Late Harvest* (1996), as well as novels and stories. Berry argued famously for the importance of putting culture back in agriculture, and for that idea alone I admire him. Scott also aims to connect culture and agriculture. He attends regional conferences and gives workshops right at Laguna on the subjects of "sustainable living" and "nature awareness." In fact, Laguna feeds the community a rich feast of ideas along with kale, turnips, cabbage, and mushrooms, and Scott helps give people a sense of connectedness to the land.

The slogan on the button that Scott wore on the winter day we met read "Inner peace is world peace," and as I learned, it is peace he craves as much as the adrenaline rush that farming can provide. "I'm addicted to this lifestyle," he said. "But I don't want the farm to run me. I want to run the farm." And he runs the farm with a lot of help from his wife, his coworkers, and the community. More than four hundred citizens paid to belong to his CSA. The acronym usually stands for Community Supported Agriculture, and there are hundreds, if not thousands, of CSAs all over the country. But Scott likes to describe his CSA as Community *Shared* Agriculture. The concept is more than one hundred years old, perhaps even older. Food-buying cooperatives have existed ever since the early days of the Industrial Revolution, when skilled factory workers banded together to buy basic necessities and thereby survived. In 1844 in Rochdale, England, for example, a group of workers who would become famous in history for their foresight and solidarity formed a food cooperative. They rented a building, bought butter, sugar, flour, and oatmeal, and divided them among subscribers, who had paid one pound sterling to join. In the late 1960s and early 1970s, hippies and radicals reinvented that idea and banded together to buy brown rice and vegetables at wholesale prices. Sometimes in the rebellious spirit of that era they called their groups "food conspiracies." Indeed, they were conspiring to undermine the stranglehold that giant food corporations—like the generic-sounding General Foods— have on society. The Park Slope Food Coop in Brooklyn, New York, carries on the illustrious tradition of the Rochdale Workers. Founded in 1973, it has 13,900 members, and it is the largest member-owned and -operated food co-op in the United States.

At Laguna Farm, the money from subscribers at the start of each year gives Scott almost all the cash he needs for equipment, seeds, and workers' pay. In return, the subscribers receive weekly allotments of fresh fruits and vegetables. What impressed me most about Laguna wasn't Scott himself, or the farm, which was no work of art or thing of beauty in my eyes, but rather the subscribers. These people were eloquent on the subject of vegetables, and committed to local, organic, and sustainable farming. Martha, who was raised on a farm in the Midwest and now makes her home in Sebastopol, told me, "We're blown away by these carrots. They taste the way carrots taste in your wildest imagination." Barbara, who came from Chicago, said, "We need to have farms like this one, close to home. This is the way we need to go in the future." Michael Traugot, a student of agriculture at the University of California at Davis, said, "I like the fact that the produce here is not flown in or trucked from far away. I also buy here to help prevent urban sprawl." Irmgard, born and

raised in Germany, articulated the feelings of a great many of the
others when she told me, "It's a political statement to buy from a
local farm. It's definitely a western Sonoma County attitude, and
I like to think it's spreading."

DOES CALIFORNIA LEAD THE WAY?

Soon after I visited Laguna, the *Economist* magazine published an
article—reprinted in *The Santa Rosa Press Democrat,* the local
daily newspaper—entitled "Voting with Your Trolley," which
made fun of trendy consumers in England and elsewhere. The
article ridiculed the claim that organic and local foods were better
for people than conventionally grown produce, and it lampooned
the notion that one could "change the world just by buying certain foods." It concluded with a sermon: "Conventional political
activity may not be as enjoyable as shopping, but it is far more
likely to make a difference." The members of Scott Mathiesen's
CSA didn't agree with the *Economist.* To them, the purse had
power, and they were prepared to use it. By shopping at Laguna
and buying fresh local organic produce, they felt that they were
making a political statement that would be heard by corporations.
They also told me that they thought their actions as consumers
would encourage farmers to grow more organic produce and that
that would encourage more farms.

Many citizens of Sebastopol and its environs like to think that
the concepts of local and organic food and farming originated in
Sonoma County, much as many Californians like to think that
all good things American—including protection of the environment and concern for the quality of air and water—began in

California. These notions do not sit well with me, perhaps because I'm not a native Californian, and perhaps, too, because I admire forward-looking thinkers, like Wendell Berry, who lived and worked in other parts of the country. Granted, California is exceptional in many ways. Carey McWilliams pointed this out in *California: The Great Exception* (1949), though, oddly, he didn't discuss Hollywood and the film industry, which gave the state much of its distinctive character and personality. The rise of Silicon Valley in the 1980s also made California exceptional, and for decades now anyone who lives in the East and shops for vegetables in the winter might think that California is an eternal cornucopia, a place that is not subject to rules about seasons and crops. Remember that Allen Ginsberg, that quintessential New Yorker, was so stunned by the produce that was available in Berkeley when he arrived in the mid-1950s that he was inspired to describe his near-orgiastic shopping experience in "A Supermarket in California" (1955). Avocados seemed miraculous. They still do to many New Yorkers who visit the West Coast.

From my perspective, however, California isn't the only place that has given birth to forward-looking ideas and values. It is simply one of many. Community-supported agriculture began in the East. The fathers of organic farming in America were also from the East. New York was the first city in the United States to ban trans fats, though California was the first state to do so. I was delighted, I must say, that when I asked Joan Didion, the California-born writer who understands this place as well as any contemporary American writer, whether California is the locomotive or the caboose of the train, she paused, reflected, and then concluded that it was not ahead of all other places. "When my husband and I lived in L.A. in the mid-

1960s, people would say that cults started in California, and that they'd spread to the rest of the country," she said. "I didn't think that was true then and I still don't think so. I don't think that California leads the way. I used to think that if you wanted to know the future of America, go to New Orleans or to Miami, and I did go there. But I don't know anymore where to go today to see the future of America, and so I don't know what to write next."

Of course, there has almost always been a cult of health food in California, and plenty of health food aficionados. Writers such as George Orwell and Saul Bellow made fun of California's vegetarians and its "fruits and nuts." But health food fanatics also exist elsewhere. My own parents farmed organically before they came to California, and they ate healthy food on Long Island about fifty miles east of Manhattan. My father adopted the gospel of organic farming as preached by Robert Rodale, who insisted in *How to Grow Vegetables and Fruits by the Organic Method* (1961) and *The Basic Book of Organic Gardening* (1971) that growing organically was almost child's play. Moreover, Rodale viewed organic as revolutionary. He believed it would take Americans "away from the centric super-industrial state toward a simpler, one-to-one relationship with the earth itself." Rodale's ideas fed utopian dreams of the sort that my father pursued all his life, even while working as a lawyer.

My mom's well-worn bible was Adelle Davis's *Let's Eat Right to Keep Fit,* which appeared in 1954, just as I was entering my teen years. As a result, that's when I began to be fed—in accordance with Davis's ideas about nutrition and health—wheat germ, molasses, oatmeal, eggs, and vitamins. I of course preferred hamburgers, fries, and cherry Cokes—everything Davis proscribed. After Davis died in 1974 at the age of seventy, my mother vowed to carry on her work, and in California she taught cooking classes à la Davis to students of the Nonesuch School in Sebastopol. A dozen or so teenagers used to gather in her kitchen to learn to cook with brown rice, tofu, sprouts, and yogurt, as well as with the fresh produce my father grew. "First feed the face, then talk right and wrong," my mom always said. Once her students were well fed, she'd shock them with tales about the greed of the American food industry and the horrors of bleached flour and processed food. Much of what she said she'd learned from Davis. At the start of the twenty-first century, I heard the same ideas all over again from writers who seemed to think they had originated them.

My parents showed me by their own example that to become a Californian wasn't as difficult as it might have seemed. They did it effortlessly: growing and smoking marijuana; making their own peach brandy; doing yoga; getting massages. Like their friends and neighbors, they worked hard and played hard. They also taught me not to use California as a yardstick to measure the rest of the world, and not to forget that California was sometimes a cocoon.

To get a sense of what was happening on farms elsewhere and see whether California was an exception, I made it a point to talk long-distance to two friends from college: Liz Henderson in upstate New York, and Allen Young in western Massachusetts. Both of them have farmed since the 1970s. They confirmed my assumption that what was happening in California was also happening in their communities.

Allen Young grows almost all his own vegetables in a big garden, and he has written about farms in his part of the world in a book entitled *Make Hay While the Sun Shines* (2007). He loves to eat straight out of his garden in the summer, and he's just as happy in the middle of winter, when he removes the snow and straw protecting his carrots from freezing. Fresh carrots in February are heavenly, and he raves about them when he e-mails or telephones me.

In New York and Massachusetts, Liz Henderson has for decades played a big part in the organic food movement and the movement for social justice in agriculture, and she wrote about her experiences in *Sharing the Harvest: A Guide to Community-Supported Agriculture* (2007). Liz has always been a radical. I knew her from New York, where I attended Columbia and she attended Barnard. We loved the theater, and we both took part in the protest movements of the 1960s. Liz studied Russian literature—and spoke perfect Russian—and she might have had a career in academia. But rural life called to her. When I talk to her now, she rails about the social and economic injustices of private property, and praises communities that support farms and farms that support communities.

To gain an objective perspective about the differences between West Coast and East Coast agriculture, I also compared notes with Dan Kaplan, the manager of Brookfield Farm in Amherst, Massachusetts, where he grows crops on thirty acres and supplies food to four hundred shareholders, three-quarters of whom come to the farm to pick up their produce. The produce for the remaining shareholders goes to Boston. Dan farmed in California soon after he graduated from Tufts University in 1987, and he also worked on farms in England, Germany, France, Switzerland, and Austria. As he knows, there is a long history of organic farming on small farms in Massachusetts and Pennsylvania that goes back to colonial days. As Dan sees it, the differences between European and American agriculture outweigh the differences between California and, say, Massachusetts.

"Probably because they have much less space, Europeans have a different sense of land use than we do," Dan said. "Like us, they have a capitalist economy, but it's tempered by social controls. There isn't the same kind of urban sprawl in Europe, either. They have many more small-scale farms than we have here in the East, and farm animals are everywhere." Like the young California farmers I know, Dan has a sense of idealism and social responsibility and a commitment to sustainability, which he defines as the "ability to last over a long period of time." He also appreciates local markets. "Of course local is relative," he said. And with a certain wry sense of humor, he added, "I'm local for *me*. New England is local, but New York feels far away, and Maine is out of the picture."

Organic and local are clearly ideas whose time has come, but it's clear, too, that these ideas belong to no one particular region. On a trip to New York, I discovered the lively, boisterous farmers' market in Union Square that has been there for decades. I met farmers from New York, New Jersey, and Pennsylvania who seemed to be as pioneering as farmers in California. I came away thinking that in California we are not *better* at farming than Americans elsewhere. We have our own particular rows to hoe, our own agricultural and cultural problems. By paying attention to our own piece of the earth, our water and sky, we may well discover paths for others to adopt, but humility would serve us better than swaggering and boastfulness.

After six months of exploration I felt that I had seen and heard all there was to see and hear, and that I had come to the end of my farm odyssey. I'd been to Valley End, White Crane Springs, Quetzal, and Laguna. I'd learned about CSAs and sustainability, and I'd listened to debates about the pros and cons of organic and local, big and small farms. Indeed, I did not know what else there might be to learn about farming. I made ready to fly to England to visit two old friends—Doris Lessing, who would win the Nobel Prize for Literature just a few months later, and Susan Seifert, the head teacher at a school in London. Then, just as I was packing my bags, my friend and colleague Noelle Oxenhandler, who wrote beautifully about parents and children in *The Eros of Parenthood* (2001), called and said that if I was writing about farming, I *had* to visit Oak Hill Farm in Glen Ellen. And with that, my life took an unexpected and dramatic turn.

2

OAK HILL HISTORY

OTTO AND ANNE TELLER

I had been to Glen Ellen before, but not for a long while, and I couldn't remember precisely how to get there. In fact, Glen Ellen wasn't far from home—at most thirty minutes by car. As the proverbial crow flies, the journey wouldn't have taken more than a few minutes of rapid flight. Had I been able to fly, I would have gone over Sonoma Mountain, the highest peak around here and a sacred space for Native Americans. But air travel was not an option. I would have to drive. And although Glen Ellen wasn't inaccessible by road, it wasn't easily accessible. That has been, and still is, part of its charm. John Lasseter, from the movie company Pixar, who made a fortune on such computer-animated movies as *Toy Story* and *A Bug's Life,* built a mansion in Glen Ellen and, like other self-made men, leads the life of a country squire. If you had the money for it, Glen Ellen was the place where you could live out your wildest fantasies and become the star of your own movie. Named after Ellen Stuart, who, with her husband, Charles, settled there in the 1860s, the valley had in many ways not changed since the days of the American Civil War. The Stuarts' stone barn was still sturdy. Their two-story house had weathered the elements for nearly 150 years, and the bridge that crossed Stuart Creek could still support a heavy load. The Stuart Ranch now belongs to the Sonoma Land Trust and will never be developed commercially. Time here will continue to stand still.

I have already discussed Jack London in the introduction to this book. There I describe one side of him, his "good side." But London was profoundly divided, and now it would be helpful to describe his "dark side." After his initial purchase in Glen Ellen, he went on buying land until he owned more than one thousand acres, which he dubbed Beauty Ranch and which his second wife, Charmian, inherited upon his death in 1916 at the age of forty. His anarchist friend Emma Goldman, who called him "the only revolutionary writer in America," referred to his place as "Dreamland," but it was also a nightmare land for London. His dream house, Wolf House, burned to the ground in 1913, just before he was to move in; though arson was suspected, no one was ever charged.

He drank heavily, though his doctor had warned him not to drink, and during the last year or so of his life he subsisted on a diet of half-cooked duck, which couldn't have been good for his health. London had wanted to create a paradise in Glen Ellen. His ideas are inspiring, but his experiment failed, and his life offers a cautionary tale to dreamers of big dreams. Moving to the country and farming organically isn't as easy as it may seem, and it isn't for everyone. The rural life presents rigors and obstacles even to the fittest of men and women. To Kevin Starr, the California historian and for many years the California State Librarian, "the Sonoma chapter of Jack London's life, his last chapter, dramatized a modality of California madness." At the time, few Californians recognized either the madness or the nightmare. They preferred to think that London at Beauty Ranch embodied the American Dream. They read his promotional essays, and they followed his example—moving to the country, buying land, planting grapes, and building mansions. "The pioneer has done his work in this north-of-the-bay region," London wrote in a 1911 essay. "All is ready for the inevitable rush of population and adequate development." He added prophetically that the region would "someday support a population of millions. In the meanwhile, O you homeseekers, you wealth-seekers and, above all, you climate seekers, now is the time to get in on the ground floor." The poetic advertising copy came from a man who also called for equality of opportunity and the end of class inequalities, and it was hard to resist. Homeseekers rushed in, cut down trees, and took all the water they wanted, depleting natural resources.

Glen Ellen and Jack London have become inseparable in history and legend, and tourists have flocked to Jack London State Historical Park, where they can view the ruins of Wolf House and tour the cottage where he wrote *The Iron Heel,* his futuristic novel about a dictatorship in an America run amok. Other writers also settled in Glen Ellen. Nearly half a century after London's death, Mary Frances Kennedy Fisher made Glen Ellen her home because it reminded her of Provence, where she had spent some of the best years of her life; she memorialized her experiences in France in two delightful books, one about Aix-en-Provence and the other about Marseille, published together as *Two Towns in Provence*. Glen Ellen, the little village off the beaten track, had tugged at my imagination long before I ever heard of Oak Hill Farm, or of Anne Teller, its owner. I learned this by going to the farm's web site. Here was a farm with the latest technology!

"Welcome to Oak Hill Farm of Sonoma, 45 acres of productive farmland set on 700 acres of protected wildlands nestled against the western slope of the Mayacamas in Glen Ellen California," the web site reads. "We have been growing flowers and produce using sustainable agricultural practices for more than 50 years, and in this temperate Mediterranean climate we are privileged to grow more than 200 varieties of flowers, shrubs, orchard fruit, herbs, and field-grown fruits and vegetables." I liked the farm just from the taste of it in cyberspace. I liked the color photos of the fruits and vegetables, and I liked the image of Anne Teller walking with Otto Teller, who, the site explained, was "a renowned conservationist who died in 1998." I liked the diversity of crops at Oak Hill and the setting in the Mayacamas Mountains, which I had explored on foot and knew to be wild and rugged, with spectacular views from the peaks.

I knew that there are several ways to get there, and I traced them in my head: north to Santa Rosa and then east and southeast on the Sonoma Highway, which leads through wine country; alternatively, south to Petaluma and then west and northwest on half a dozen different roads that zigzag through valleys and over mountaintops. Or I could go over the mountain on Bennett Valley Road, the ultimate back road, with twists and turns that lead through oak forests and fields covered with rocks and boulders.

I chose Bennett Valley Road, and as I drove I kept checking the mileage and the temperature on the dashboard of my red Volvo. I wanted to know not only the total mileage but also the mileage for each leg of the journey. I wanted to see where the temperature rose and fell, and where microclimates began and ended, and I learned a great deal on that first trip.

The route took me past the Crane Melon Barn and past fields of hay and sheep in the pasture on Petaluma Hill Road, which serves as a dividing line between the suburban and the rural side of this area. For the next six months or so, three or four times a week, often at 5 or 6 A.M., I would make this journey from my side to the other, which, with its milder climate and slower pace of life, always felt like another world. I would drive past the road that leads to Jack London State Historical Park, then through the town of Glen Ellen, and past the house where M. F. K. Fisher lived. I grew to love the journey, and, little by little, it stamped itself on my memory until I could go there, in my head, whenever I wished—taking the hairpin turns, holding the steering wheel tightly on the stretches with no shoulder, my foot on the brake on the long downhill.

Oak Hill Farm lies at the heart of the Sonoma Valley, though it does not make that claim for itself; indeed, it does not announce its presence at all. Although the farm runs along Sonoma Highway for more than a mile, there is no indication that a farm exists beyond the gently sloping hillside dotted with oak trees. Driving past in a car, you might think that woodland continues all the way to the top of the mountain. Only where the road takes a sharp turn—where a huge fallen tree lies on its side—do I see a sign with the image of an oak tree and the words "Oak Hill Farm." It would be easy to miss the entrance. I

The oaks at Oak Hill Farm and throughout the Valley of the Moon give Sonoma County much of its personality and identity and serve as a reminder that the region was once covered with forests, salmon once swam in the streams, and bear once roamed the mountains.

drew to a stop in the middle of the road and waited for the oncoming traffic to pass.

Then I turned left, driving up a narrow road at ten miles per hour, as the speed limit sign indicated. And there it was: a big red barn, with a bright green roof. It was obviously old, but it had been well taken care of, and it had an air of unpretentious dignity about it. I experienced what felt like love at first sight. It might have been that. But at the age of sixty-five, I had come to distrust love at first sight. And yet I did immediately feel that I belonged here, even before I met Anne Teller. I would feel a deep sense of kinship after I met and got to know her and the twenty or so people who live at Oak Hill in houses spread across the property, the people who tend the fields and orchards, repair the old tractors and burst irrigation pipes, sell apples, raspberries, zucchini, and corn in the Red Barn Store, keep the books, cut the flowers, make bouquets and wreaths, and sweep the leaves that fall from the old eucalyptus trees. But even at first sight I felt enclosed and protected within the Oak Hill world that surrounded me, and I wanted to embrace it in return. Of course I didn't blurt out my feelings on that first day. I wanted to see if the place was really as spectacular as it seemed to be. Was the beauty skin deep or was there also underlying beauty not immediately apparent?

O PIONEERS

Patrick McMurtry was not the first person I met at Oak Hill. Nor was he the oldest person living on the property. But he had lived there longer than anyone else—longer even than Anne Teller—and so I will let Patrick be the first Oak Hill resident to speak in this book. Anne dubbed him "the historian of Oak Hill," and rightly so. Equipped with a good memory, Patrick also appreciated facts and the sweep of events. Like most good historians, he had a knack for telling stories vividly. To go by his enthusiasm, body language, and facial expressions, he might have been talking about events as momentous as the American Revolution or the Civil War. His stories happened to be about Oak Hill, about himself and his own family, none of them famous. But ancestors of his had played a dramatic role as pioneers in nineteenth-century California. He told his stories with the conviction of a great national historian describing wars, plagues, and revolutions, and in his rendition his family became emblematic of other families. Like many Americans, the Mc-Murtrys were caught up in the wave of social change that transformed America from wilderness to industrial nation, and from a rural to an urban and suburban society.

Of course, Patrick's ancestors had come from Europe, and they belonged to that generation of early pioneers who put their stamp on California. They farmed, raised chickens and cattle, grew grapes, and cut down trees, milled them, and sold the lumber. His grandparents made money, built houses, and sent their kids to college. Those kids—Patrick's parents—turned their backs on farming and their rural roots when they grew up.

"My father worked for Shell Oil, and my mother worked at the high school," Patrick said. "They became party animals and alcoholics, but a great-aunt who had a farm in Paradise, California, continued the family tradition, and I learned about agriculture from her. She lived to be 103, and all her life she was up at dawn and went to work picking fruit, canning and drying fruit, and making pies, jams, and preserves."

Born in 1947, Patrick watched the rural world vanish. In the 1950s, he witnessed the strange transformations of the American society of the post–World War II period, which forever changed the ways people worked and played, ate, drank, entertained, and existed. Sonoma might have been San Diego, Syracuse, Seattle, or Savannah. Everywhere was nearly the same as anywhere else. "We lived on TV dinners, and everyone had a little table in front of the TV, and we all ate there and not at the dining room table," Patrick said of his own family life. He might have been speaking of my family. "At school they showed us movies about how wonderful DDT was, and back then people didn't seem to care where their food came from or what chemicals were in it."

Patrick graduated from high school and college and went the way of many a young man of his generation. He lived in a commune, grew marijuana, and protested against the war in Vietnam. "Those were trippy times," he said. "There was Elvis, the Beatles, the hippies, and Abbie Hoffman's *Steal This Book*, which I actually went out and bought." Patrick laughed as though it was yesterday and he could still smell the pot and feel the passion of that time. The 1960s had arrived with a roar and changed the cultural landscape of the Valley of the Moon. "It was wild," Patrick said. "The Hells Angels congregated here; and up on Sonoma Mountain, Alex Horn, a follower of the Armenian-born mystic G. I. Gurdjieff, had a farm. Hippies moved up there; Horn took their money and put them to work, which is pretty funny."

Oak Hill's founder, Otto Teller, belonged to an older generation than Patrick's—the "Greatest Generation," some call it—but he, too, felt the vibrations of the 1960s. Born in 1908, when a majority of Americans lived in farming communities, he died in 1998, when city life had engulfed so much of the landscape. That transformation of the country from rural to urban alarmed him, but it also energized him. For half a century he fought battles on behalf of nature and wildlife. He was born on a farm and vineyard near Cleveland, Ohio, graduated from the University of California, Berkeley, and served in the Army Air Corps during World War II. An early convert to organic farming, he took up Rachel Carson's ideas and rejected chemical fertilizers. Though he loved his Jaguar and might wear an ascot, he aimed for simplicity and, before it was popular to do so, experimented with solar energy and wind power. "Country slicker" was a phrase he used to describe himself.

Young, idealistic Sonoma County environmentalists like Joan Vilms admired his passion, commitment, and generosity. They congregated around him, and he took them under his wing. Some called him "Mose" because they saw him as a Moses leading them into a promised land where nature would be revered and protected instead of being trampled, raped, and ripped apart, as had been happening in the Valley of the Moon ever since Europeans first arrived. "I learned a lot from him," Vilms, a California transplant from New Orleans, explained. "He taught me that nature comes first, and that it's essential to create healthy ecosystems and lighten the human footprint on the planet. Otto was imperious and blustery at times, but he was right, and he was ahead of his time."

Otto bridged the gap to Patrick's generation, and for a brief time marijuana and grapes existed side by side in the Valley of the Moon. When Otto bought an old vineyard named Old Hill and sprayed the vines with liquid seaweed, the plants went wild. He sold the grapes to Ravenswood, where winemaker Joel Peterson turned them into award-winning Zinfandels. As Otto aged, Patrick worked for him more and more. He worked overtime when Otto, who loved to read, went blind and could no longer read a newspaper or a book. When he couldn't see well enough to drive a car or accurately dial the numbers on his telephone, Patrick became both his chauffeur and his reader.

"Otto was a one-man political action committee," Patrick said. "He created Trout Unlimited and the Salmon Foundation, and he also enlisted old friends like Bing Crosby and Arthur

Godfrey in his causes. He worked to preserve watersheds around here and to save the streams, which had trout and steelhead when he arrived. The trout and steelhead were the canaries in the coal mine, he would say, and when they began to die, he knew that it was not a good sign for the water, the earth, or human beings."

Then came Anne's arrival at Oak Hill in the 1970s. She was Anne Bucklin then. She was young, bright, and beautiful, and she saw the beauty of Oak Hill. With her marriage to Otto, the slow, sometimes painful, and even erratic evolution and growth of the farm began. In the years that followed there were crops that worked and crops that failed, people who stayed and people who didn't, and always the changes of the seasons and scourges of weather, from droughts to flooding, while new moons and full moons illuminated the Mayacamas Mountains and the valley floor. "In the old days the Red Barn Store occupied only half the space it occupies now, and the produce was much more limited," Patrick said. "These days you'll see twenty different kinds of tomatoes and all kinds of squash—dozens and dozens of vegetables—but back then there was just one kind of tomato, some zucchini and corn, and maybe eggplant. You took what you wanted, put money in a tin can, and that was that.

"Now it's very different, though in some ways you might say it's still the same. Oak Hill has not lost its original glory. In winter it's slow, as always, and I won't see much of Anne or anyone else. Some of the Mexicans go back to Mexico. And then spring comes, everyone gets in gear, and I hear the tractors again plowing, and it's busy, busy, busy, planting and sowing seeds. Summer comes before you know it, and that's when Gael—the woman I live with, who works in the Red Barn Store—develops muscles

Anne Teller is an eloquent spokeswoman for organic farming as well as the protec tion of the environment, and she provides Oak Hill with its overarching philosophy and vision of the land and its inhabitants.

from lifting heavy boxes of produce. Then, when the ugly Hub-bard squash come in, I know it's fall. One day I'll go outside to pick an apple from a tree laden with apples, and then the next day there won't be a single apple left."

Patrick had me in the palm of his hand. I could see the drama and colorful characters of Oak Hill unfolding before my eyes.

"In November the farm always begins to wind down, and the people who work here aren't as stressed, but it's still busy all the way to Christmas. There's always a human drama going on here. People can be touchy and temperamental. I don't ever suggest anything to Chuy, who is in charge of growing and harvesting flowers. Lynn, the office manager, has a mind of her own, and Anne always has an opinion about everything. Paul is a hell of a farmer and a bit obsessive at times, but he and Gael can get into a pulling, pushing thing. Candi, who lives with Paul, always sides with him. There's Miguel, his wife, and their kids. There's Sam Josi, the grandson of Anne's third husband. Laptop boy, I call him. He came and looked at the farm through his computer software program and his mathematical formulas about profit and loss, and he never touched the soil. With all these personalities, it can get melodramatic around here."

THE RED BARN

In Otto Teller, Oak Hill had a legendary founder who left a living legacy. Today, in addition to its unofficial historian and raconteur, Patrick McMurtry, the farm has a large cast of characters, all from different backgrounds and cultures, and all pulling this way and that. And yet they are a loyal bunch, and, pulling together, they succeed in producing quality fruits and vegetables.

This wasn't just any farm. It was a farm with a face all its own. Here I decided to plant my feet, make a lasting commitment, and cast my fate. It was exactly what I had been looking for, and I could not have imagined a more perfect farm if I had tried.

On the occasion of my first visit, I saw cars arrive and shoppers going into the Red Barn Store with backpacks and bags of canvas and paper. I followed the shoppers and, like them, looked at the produce, and I drifted into conversation with a woman standing next to me. She defined herself as a "locavore." "A what?" I asked, not having previously heard the word. "A locavore is a person who shops locally," she said. "That's precisely what I'm doing now." And I watched as she selected the vegetables she planned to cook for supper.

The Red Barn Store is a veritable paradise for locavores. For nine months of the year, from April to Christmas, when it closes for winter and a much needed break for the staff, Gael del Mar, Patrick's girlfriend, runs the store with help from two young women, Estefania and Courtney. In many ways the Red Barn Store drives the farm. The shoppers I saw arriving were insatiable for the organic fruits and vegetables on hand and couldn't seem to get enough of the items they wanted. When would the tomatoes arrive? a young woman wanted to know. Why wasn't corn in the store? another asked. It would all be here when it came into season, Gael explained, but for now they would have to wait. Why not shop, cook, and eat what was available, she suggested to the importunate buyers, expressing much the same approach as Henry David Thoreau, who urged his contemporaries to "live in each season as it passes" and "open all your pores and bathe in all the tides of Nature, in all her streams and oceans, at all seasons."

This was clearly a new concept to the young woman who had asked for corn and was obviously accustomed to buying whatever she wanted at almost any time of the year. "Why don't you have strawberries?" she asked. "I saw them in Safeway." Gael replied, "We don't grow strawberries here." With that, the young woman took Gael's suggestion to buy what was in the store and in season, and she filled her basket with beets, fava beans, celery, kohlrabi, radishes, Savoy cabbage, and several bouquets of flowers. The older woman, who had introduced me to the word "locavore" and was now paying with a check at the counter, turned to the younger woman and said with a smile, "Welcome to the world of the locavores."

Gael del Mar, a California native, runs the Red Barn Store at Oak Hill, which is a destination for local shoppers and open to the public from spring until Christmas.

Just then another young woman arrived, sporting a pierced nose and with her hair in dreadlocks. She had a beautiful mouth, and when she said hello to Gael, I heard that she spoke English with a French accent. I had to know her name. "Genevieve Rousseaux," she said. She came from Quebec, had grown up on meat and potatoes, and had later changed her diet radically. She was at the Red Barn to buy vegetables and huge bunches of brightly colored flowers. She was planning to prepare raw food to sell at a three-day reggae festival. Genevieve explained that she did not bake, sauté, fry, boil, grill, roast, or toast anything, and that she herself ate no cooked food. What's more, she had a thriving business selling raw-food dishes. "When I set up my booth, it's all about the visuals," she said. "It's all about what attracts the eye." Everything about *her* certainly attracted the eye, I thought to myself, as she roamed freely around the store buying green, red, and yellow flowers to attract the eyes of the reggae fans during the coming festival.

"I play a lot of reggae in the store," Gael said. "I play the blues, Cuban music, and soul, too." And, right on cue, Marvin Gaye's voice filled the Red Barn. Shoppers began to sway their hips back and forth. Genevieve certainly did, and I might have continued my conversation with her if Anne Teller hadn't arrived just then. She was wearing jeans, dark sunglasses that obscured her eyes, and a fedora of the kind that Otto might once have worn. "What can I tell you?" she asked, as we drifted into the sunlight, away from the sounds of Marvin Gaye and toward those of a tractor in the distance. At that point I intended to write about Otto Teller. The Oak Hill web site description of him had intrigued me. In the photos he looked gentle, and I liked the bigness of his face, his strong chin, and the twinkle in his eyes. I wanted to know more about Otto, now that I knew so many new farmers, young farmers, and young environmentalists.

Otto had a long history. I wanted to learn all I could, and Anne was eager to tell me about him. "He came for the fishing," she said. "The streams were full year-round, and he thought it was paradise. He came for the Millerick Family Rodeo, too. That was before World War II. After 1945 he bought Magnolia Farm, on Eighth Street East in the town of Sonoma, which had been used to experiment with semitropical fruits and plants like figs and palms, which did very well. He ranched sheep, tired of sheep, and got into the flower business. After we married in 1977—and commingled our chickens—we added vegetables to the mix, but at first it didn't work." Anne had a sense of humor; like Patrick, she had a feel for the sweep of history and an idiosyncratic way of putting things. "Commingled our chickens" was unusual. I'd probably never again hear anyone use that expression to describe a romantic relationship between a man and a woman. Anne could be earthy, too, and she enjoyed recalling many of Otto's expressions: "It's as cold as a well digger's ass"; "You're as useless as a glass eye at a keyhole"; and when a friend or acquaintance was headed for the city, "Remember me to the flesh pots."

Anne seemed to have nothing to hide and to want to tell me everything she knew about Oak Hill. "There's a secret pasture on the hillside where the outlaw Joaquin Murrieta used to sequester his cattle," she said. "There's water up there, too, and it's a perfect place for a man, wanted by the law, to lie low." Anne and Otto shared a passion for the environment, she told me. In 1981 they gave their land—all seven hundred acres—to the Sonoma Land Trust, an organization that protects open space and creates natural corridors for wildlife. (In fact, Otto founded the Sonoma Land Trust.) Under the terms of easement, Oak Hill was allowed to farm in the valley floor. But it could not develop the property for commercial purposes, build houses for sale, or pave roads. It would be farmland forever. Several nearby properties, including the Bouverie Preserve at Audubon Canyon Ranch, where M. F. K. Fisher had lived, formed a green belt where development was prohibited. "Otto left quite a legacy,"

Anne continued. "He loved the natural world, and he had a sense for 'the natural' before it became a buzzword. He knew instinctively that chemicals were to be avoided. Then, too, he didn't want to build castles or mansions of the sort that Jack London built; he would have thought that Jack London was an egotist."

Almost as an afterthought, I asked Anne about herself, and she told me about her ancestors, some of them Mexican and Guatemalan, who had owned a coffee *finca;* about her early passion for gardening and farming; about her education at Smith College and the University of California at Berkeley; and about her first marriage, children, and family life in San Francisco, followed by her divorce from Mr. Bucklin, whose last name her children inherited. Her youngest child, Will, manages the family winery next door. Her younger daughter, Kate, followed in Otto's footsteps and fights to protect the environment in California, Oregon, and the Teller Wild Life Preserve in Montana. Her older son, Ted, graduated from the University of New Mexico with an MA in social work. He managed Oak Hill for six years—stormy years—before returning to New Mexico with his wife, Wendy Westerbeck, who belongs to one of Sonoma's storied families. Anne's older daughter, Arden, works in San Francisco for the school district, removing concrete and putting in gardens where students can learn the ABCs of agriculture.

Anne suggested that I might want to wander about a bit. I told her I'd like to see the fields above the parking lot. Several roads led up the hill behind the Red Barn. Signs read "Keep Out" and "Private," and naturally I wanted to go beyond them. But on that first day I did not manage to get very far from the barn. Anne pointed to the iris and the godetia—"a tapestry of flowers and

Otto Teller, one of the founders of the environmental movement in Sonoma County and a pioneering ecologist throughout the American West, with Anne Teller, his wife, who has carried on his traditions and advocates for responsible stewardship of the land at Oak Hill.

weeds," she called it. We strolled side by side through fruit trees and across a plot of land planted with radishes that, Anne explained, would not be harvested and sold. The reason for growing the radishes was to repair the damage inflicted by a virus. Growing a crop to mend the soil—I loved that idea.

"We don't use chemicals," she said. "We don't have fences, either, as you can see, in this day and age of fences. We strive for balance. We manage to get along with most of the wild animals, though the deer do damage now and then. We have to buy compost because we don't have enough biomass here to make our own. We have our own bees and a beekeeper. Stewardship is part of my responsibility. What we're doing with the land seems to be the best thing to do right now, and my family will be stewards after me. I don't want to grow grapes. At Oak Hill we're committed to diversification, and now we're 75 percent in vegetables and 25 percent in flowers, a change that would probably surprise Otto."

It sounded good to me. Perhaps too good. "Is Oak Hill profitable?" I asked. Could she and the rest of the farm staff do all the wonderful things they did and still make a profit? "We want to make money, and we do," Anne said. "But profit is not number one. It's built into the equation. The farm has evolved, but not by design. My style is to take on almost anything and nearly everything without knowing precisely what I'm doing, and I often regret it. We have all learned here from experience."

I had started my odyssey six months earlier looking for the quintessential farm and eager to have an aesthetic experience. At Valley End I had walked into the landscape and felt myself becoming a part of the picture. I had also walked back out of the picture. And now I had Paige Green's beautiful photos of Valley

End and could look at them anytime. I hadn't been looking for more beauty, but I had found it again at Oak Hill. I had found the bright Red Barn, resounding with farm life—and real live locavores. At Oak Hill, I had discovered, culture was back in agriculture, precisely where Wendell Berry wanted it to be.

I was scheduled to fly to London. I had my ticket, and my bags were packed. I knew I had to make the flight. I could not stay, though I wanted to. I was afraid that the farm might not be here when I returned, or that Anne Teller might close the door that had opened and that Oak Hill might not be available to me upon my return. Anne was clearly an eloquent spokesperson for organic farms, and I did not want to let her go, either.

I had gotten a taste of the farm and a sense of the place, and I wanted more. I was greedy and felt like the edgy shoppers who wanted their favorite vegetables this instant, without having to wait. "Can I come back?" I asked. Anne removed her sunglasses, and I could see her eyes for the first time that spring day, the first warm day in weeks. "Come back when the tomatoes are ripe," she said. "When is that?" I fired back. "Mid-July," she said and climbed into her truck and drove off. Mid-July looked far away. I wanted something to hold on to now. I refused to go away empty-handed. I had harvested a great deal of information and stored it away in my head, but I wanted something tangible, too. I returned to the Red Barn and in a kind of frenzy gathered beets, radishes, and chard and brought them to the counter for Gael to add up. "They're on the house," she said. And, reaching for a box of Oak Hill organic raspberries, she said, "Take these home, too. They're in season, and you've got to eat them now."

3

DEPARTURES AND RETURNS

TEA WITH DORIS, TELLY WITH SUE

In London and Leeds I continued my food and farming odyssey, though I also gave a paper about Doris Lessing at the Second International Doris Lessing Conference and visited Doris herself at her flat. On the cusp of ninety, she was still writing — and just then she happened to be writing about farming, no less. "I think it's going to be my last book," she told me. "I don't have the energy anymore. I've written a novel about what would have happened if there had been no World War I. I've made my father an English farmer, which is what he always wanted to be." Later, taking a train from Kings Cross that crossed the lush English countryside, I could see why Doris's father might have wanted to be a farmer. Long after the industrial revolution, urban sprawl, and highways had divided England's green and pleasant land into pieces, it was still gloriously beautiful. It rains here in the summer, so of course Doris's father wouldn't have had to irrigate as much as farmers have to do in California. And in England there are still market towns and villages close to farms, so dairy products and produce don't have to be trucked long distances.

Doris served me tea and biscuits in her kitchen, and later in the afternoon we shared red wine, Cheshire cheese, crackers, and green olives at the café next to the London Review Bookshop. Here we talked about food and farming in California and in Southern Rhodesia, where she was raised. Over the years I have learned a lot about cooking from Doris. She introduced me to her favorite herbs—including tarragon—and taught me how to make chicken with onions and carrots, how to steam vegetables, like broccoli and cauliflower, and how to use the liquid at the bottom of the pot to make soups. She had also always taken pride in the wonderful English flowers she grew in her garden.

While I was in London this time I stayed with Sue Seifert, who lives in Finsbury Park. Most afternoons I ate out, either in that neighborhood or in Haringey. In the windows of the restaurants to which I gravitated, there was usually a sign that said "Halal," which my English friends told me was the Arab equivalent of kosher, though I was sure that might have been debated between Jews and Arabs. The food served at these restaurants— dishes such as roasted chicken with carrots and aubergines—was spicy, colorful, and inexpensive. Smoking had just been outlawed in pubs, so I no longer dreaded bellying up to the bar and ordering a pint. Pub air was cleaner than it had been in a century, and it occurred to me that if the Brits could ban smoking in public, they could ban pesticides and herbicides, too, and make organic a dream come true in this country as well.

At night I cooked for Susan, her daughter, her daughter's boyfriend, and their friends. When I shopped at the Tesco in Finsbury Park—I told myself I was conducting research for my book—I noticed that the global economy was very much in evidence. In the produce section at Tesco there were fruits and vegetables from around the world, including bananas from Costa Rica, limes from Brazil, oranges from South Africa, pomegranates from India, watermelon from Spain, tomatoes from Holland, and assorted fruits and vegetables from as far away as Uganda. But there was also produce from the British Isles. "Local" has made its way here, too. The Tesco spinach was grown in West Sussex by George Gagg; the package had a photo of him, along with a description of his farm "in an area of outstanding natural beauty." The British, too, want to buy beauty along with their produce; and they, too, are beginning to promote their local farmers. These days there are even farmers' markets in Finsbury Park and Harangey.

One afternoon I peered through the window of the halal butcher shop on Stroud Green Road and eyed the goat leg and shoulder. I love goat. When I lived in Mexico, I subsisted on it, along with guacamole, corn tortillas, and salsa verde. But I had never cooked goat myself, and I did not feel up to the culinary challenge that day, either. Instead, having made ratatouille many times, and having recently seen *Ratatouille,* the feature-length cartoon about a rat who becomes a gourmet chef in Paris, I bought the necessary ingredients for that dish: eggplant, onions, tomatoes, garlic, peppers, and zucchini. I cooked them all in olive oil with the oregano I found in Sue's kitchen. Then we turned on the telly and ate while watching prime-time soap operas: *Eastenders* and *Coronation Street.* Some things do not change.

I first lived in Manchester, England, from 1964 to 1967, and since then I have been back again and again. For forty years I have taken part in the revolution in English cooking, diet, and restaurants, and I have watched as English men and women began to eat more foods from former outposts of the empire, as well as foods cooked by their longtime adversaries the French. Fish and chips gave way to coq-au-vin, and steak-and-kidney pie to curries and tagines. I give a great deal of the credit for this culinary revolution to Robert Carrier, the innovative British chef whose cookbook *Great Dishes of the World* I bought in 1967 in paperback and still treasure because of its wide-ranging content and inspiring words. "The history of every nation lies visible on its table," Carrier wrote, adding, "Civilization itself, in fact, is founded upon food."

In the 1960s, when I often visited Leeds to see Professor Arnold Kettle—a dynamic teacher and expert on the English novel—I usually considered myself lucky if I could find a good fish and chips shop. Now I was pleasantly surprised to see Chinese, Italian, and Indian restaurants in the heart of Leeds—and Browns, too, the chain that serves excellent fish and fresh vegetables. Before I flew back to the States, I had the opportunity to visit a tiny vegetable garden in a place where I would not have expected to find one—at the Montem School, where Susan Seifert is the head teacher. "I wanted the students to have a *proper* English garden and to see where vegetables come from—the earth," she said. "We've been planting potatoes, cauliflower, rocket, peas, lettuce, raspberries, apples, and courgettes ever since 2002." On July 4, which is not, of course, a holiday in England, the students, with help from the gardener, harvested the potatoes they had grown; and on July 5 they roasted them with garlic and wolfed them down. After my two-week so-journ, I went home with a sense that California isn't an island unto itself, and that local organic food has a future in England.

SMALL IS STILL BEAUTIFUL

Once I was home again I called Oak Hill and arranged to go there the next day. The farm was still there, of course, alive and well, and the Red Barn was going strong. The tomatoes Anne Teller had described—and that so tempted me—had not come in yet, I learned from Lynn Thomas, who knew as well as any one what was in season. Lynn had worked unhappily at a cor-porate winery and found Oak Hill much more to her liking. She could get up from her desk and walk outside and pick or-ganic raspberries when they were ripe. Now July's crops were beginning to flood the Red Barn, and Lynn told me that Gael had her hands full, so I wanted to feast my eyes on the abun-dance of summer.

On my first visit I had seen Oak Hill's products of late spring—the flowers, a riot of colors, combining greens and or-anges, reds and yellows, artistically displayed at the Red Barn Store. I had also seen the spring produce in all its diverse shapes and in almost all sizes—though small clearly predominated. After all, small is often thought to be more beautiful than large, and on this small farm, nothing was allowed to get too big.

I'm eager to show you the fields at Oak Hill, and I imagine you're eager to see them. But please bear with me. I want to make a few comments about "small," because "small" is a big part of the story. In many ways it's as important as "local" and "organic," and it has a curious history as well as contemporary relevance. At Oak Hill, where almost everyone is a serious reader, E. F. Schumacher's book *Small Is Beautiful* (1973), which popularized the idea of sustainability, is well known. Curiously, or perhaps predictably, a great many young people I meet— members of the so-called Google Generation—have never heard of Schumacher or read *Small Is Beautiful,* though these same people are fond of saying "small is beautiful" as though it were a kind of mantra. Schumacher's ideas have become much more integrated into popular thinking than he or anyone else could have predicted.

Of course, a preference for the small goes back further than Schumacher. Frank Marryat, a European visitor to California in the first half of the nineteenth century, longed for small vegetables because he thought them tastier, and when he found small peas he was ecstatic. In his classic of frontier life, *Mountains and Molehills,* which was first published in 1855, he criticized the gargantuan New World vegetables that he claimed were tasteless. "Vegetables attain an unusual size in California, owning to the rich qualities of the maiden soil," he wrote. "But I have observed an insipidity in everything that has thus matured, and size is attained at the expense of loss of flavor. Onions and tomatoes as large as cheese plates are common. Melons have attained the weight of fifty pounds . . . potatoes reach dimension unheard of elsewhere." Very possibly Marryat exaggerated, as did so many other tellers of frontier tales, including Bret Harte and Mark Twain. Marryat explored Borneo before exploring California, and he had an eye for the exotic. In his view, California was no less fantastic a place than Southeast Asia. Sadly, the notes he made while in the fields and forests of California burned up in a

San Francisco fire, which necessitated his relying on memory to write his book. I took no such chances. I typed my notes on my computer every day and stored them in a safe place.

Today, more than 150 years after Marryat, farmers in California are picking fruits and vegetables before they grow too large, at the point when they have the most flavor. Just by looking, a farmer can tell when it is time to pick. When I went to the Red Barn in July there were baby carrots, baby zucchini, and bite-sized cherry tomatoes, the first of the tomato crop. They were delicious, and they awakened my taste buds.

On this second visit of mine to Oak Hill I wanted to get beyond the Red Barn and see the fields, and walk them, too—get down on the ground, and get dirty, which I knew would inevitably happen. Anne had told me that the man to see about the vegetables was Paul Wirtz, and the man to see about the flowers was Jesús Soto, or "Chuy," as everyone called him. To me, however, he was always Jesús. Each and every one had his or her own bailiwick, and there was a kind of loose hierarchy. Some had more responsibilities than others. Anne, Oak Hill's owner, knew what went on in the fields—she knew the big picture—but she didn't oversee everything day in and day out. E. F. Schumacher, the British economist who believed in decentralization, would have approved. Here was a farm without a CEO or a towering boss, a farm whose operating culture tended toward the democratic, with meetings and discussions that involved everyone. The relative smallness of Oak Hill lent itself to democracy, much as small New England towns did in colonial days and still do today.

The meetings at Oak Hill provided a space for everyone—from Jesús and Miguel to Paul and Anne—to express what was

bothering or troubling them, and these meetings usually miti-
gated the kind of rupture that took place in the middle of the
summer at Sharon Grossi's farm in Capay Valley. I was not there
to see that, though I had seen it coming, and Sharon told me
about it afterward. She had fired Leno, her foreman, and in
protest he wanted the whole crew to leave in solidarity. Another
worker warned Sharon what was afoot. She met the farmworkers just as the sun came up, told them what had happened with
Leno, and persuaded them not to leave with him. Her speedy in-
tervention prevented the walk-off and saved the season for her.

FARM SECRETS

To get to know Oak Hill, I wanted to start with the vegetables.
Fruits were also coming into season, but I craved vegetables—
and this is no exaggeration. So I called Paul and met him one
Sunday at noon at the Red Barn, always both the starting and the
ending place of a day. It was eighty-nine degrees Fahrenheit, and
Paul was expecting an onslaught of what he called "serious heat,"
which could be hard on the "tender crops," especially arugula
and other lettuce greens. Every morning he would turn on the
radio, do push-ups and sit-ups, listen to the weather report, and
prepare to take dramatic action, if necessary. If the temperature
went over one hundred degrees, he would turn the irrigation on
at full blast to cool things down. I took a close look at Paul. I
knew he had to be a farmer: he had dirt under his fingernails
that would not be easily dislodged, and he wore a beard, glasses,
a red T-shirt, and, for protection against the sun, a baseball cap.
The cap he wore that day said "Ocean Spray." It was his favorite

Born in Wisconsin and the son of traditional cranberry farmers, Paul Wirtz stands in a row of crops on a bright spring day at Oak Hill just moments after he has fixed a leaky irrigation pipe—one of his many responsibilities.

because his parents had grown tons of cranberries that they sold to Ocean Spray in Wisconsin, where he was born and raised. (A sister and brother-in-law were continuing the family business there.) Paul owned a dozen or so caps, among them one that bore the green and yellow colors of the Green Bay Packers, Wisconsin's only professional football team; another was from the California company Golden State Lumber.

Metaphorically speaking, too, Paul wore more than one hat; he was a manager of materials and men as well as the man in charge of planting, cultivating, irrigating, and harvesting vegetables. While he had adapted to California and become a Californian, part of him was still attuned to Wisconsin, where his roots ran deep. He was remarkably thin; like the lean carrots he grew, there wasn't an ounce of fat on him.

Paul struck me as quiet-spoken and gentle, but I got the impression that he didn't want me hanging about and asking questions. Certainly he had plenty of work to do, and it could have been no more than that I was a distraction. He suggested that I investigate some of the farms nearby, and he mentioned Bob Cannard's Green String Farm on Adobe Road; an old dairy on Highway 121; a place called "The Patch," near the town of Sonoma; and the strawberry fields on Watmaugh Road. Was he giving me the brush-off?

Maybe so. In the 1970s and 1980s I had written for newspapers and magazines about the cultivation of marijuana, that billion-dollar industry, and about its impact on the economy. At nearly every place I had gone—including chambers of commerce and Ford dealerships—I had been told, "There's no marijuana here. You'll find it up north." Those who told me that were lying through their teeth. I know they were raking in the cash from selling vehicles, tools, and land to the pot growers who paid on the spot with one-hundred-dollar bills.

It's not that I suspected Paul of growing pot. He had too much else on his plate. But I wondered whether he might have another secret that he didn't want me to discover. I believe that every farm has secrets. It's in the nature of a farm to have secrets, much as families inevitably have them. And a family farm would have a surplus of them. That it was a family farm struck me soon after first seeing Oak Hill, even though the place held more than one biological family. When I shared this thought with Paul, he didn't disagree. "It's certainly small enough to be a family farm," he said. "And it feels that way, too." He knew. He'd grown up on the family farm.

Anne Teller has redefined the meaning of the family farm at Oak Hill. She assembled a ragtag group of individuals who would otherwise have remained strangers to one another. At the time I got to know the Oak Hill family, it included a feisty Irishman named Fred Davison, who spoke with a brogue and kept the farm vehicles running smoothly. When I found him repairing the engine of a truck on St. Patrick's Day, he quipped that working was part of his religion. A charming Frenchman named Serge Labesque kept the bees buzzing, though that job, given the global honeybee crisis, was getting harder. The cultural mix of people from all over the world is part of what makes Oak Hill work. Certainly the farm has a style all its own. Gael explained Anne's gentle yet firm way of running Oak Hill. "She urged Paul, Jesús, and me to run our own areas independently of one another and without pushing up against one another. With her support and encouragement we have learned to be self-reliant and autonomous, and at the same time to be cooperative."

In the nineteenth century, crimes on farms—fights over horses, pigs, or water rights—were commonplace, as I knew from reading history. Today, such crimes are infrequent. Today, what a farmer might want to hide isn't necessarily a murder or robbery. It might be any number of things: an undocumented worker, how much water came up from the ground, how much money the farm brought in. It also might be a crop failure, which could be embarrassing and therefore something you might want to conceal. I knew that from my dad's experience, and from my own. Bolted lettuce and wilted bok choy could be shameful. I had tried to grow okra, hadn't succeeded, and had never wanted anyone to know.

On their farm in Wisconsin, Paul's grandparents had raised several crops. His own parents had just one crop—130 acres of cranberries at Elm Lake Cranberry Company—100 percent of which they sold to Ocean Spray, the giant company. Over the years, Elm Lake became more productive, more efficient, and better able to manage resources like water. Paul's sister and brother-in-law took over the business and continue to use chemical fertilizers, but they use fewer of them than Paul's parents did, and they monitor the use carefully and with precision. Paul told me that he favors organic cultivation of crops, but he doesn't berate agribusiness. I was surprised at how tolerant he was of different customs and ways of farming. I thought his background might be the explanation: he had attended the University of Wisconsin, where he graduated with a BA in fine arts, and he had come to California hoping to make a life for himself as an artist. Instead, he had drifted into agriculture, leased a plot of land, started his own business, Paul's Produce, and made a name for himself growing radicchio, frisée, and other winter chicories, as well as fennel and purslane, before any of these greens had come on the market in a big way. He also worked wonders with old standbys like celery. "It was a mindblower how good celery could taste if grown organically," he said. "Celery helped to sell me on organic." Paul was modest, but he'd been a pathfinder in the world of produce.

Paul had absorbed a lot about farming growing up around his parents, who always had a vegetable garden, and his grandparents, but he had known that there was a lot more to learn. So he studied agriculture with Bob Cannard Jr., one of the fathers of modern organic farming in California. Nearly everywhere I've been in California and throughout the country, people who know about food, farming, and the environment praise Cannard. "Oh, Bob Cannard," my friend Liz Henderson said, when I mentioned his name. "He's famous for his agricultural innovations." One Sonoma grape grower called him "a warrior for the earth." Another said, "He's beyond a farmer; he's the Vegetable King." Anne Teller called him "our alter ego," meaning that he was a superhero fighting corporate evils. Paul was less grandiose. "From Bob, I learned to focus on the health of the soil and how to achieve it," he said. "Bob does things I don't do. He intentionally grows weeds alongside his vegetables, and from my point of view weeds slow down crops. I've had disappointing yields with weeds. But Bob says that weeds are the stewards of the land, and it's true that some of the weeds that spring up—nettles and amaranth—provide an accurate indication of whether soil is healthy or sick."

After thirteen years of running Paul's Produce, from 1987 to 2000, Paul was ready for a change, and when the opportunity presented itself to work for Oak Hill, he leapt at it. "I was burning out," he said. "I was growing the vegetables and doing the bookkeeping, too. It was too much for me and would have been too much for any human being. Anne's son Ted hired me. Oak Hill needed work when I arrived." One of the problems was water management. Paul had to tear out parts of the old irrigation system and put in new ones. Today, the big well produces a tremendous amount of water. In the summer months it pumps water for days without stopping or giving out. Soon after Paul arrived, he also ripped out the old perennial plantings and put in more row crops. Flowers had been the focus, and that changed under Paul. For vegetables, he needed more fertile, balanced soil than is needed for flowers alone. He added tons of compost, which he bought from Jepson Prairie Organic in Suison, California, and he grew cover crops, too, and asked Bob Shafer, a local soils consultant, to analyze the soil at Oak Hill. Paul also purchased new equipment for tilling the soil and for seeding and cultivation. At the same time, the farm went through a kind of agricultural revolution that changed nearly everyone and everything. Anne Teller had to put together a work crew and figure out how to pay everyone decent wages, since everyone was working very hard.

"Wow!" was all I could say after Paul had told me his stories. The tasks seemed enormous—and unending. Paul and I had been standing, all this time, under the shade of the eucalyptus and Douglas fir trees in front of the Red Barn. Cars were pulling up; shoppers were getting out, going into the store, and coming out with fruits, vegetables, and bright smiles. But I still had not gotten beyond the signs that said "Private" and "Do Not Enter." I feared that I might have to leave without a glimpse of a field, a tomato plant, or even a tractor. Then Paul suggested that we get in his truck, a 1992 Chevy 350 flatbed, and drive to the ten-acre parcel—land that Oak Hill now leases—where he grew vegetables when he ran Paul's Produce.

So we drove from Sonoma Highway to Madrone, past the vineyards at Valley of the Moon Winery, and on to Arnold Drive. Listening to Paul in the cab of the truck, I realized that he could be poetic as well as practical. Though he had not become an artist in California as he had originally planned, farming provided an avenue for his artistic temperament. "Farming, like painting, is about the creative process," he said, his hands on the steering wheel, his eyes peering through the windshield. "I've done tai chi, too, and from that I've learned mindfulness. To farm successfully you have to be mindful. You have to pay attention to all the details. Tai chi also taught me that what I yearn for is simplicity, but that has proved to be elusive."

Throughout the growing season, Paul writes about the farm in a running column called "From the Fields," which goes out via e-mail to chefs and produce managers at local stores. "Spring plantings are doing great," he wrote in one of the columns I read, and I could hear the enthusiasm in the sentence. He could also be practical: "Today we transplanted our first Purplette & Walla Walla Onions. We're adding Lettuce Mix, Braising Mix & Arugula this week. The Braising Mix is Asian greens—Mizuna, Ruby Streaks, Arugula & Golden Frill—grown up to about 6" & packed neatly in rows."

On the ten-acre parcel, which is flat as a pancake, Paul had planted willow trees to provide shade for summer salad greens. This was bottomland, and the soil was rich. He also makes a potent "tea"—a mix of molasses, powdered fish, earth worm castings, and one or two additional, secret ingredients—that he feeds the plants soon after starting them from seed in the greenhouse, the *casa plástico,* as the Mexicans call it. "You need active microorganisms to break down the nutrients so they get from the soil to the plants," he told me. As we walked through the fields, he explained that most of them were cultivated by machine. The broccoli plants were near the end of their life cycle; it was too hot now for broccoli, which turns yellow and tastes bitter late in the season. Customers don't find it attractive and won't buy it, so it's plowed back under, returned to the soil from whence it had sprung. Waiting in the greenhouse to be planted in its place were celery, Brussels sprouts, cauliflower, leeks, and the last of the tomatoes. The bulk of the tomato crop was already in the ground and maturing in the hot July sun.

Everything I was seeing and hearing and smelling confirmed my first overwhelming sense of kinship with this farm. I was finally ready to pop the big question. I asked Paul if I might work at Oak Hill, and, after pausing a moment, he looked at me and said, "Yes." I didn't know how long I would work or what exactly I might do. I did not need or want to be paid, and I didn't give a thought to health or safety. All I knew was that I had to work at Oak Hill and be a living part of it. It was a part of my destiny. Like fools and lovers, I wanted, with all my being, to rush in.

Paul must have seen and heard my intensity. He explained that it would make sense for me to work at Oak Hill with Miguel and the crew that worked under him. The two brothers, Silvano and Servando Calderon, who tended the fields at the ten-acre parcel, were an odd couple. Though they put in long hours and did the jobs they were required to do, they didn't seem to like one another, and I figured that working around them wouldn't be as pleasant as working with Miguel. I could show up at 6 A.M. and still go to work that week, Paul said. "Six A.M.," I muttered to myself. I think I even gulped. Working at 6 A.M. would mean getting up at 5 A.M. But if I wanted to farm, I would have to adopt farmers' hours. Paul worked twelve to thirteen hours a day, and he'd be doing that all summer long. I knew that

In the foreground, baby tomato plants that will yield tons of tomatoes; in the background, the trees that Paul Wirtz planted to provide protection for crops from the sun in summer, when temperatures can reach 100 degrees.

was beyond me, but I thought I could do a decent day's work. We drove back to Oak Hill and shook hands to seal the deal we'd made, and I went into the Red Barn to shop for supper. I had come back to where I had started two hours earlier.

VOTING AT THE RED BARN

The Wailers, not Marvin Gaye, were blasting on the sound system. Gael was at the cash register, and shoppers were filling their baskets with cherry tomatoes, salad mix, and flowers. I noticed the poster on the wall that featured a woman wrapped in the red, white, and blue of the Stars and Stripes while sowing seeds in a field, along with a quotation from Wendell Berry: "Eating is an agricultural act" and the slogan "Vote for Small Farms and Local Food, Join Slow Food Movement." Obviously the Red Barn also served as a voting place. When I commented on this to Gael, she said, "It's a sanctuary, too." And, between adding up purchases on her machine and chatting with the customers, she told me her story.

"I've crawled my way up the state of California, and every place I have been I have seen crops ripped out of the earth and tract homes put in," she began. "In Orange County I saw the orange groves go, and in Santa Barbara I saw the end of avocados. My grandfather had a dairy, and my great-aunts and great-uncle all had fruit trees and chickens, and then my parents and their generation got into modern life, followed Betty Crocker, and bought margarine because the advertisements said it was better than butter. I went to elementary school in Long Beach, to the University of California at Irvine, and to Australia to lose my virginity and to find myself. I came back here and didn't want to return to Orange County, so I settled in Santa Barbara, where I worked for César Chávez and the United Farm Workers. I took LSD and was introduced to health food stores that smelled of patchouli and wet socks. Six years ago I came to Oak Hill and started to eat vegetables, which I only ate as a kid because I had to, to get dessert. In those days vegetables didn't taste good. At Oak Hill, I remember, I bit into a broccoli spear and it tasted soooo gooood."

Gael was a savvy saleswoman and an adept captain of Oak Hill's flagship, the Red Barn. She's part hippie, part sage, part shopper's guide, handing out recipes and suggesting ways to steam, sauté, and roast vegetables, recommending that kohlrabi be sliced thinly and added, along with sliced beets and carrots, to a salad. Gael accepts credit cards, checks, and IOUs. She kibitzes with customers she knows well. She got into an exchange with a man wearing a T-shirt that said "SPAM" in big, provocative capital letters. To a woman who was getting married, she gave a gift, a bouquet of zinnias. When a woman from Chicago, who was in California on vacation, wanted four baskets of raspberries later in the week to serve at a dinner party, Gael promised to set them aside. There was no anonymity here; shoppers talked about the heat and the price of gas, but they also shared their hopes and dreams, and so did Gael.

She also spoke her mind on all kinds of subjects, including the 1960s and people from that era who now, in the twenty-first century, just want to "think positive thoughts and refuse to be politically active." The "food Nazis" she doesn't care for, and she described herself as a "carnivorous vegetarian"—a contradiction in terms, but Gael isn't bothered by contradictions.

Oak Hill sells cut flowers as well as dried flowers and wreaths. Here, in what's called the upside-down garden, colorful flowers dry hanging from the barn rafters.

When she smiles, her smile is genuine, not merely a smile that the job requires. During a lull in shopping, while no one was in the Red Barn, Gael showed me around: there was a large room to store vegetables and fruits, and a walk-in cooler. "I have kept detailed, accurate records for the last five years," she said. "I know what we sell and what we've been selling. Our 250 customers are our best friends, and they're excellent spies, too. They tell us the cost of basil in Safeway and what garlic is going for at Sonoma Market, and we adjust our prices accordingly."

We went upstairs to the second floor, and then the third, and here flowers were hanging by their roots to dry, and colorful, pungent wreaths hung on the walls. "They call this the upside-down garden," Gael said. "Jesús does the floral designs, and he's a real artist. Everyone here is an artist. My boyfriend, Patrick, is. So am I, and so are Candi and Paul. Oak Hill is a mind-boggling place; art really matters here."

Of course, she was right. Everything about it was artistic. The fields Paul had shown me were aesthetically pleasing, the heirloom tomatoes were art, and the Red Barn, inside and outside, was a work of art. I felt that I would fit in—that I, too, could be creative here, and that Oak Hill would inspire me.

4

FARMWORK, FARMWORKERS

WHISTLE WHILE YOU WORK

In July and August I spent day after day in the fields. All my days were field days, and I felt as though I were on new ground. It was summer, and I did not have to go to my job on campus. I was free to work, and to work for free. I felt I was being handsomely paid in the produce I carried home at the end of each day and in the experience, which was exceedingly valuable to me. I was a fortunate man. I knew that all over California, wanna-be farmers and wanna-be grape growers from faraway cities were paying ranchers and grape growers for the opportunity—and the privilege—to work on their farms, ranches, and vineyards. I did not have fees to pay, and, unlike the field hands, who worked ten-hour days, I was free to come and go as I pleased. Of course they could choose not to work, but then they would not eat. I worked hard for the fun of it. The work was labor-intensive but not backbreaking. We didn't use short-handled hoes, which I knew were killers and had been outlawed. When we cultivated the fields and chopped weeds, which proved to be work I enjoyed, we used long-handled Hula Hoes, which were designed to take backache and muscle strain out of hoeing.

I had worked in construction eight hours a day when I was in my teens, and again in my thirties, when I first came to California, so I knew how onerous physical labor could be if one had to do it to make a living, eight hours a day, five days a week. This work wasn't onerous. At the end of the day, after working in the fields, I felt exhilarated and clean at the core of my being—all toxins removed from my body—though I was covered with dirt. Earth was lodged under my fingernails. I lost weight and enjoyed the feel of a tauter, leaner body. I felt younger and more energetic, and I developed a deeper connection to the earth and a more meaningful sense of place than I had had for years. In the 1950s, when suburbia came to Long Island, I felt displaced. Now, in the Valley of the Moon, I felt reattached to the earth and infused with a new appreciation for the land and the soil. Belonging was uplifting. Oak Hill was good to me, good for my body and good for my soul. I was a new man from the outside in and the inside out. My friends and family noticed the change, too.

About the time I began to work in the fields at Oak Hill, I had gone for a physical exam, and now the lab tests came back with disquieting news. For the first time in my life my blood sugar count was high; my physician warned me that I was pre-diabetic, and he wanted to put me on medication. I didn't want to start down that road and persuaded him to hold off on the prescription drugs. I wanted to see if changing my diet would help. I immediately stopped using sugar. I stopped eating white bread, white rice, pasta made from white flour, and all sugary desserts. No more potatoes, either, though I loved them, and after a short while I found I no longer missed them. I switched to complex carbohydrates and ate more vegetables and fruits than I had ever eaten before. I love bitter greens, and now I ate more of them, not just for supper but also in omelets at breakfast. At the peak of summer I was eating two or three peaches a day, and when pears came into season, I ate them for breakfast, lunch, and supper. Oak Hill's organic produce fit my new regimen perfectly. In four weeks the new diet and working brought my blood sugar count down from 151 to 114. I was out of the danger zone, my doctor told me.

Oak Hill not only brought me better health, it also brought me out of my office and away from my computer, into the open air. I felt focused and in the present, with tasks at hand and the need not to become distracted.

I was not the only one to appreciate the beauty of the place or to feel that physical labor was good for body and soul. Miguel Barrios, the foreman of the crew I worked with, had worked in fields in Mexico and the United States nearly his entire life, and he liked the routine and rhythm of picking vegetables. He said he would not want to trade his line of work for an office or factory job, and I believed him. He whistled while he worked, and he sang songs; he and the other men in the fields also carried on animated conversations in Spanish while they worked. Much of what they said was lost on me. When I lived in Mexico, I knew conversational Spanish quite well, but I had lost much of the language, and I didn't recognize the slang or the technical farming terms they used. But I saw that they laughed a lot and that they

Born in Mexico and now an American citizen, Miguel Barrios runs the crew that tends the vegetable fields at Oak Hill. Though he works longer hours and harder than anyone else, he enjoys every day, delighted not to have to sit and toil in an office.

worked side by side as a team. No one barked orders. Miguel certainly didn't. But he set the pace, and he worked faster and more efficiently than anyone else, so we tried to keep up without competing with one another or becoming sloppy or careless in the fields.

I had long questioned the idea of the happy, contented lot of the farm laborer. After all, many farmworkers had followed

César Chávez and joined the United Farm Workers. They marched, and then, beginning in 1967 and on and off for several decades, they asked consumers to boycott table grapes. Oak Hill has its share of economic inequalities. Not everyone is paid the same wages for the same kind of work. But it is not a factory in the field, not a plantation like some of the farms in the great Central Valley I had seen, with a big white house with pillars and shacks hidden out back. There is a great deal to be happy about if you work in the fields at Oak Hill. You make ten dollars an hour—more than minimum wage—and you have decent housing with hot and cold running water, a shower, and a bathtub. At Valley End, some of the farmworkers live with Sharon Grossi in her home. She doesn't keep them at arm's length. At Star Route, Valley End, and Oak Hill, the men labor in fields that don't have pesticides and dangerous chemicals. Rachel Carson's message has reached them, and they prefer not to jeopardize their health and choose as often as possible to work on organic farms. If there is one major improvement they could use, it would be additional health care. Several farmworkers told me that if César Chávez were alive and organizing in the fields now, he would make health benefits his number one priority.

Born in 1950 in Mexico, Miguel Barrios has worked in agriculture ever since he was a boy on the farm where his family grew beans and corn, the staples of the Mexican diet. His family's farm had no heavy machinery; a team of oxen pulled the plow, and you walked behind it. Miguel had grown up quickly; when he was still a boy his father was struck by lightning and killed instantly. At the age of twenty-one, he came to the United States—to Texas first, then to Southern California, and finally to Oak Hill in 1990. He become an American citizen, though how he passed the test I can't imagine. He speaks barely a word of English.

Miguel's story is common enough; millions of men and women have stories like his. He is one of many, and in many ways he wears a cloak of invisibility—much like the invisibility that Valde and his son, Jesús, took on when they wore their hoods in the fields at Oak Hill. Those hoods seemed emblematic of their status in society and their place in our culture. They are very different from the kinds of clothing that students on campus wear. Unlike farmworkers, undergraduates on my campus— men as well as women—are quick to shed every possible layer and show as much skin as possible. They want to see and to be seen: tattoos, pierced ears, pierced noses, and pierced tongues, bellies, and thighs. So, going from the campus to the farm, I was surprised by the farmworker habit of covering up the body in both summer heat and winter cold. At times I thought they might actually be seeking anonymity, though my friend Uriel assures me that this isn't the case. Mexicans cover up to protect themselves against the sun, he insists, not to hide.

I didn't want to make Miguel and his compatriots into invisible men, and I told myself *not* to think of him or them as "Mexican." I listened to them closely and watched them carefully. In a sense, I took photos of them—but without turning them into picturesque subjects. I saw their individuality, recognized their own unique rhythms of work and speech, and grew to appreciate their grace and beauty in the fields. Miguel Barrios was Miguel Barrios, just as Paul Wirtz was not the "German Catholic Farmer" from the Midwest but Paul Wirtz.

Of course, it was hard not to see Miguel and the crew as Mexican, since Mexico was written all over the way they looked,

Jesús Barrios, who is still a teenager, works alongside his father, Valde, to harvest baby carrots that will be washed, sorted, and sold later the same day to eager customers.

dressed, and spoke. In California, ranchers and farmers often talk about "the Mexicans" who work in the fields as though they were part of a herd and all the same—nameless, faceless, and anonymous. In Sonoma, Anglos talk, too, about the time in the 1970s before "the Mexicans" arrived in large numbers—"the Mexican invasion," some call it—and changed the face of the landscape. Some Sonomans are blatantly racist; they believe that Mexicans are dirty and bring disease. I have heard that comment. They are responsible for the contamination of vegetables—for the scare when *E. coli* contaminated the spinach, for example—because they use the earth as a toilet and don't wash properly. They ought to be allowed to work here, I was told, and then shipped back to Mexico when the job was over. But such views are the exception, I found, not the rule. As Paul pointed out, the workers at Oak Hill are conscious about cleanliness; they know the importance of health and safety in the fields. I followed their example and always washed my hands before sorting vegetables and fruits.

The arrival of large numbers of Mexicans in California in the early 1970s marked a historical tipping point. Without them, agriculture as it now is would not exist in Sonoma and elsewhere in California, for they provide a steady supply of unskilled laborers eager for employment. Because of their illegal status, they are often at a disadvantage vis-à-vis their employers and in no position to bargain for higher pay and better working conditions. Before the early 1970s, much of the agricultural labor was done by white workers, most of them poor, who toiled in the fields and the canneries and traveled with the crops. Some of these white workers were from Oklahoma, but, despite the fact that most of them were not, they were still all called "Okies." They, too, were stereotyped and wore a cloak of invisibility.

Immediately after World War II, only a handful of Mexicans trickled into Sonoma Valley. (How many, it's hard to say, since many entered the country illegally, and no one kept accurate records.) Of course, there were men of Mexican ancestry in Sonoma as early as the nineteenth century, men such as General Maríano Guadalupe Vallejo, one of the most important figures in nineteenth-century California history. Vallejo was a founding father of Sonoma and is to this day a looming presence. His former home, built 1851–1852, is a historical landmark, and parts of his vast ranch and the ranch house now belong to the state of California and are tourist attractions. For decades, he was the wealthiest and most powerful figure in the entire region. Raised in California, where he was born in 1807, he was three years old when Mexico declared independence from Spain in 1810. And he was a teenager a decade later, when Mexico finally won its independence. Vallejo held sway in Sonoma until Yankee rebels seized control of the territory in the notorious Bear Flag Revolt of 1846. Vallejo saw the handwriting on the wall and joined his adversaries, who had taken him prisoner briefly and toppled him from his position of authority. He changed sides quickly and effortlessly, and I wondered if perhaps he'd conspired with the Americans to overthrow Mexican rule. He was a Californio, along with thousands of other Spanish-speaking inhabitants of Alta California, a region onto itself that was annexed by the United States in 1848, following the Mexican-American War. I thought of Vallejo as one of the cultural ancestors of my own California. In a real sense he paved the way for later immigrants who rushed into Sonoma, including Miguel Barrios and the crew at Oak Hill.

I'll leave the last word here to Professor Dan Markwyn, a friend and a scholar of California history, who talks about the controversial general as though he knew him personally. "Vallejo was a tough customer in his youth and an avuncular figure in old age. He was a collaborator and he knew how to cooperate, and he went on recreating himself all his life. Near the end of his days he gave a rousing speech on July 4, 1876, in which you can see he'd become an American patriot."

VINEYARDWORKERSDAUGHTER.COM

To look at her, you wouldn't suspect it, but Vanessa Robledo is the descendant of Mexican farmworkers who worked in orchards and vineyards. She doesn't hide her past; her e-mail address is vineyardworkersdaughter.com. Like her six brothers and her older sister, she is proud of her heritage and her family's roots in the earth. Her great-grandfather Luis came to California in the 1940s as part of the Bracero Program, which was sponsored by the U.S. government to bring men in need of work to farms and ranches in need of inexpensive labor. Luis Robledo and workers like him were indispensable for American industrial farming—and at the same time they were easily disposable; after they finished the jobs they were hired to do, they'd be sent home. Vanessa's father, Reynaldo, settled in Sonoma in 1968, and her mother, María, followed from Mexico soon afterward. María cooked for nearly a dozen men every day, while Reynaldo and his brothers and cousins worked in the fields. They all worked hard. That's what Americans did, they were told, and it was true. Americans even worked on Sundays, when from a Mexican point of view they might have been in church, taking a siesta, or sitting down to a meal with the whole family. This was a strange country, where work seemed to be everything. But the Robledos adapted to America. They made money, bought small parcels of land here and there, and then planted grapes and made wine. Their winery was the first to be owned and operated by descendants of immigrants from Mexico. They became an American success story, and they were also an exception in Sonoma. On the social ladder they were far above the Mexican farmworkers at Oak Hill. But if they could climb out of fields and vineyards, then perhaps other migrant laborers could do the same.

"We make wine as good as people from any country," Vanessa said on a spring morning when I visited the winery. "Mexican fieldworkers walk the vineyards every day, hot or cold, rain or shine. They know everything about grapes; their hands have put this place on the map." To honor their ancestors, the Robledo family made a wine with a label that read "Los Braceros" and showed a picture of a farmworker standing in a field, hands on hips. Mexican president Felipe Calderón traveled to Sonoma to meet the Robledo clan and congratulate them. "I was honored that he came to our winery," María said. "I feel as though I have two countries—Mexico and America. You can't forget what you've left behind and where you've come from, and if it's important to have a sense of pride, it's also important to have a sense of humility and help those less fortunate than you."

María's mole sauce with traditional chilies and chocolate, made in the Michoacán style, is one way she keeps her heritage alive, and everyone in the family loves it. "My mother goes into the kitchen, plays Mexican music, wears a Mexican apron, and goes into a meditative Mexican space when she cooks mole," Vanessa said. The mole recipe was handed down from one generation of women to the next, and each generation added an ingredient to—or subtracted one from—the mix of chilies, cinnamon, cloves, ginger, pimentos, onions, garlic, tomatoes, tomatillos, peppers, and tortillas. María added prunes and used less chocolate than her mother had, and while her mother had ground the ingredients by hand with a metate, María uses an electric blender. "I cook to bring people together," she said. "I'm learning to make food healthier because I don't want my children to be plump." When I asked her to express how she feels about America, she said, "This is a land of opportunity, and we've made the most of them. We've worked hard, and hard work has kept us together. But don't close the book on us; the Robledos are an unfinished story; there are more chapters still to come."

HAVE FELCO—WILL TRAVEL

On the day I first worked at Oak Hill with the Mexican crew, we started at 6 A.M. Outside the Red Barn it was chilly and overcast, and the men wore baseball caps—one said "New York Yankees"—and jackets or hoods that covered heads and faces. One man wore a sweatshirt with a picture of the Virgin of Guadalupe. I barely uttered a word to them, and they barely uttered a word to me, though we nodded to one another, as though to say, "Yes, I see that you exist." That was all. We were on the same footing, that of existing on the face of the earth. The men piled into a battered Toyota truck, and Miguel was about to drive off when I jumped into the bed of the truck and held on tightly. We drove up the hill, past the "Do Not Enter" and "Private" signs. Now for the first time I got a look at the fields behind the barn. The farm felt like an oasis in the stillness of the chill and fog. I liked the bigness around me, and the silence that blanketed the fields.

Miguel parked the truck on the grass at the side of the narrow road. Then he, Valde, Valde's seventeen-year-old son, Jesús, and the other men sharpened their long knives. Before I knew it, they were in the field, bent over, parting the leaves of plants, and harvesting zucchini. I stood there uncomfortably alone for a few moments. Apparently no one was going to tell me what to do or offer any on-the-job training. I was expected to know what to do and get going. Using sign language and a mix of the Spanish I had learned in Mexico over the years, I indicated my need for a knife, and Miguel gave me one. I bent to the work, eager to show that I was no slouch. After all, I was on probation. Paul would want to see whether I could work well with the crew and whether they accepted me. He certainly didn't want an Anglo outsider to disrupt the rhythm of the work. The vegetables had to be harvested. The law of the all-powerful market demanded it. The Red Barn Store required them, and so did the farmers' markets and the restaurants—from Glen Ellen to San Francisco—that receive produce from Oak Hill. I could see the chefs and the cooks waiting for vegetables with knives in hand.

I worked imperfectly that first day. I picked yellow squash that were too small, and zucchini that were too large, and I had my errors pointed out to me. Leave the little ones, Miguel said, scowling. "Mañana," Valde added. Even Jesús got into the act and told me when I made a mistake and picked unripe vegetables. They were the experts, and I was the novice. I took their advice, kept quiet, and worked on, knowing that they were watching and testing me. Or so I felt. After harvesting zucchini, we started on the yellow squash with Felco pruners. Everyone had a pair and wore his in a holster strapped to a belt. I would soon see them everywhere; you couldn't work on a farm without a Felco, and I thought of making a card that said, "Have Felco—Will Travel," an allusion to the TV show in which Paladin, the hero with a six-shooter, handed out cards that said "Have Gun—Will Travel."

That day we harvested fennel and several different varieties of eggplants and squash and placed them, one at a time, in cardboard boxes. It was essential not to bruise a single fruit; any that were bruised were discarded. These were no lowly eggplants. They were radiantly purple and treated like royalty. An unattractive eggplant didn't make it into a box; it was left on the ground to decompose. Next we harvested carrots. There were rows and rows of them. With a pitchfork, Valde gently loosened the earth around the carrots, and then we pulled them up and shook off the dirt; carrots that were bent, crooked, or twisted were left on the ground, but I found it hard to reject crooked carrots. It seemed wasteful. But I learned that customers want perfect or near-perfect carrots, and so I, too, selected only the most beautiful of carrots. *Zanahoria,* Miguel called them, and proceeded to give me a crash course on the names of vegetables in Spanish: *berenjena,* he told me, and *calabaza.* That led to a discussion of food, and I asked him if he ate eggplant. He said no, it wasn't part of his diet. That struck me as odd, not to eat the produce he picks. But eating habits can be hard to change, as I knew from my own experience. As a boy, I had strong likes and dislikes. Of course, I also had friends and family members with strong prejudices who refused to try anything new, whether it was lima beans or chorizo.

We piled the boxed vegetables into the bed of the pickup truck and brought them to the Red Barn. Paul had rigged up an outdoor stand to wash carrots, and after a thorough rinse to remove the dirt, we sorted them into piles of small, medium, and large carrots, which we packaged and stored in the cooler. By this time I must have passed muster, because Miguel cut a peach he'd picked in the orchard and offered me a slice, and when I finished it, he did the same with an apple. Then he invited me to ride in the cab of the truck. Miguel knew I was a writer and a teacher, and he called me *maestro*. When I asked him to call me Jonah, he shook his head and said he wouldn't. *Maestro* was a term of respect, and he wanted to show that he respected me. I called him *maestro del campo*, but that didn't sit well with him, and when I asked him how I might describe him, he said *trabajadero del campo*, a fieldworker.

As we went on with the work, I saw fields with tomatoes and basil covered with thin gauze to protect against pests, and others with celery, broccoli, beans, corn, beets, peppers, kale, chard, melons, radicchio, and garlic. The land sloped gently downhill; there were mini valleys and mini ridges all across the property, and the farm struck me as a patchwork quilt of fields, some with rows going east and west, others with rows going north and south—perhaps in reflection of Paul's carefully organized mind. After all, he said, his ancestors were German, and Germans think linearly. Not every inch of the land was used for agriculture; there were also wooded tracts, streams, ponds, and houses tucked under trees and in the shade. There was a hidden grove of lilac bushes, the apiary, and an old barn with horse stalls and an equestrian history you could smell. Of course the thickly wooded mountain was always there behind us, towering above the farm, a reminder of the wild that had once extended over the entire valley.

An hour or so after we began to pick, I watched Paul when he climbed down from his tractor and went from one valve to the next to turn on the overhead irrigation system—a bit of man-made rain that he said was better for salad greens, beets, and carrots than drip irrigation. Later in the week there was real rain—a freak rain, for it rarely rains in California in the middle of July. It started as a light drizzle. We donned yellow slickers, changed into boots, and moved into the fields to harvest cucumbers and basil, as well as more eggplant, zucchini, yellow squash, and carrots—by now I'd seen enough carrots to last me a lifetime. Then we attacked the torpedo onions, which had been harvested weeks earlier and were still lying on the ground under the oak trees to dry. The drizzle wasn't helping. We cut off the tops, put them in cartons, and took them to the storage room in the barn next to the Red Barn Store, leaving them there next to the garlic piled high in box after box.

By now it was 9 A.M. The sky had darkened, and the rain was coming down heavily, in straight sheets. We took a break to wait out the storm. Valde offered me a *pan dulce,* Miguel offered an ear of corn his wife had steamed, and I felt the rush of sugar in my blood. We listened to Mexican music on the radio, gazed up at the sky, and scraped the mud from our boots. And then, an hour after it had begun, the rain stopped, and the clouds lifted. I saw a patch of blue, then blue stretched from horizon to horizon, and finally the Mayacamas Mountains, hidden that morning, appeared in all their grandeur. It felt good to be there with the crew—working, waiting, watching the rain. I could see how good-natured and patient they were, and I could see the sweetness in their souls. They waited without getting anxious or cursing the heavens above as I might have done.

Now we turned to harvesting green beans in the muddy field, and that was hard labor that made my back, thighs, and knees ache. I had to bend over—we all did—bend down to the ground, even to our knees, in the wet, dark earth, which was as rich as chocolate, then flip the plants over without uprooting them, so that the beans would become visible and we could pull them off, one at a time, and put them in a white bucket that filled oh so slowly. Beans did not come off easily; maybe that's why they were expensive in the Red Barn. I remembered Greg Brown's song "Walking the Beans," in which he complains about picking beans in the field. Beans were backbreaking, but a bucket of beans was real money. Moreover, harvesting beans didn't deter dreams and dreaming. Kneeling close to the ground, and close to one another, we shared our dreams and our hopes. Miguel wanted a new car—a Honda Accord, because it had good gas mileage. Valde wanted to return to Zacatecas—to his own village, his ranch with its horses and cows, and his family. Someone else wanted to own land and grow crops. And I dreamed about writing my book.

Miguel harvested more beans in less time than the rest of us. He didn't seem to have a problem crouching low to the ground on his haunches, pulling beans, and moving on in one continuous motion. The stubborn beans didn't advertise themselves, and they didn't make life easy for us. None of the vegetables did; carrots of course are underground and invisible, though their tops broadcast their whereabouts. Most vegetables hide under leafy canopies; they all have protective coloration, but beans more so than any others. When we finished picking them, the field looked as though a tornado had swept through it and tossed the plants every which way.

I felt as though I'd been tossed about, too. There was more work to be done, but I'd had enough. My knees were shaking. I thanked Miguel and began to walk slowly back to the Red Barn, feeling as though I were walking back to safety.

Some of the men drifted off; Miguel and Valde got down on their hands and knees and began to weed the lettuce by hand. A man passing in a truck slowed and rolled down his window. Did I want a ride? he asked in near-perfect English. All that morning, in and out of the rain, I had noticed him in his bright red jacket as he sat on a tractor mowing weeds. Now I could see that he was wearing a large Catholic cross and a T-shirt that advertised Corona beer. What a combination! I knew this had to be Jesús Soto, the man in charge of flowers and Paul's counterpart: dark, not fair, with a Latin rather than a Germanic temperament, loquacious rather than taciturn. Jesús and Paul were the farm's twin pillars. Granted, Anne Teller created the overarching tone and philosophy of Oak Hill, but she wasn't in the fields working every day. Paul and Jesús were, and if ever any two men exemplified the dignity of labor, they did. Mostly they worked separately, but now and then they worked together, comparing notes and helping one another with problems such as irrigation. Listening to them talk in the shade of the Red Barn made me feel that the "brotherhood of man" wasn't just a hollow slogan but meant something real and tangible.

Unlike Paul, Jesús liked to talk, and he talked freely the day I met him, even boasting—it sounded like a boast—that Mexicans knew more about farming, and were better at it, than most white landowners. Born in 1957 near Las Pilas, in Zacatecas, he'd grown up on a ranch. His grandparents and his parents farmed organically, only they didn't use words like "organic" or "sustainable." In Jesús I met a fieldworker who spoke articulately on the subject of sustainable farming and his personal experience on both sides of the border. "My parents and my grandparents didn't use chemical fertilizers, pesticides, and herbicides; their

A singer, musician, and songwriter as well as farmworker, Jesús Soto was born and raised on a farm in Zacatecas, and he plans to return there. He has worked at Oak Hill for most of his adult life, and he has brought a Mexican perspective on art and culture to his adopted country.

horses provided all the manure that they could use," he said. "They raised corn, beans, and their own vegetables in a small garden. They had cows for milk and cheese, and they never pasteurized their dairy products. They fattened their pigs with corn and used lard to cook, and the cows were grass fed. They had healthy diets, and they got lots of exercise. Most of my ancestors lived to be ninety-five or a hundred years old, and for the most part, they led lives without the kinds of stress that people have here and that kills them.

"When I first arrived in Sonoma I called my grandmother and described what life was like here. She wouldn't believe me. She thought I was making it all up. Maybe the United States *is* unbelievable. The place I come from in Zacatecas is more real to me than anywhere else on earth. I'm going back there to retire on the two hundred acres I own there. It's too materialistic here, and I want to be back where it's wilder and freer, ride horseback, and do the things I didn't get to do as a young man because I came here to work and to make money. Originally I thought I would stay a while, get rich, go back, and start my own business, but it didn't turn out that way."

I wanted to see the wreaths that Jesús made, which are sold in the Red Barn Store and shipped all over the country, especially at Christmas. He led me up the wooden stairs to the top floor where herbs were drying—lavender, oregano, and sage—along with garlic and barley. These are the ingredients he uses for the wreaths, which he makes in a Mexican style that keeps alive the traditions of his parents and grandparents and his own Mexican identity. "I feel more Mexican in the United States than I do in Mexico," he said. "Especially when they point an accusing finger at me. That's when I'm most proud to be a Mexican. If someone harasses me, I say something, even if it's not in the most perfect English."

Jesús's father was another person I learned about who came to Sonoma as part of the Bracero Program before being sent back. (The Bracero Program officially ended in 1964.) Jesús himself arrived in 1979, after crossing the border legally with a visa to work for an American company. Soon after arriving he started dating a woman who taught him English; he taught her Spanish. It was a mutually beneficial arrangement. Jesús soon found his way to Oak Hill, where he worked for Otto Teller as a handyman, and they became friends. Then he went back to Mexico; the second time he entered the United States, he crossed the border illegally. In time he became first a resident and then, in 1996, a citizen of the United States. During this time he continued improving his English skills, and he learned from Otto Teller how important it is to protect the environment. Otto taught him the latest scientific organic farming methods, and Jesús considers himself a convert. "Right now we're at a critical point," he said. "If we don't change the crazy ways that we grow our food, there won't be any food to eat. People will take pills that taste like beans and corn. Maybe not you and I, and maybe not our children, but our grandchildren. I think that's very likely unless we wake up and do something ourselves, because the big monster corporations aren't going to do anything for our benefit. They don't care about the future. All they care about is making money right this minute."

I could hear the passion in Jesús's voice. And then, as though becoming aware of his intensity, he changed his tone of voice and relaxed his facial expression until he looked positively serene. "I've separated from my wife," he told me. "I'm dating a new girlfriend. I'm converting her. When I met her, she said she liked to go to expensive restaurants. 'That's not me,' I told her. I invited her to Oak Hill and showed her around. In the orchard I picked a ripe peach and handed it to her. 'Taste this,' I said and she bit into it and said, 'This is so good!' I said, 'Yes, it's a real peach—this is the way a peach is supposed to taste.'"

WORKER BEES

In addition to Jesús, Miguel, and the other Mexicans who work at Oak Hill, there is another workforce there that is no less important but largely invisible. It is an undocumented, unpaid workforce, and it is mostly unappreciated. It is also an endangered species. I'm talking about Oak Hill's honeybees, of course. There are about three hundred fifty thousand of them, living in sixteen or so colonies on a gentle slope that receives ample morning and afternoon sun and is protected from the wind and the hottest summer heat by a line of trees along the top of the ridge. The honeybees are indispensable to the farm. Without them there would be no pollination, no seeds, no fruits, and no crops to harvest. The bees have snug, comfortable houses made of knotty pine. They are waterproof houses with ventilation and fresh air, and they are pleasing to look at. In spite of the luxury accommodations and the human hands that help them, the bees are wild. They don't respect fences or walls and, unlike humans, don't pay the slightest attention to signs that say "Private Property" and "No Trespassing." In a way, the bees are nature's pure anarchists and utopians, and they are role models of a sort. By following their self-interests, they manage to serve the larger environment of which they are a part. At Oak Hill they find nectar and pollen in the wildflowers that grow on hillsides and in the valley. They buzz busily all over the farm and beyond it in a radius of three miles or so, and they always find their way back home. The honeybees transport pollen from the male to the female parts of the plants, and so they make possible the intense sex life of plants.

The man in charge of the bees—though he himself would not put it that way, as he doesn't like the idea of being in charge of bees—is Serge Labesque, who seemed to me as though he had stepped out of the pages of Pagnol's *My Father's Glory, My Mother's Castle,* which takes place in Provence. Bees and beekeeping are Serge's passion, obsession, hobby, and calling. Without bees, I'm not sure what he would do. He'd have to invent them. "It feels like I have been keeping bees all my life," he told me one warm afternoon when we sat and talked and the bees buzzed all around us. "It also feels like I'm just beginning to learn about them. For years they have been my teachers. They've taught me the importance of diversity and how all the pieces must fit together to form the whole mosaic. I have also learned that the more I know about bees, the more unanswered questions I still have. In the end I often have to say, 'I don't know.' The bees are mysterious insects, and their activities are a big mystery, too. We'll never know all the secrets about them."

Serge came to California from France at the end of the 1970s. He began to keep bees almost by happenstance, and from there he drifted into teaching beekeeping at Santa Rosa Junior College. Here he tells his students that it is important to trust and respect bees, to respect the environment, and to not use toxic chemicals. Serge is the perfect apiarist for Oak Hill. The marriage between him and the farm is one born in a heaven that believes in organic, sustainable, local farming. On the day I met Serge, he wore a straw hat and a white beard, and he moved about the apiary like a bee himself, buzzing here and there. I watched him as he took a hive apart carefully so as not to disturb the bees. I could see he respected them. I watched as he fearlessly removed a single bee from the hive and allowed it to wander along his extended index finger. I had never before seen a bee at such proximity—and without fear, too. Serge explained to me how the furry body is designed and constructed so that pollen and nectar will cling to it. Then the bee took to the air and soared into the blue.

Serge removed the honeycomb from the hive and urged me to poke my finger inside and scoop out some honey. What an invitation! I had never before gotten this close to honey in a hive. I poked my finger beneath the firm surface and there it was: rich, dark honey. I put my finger into my mouth and licked it clean, but a drop landed on the book in which I was writing notes. I scraped it off the page and licked that, too. The honey was sweet and sticky, and it had a taste and an aroma that are unique to Oak Hill. All my life I have loved honey as much as any single food, and this Oak Hill honey was as good as any I had ever tasted. Here was *terroir* at work again. With bees and honey, how bad could life be, I wondered?

But there is trouble in this paradise—not only here but all over the country. Honeybees are in crisis. Whole colonies are collapsing, their numbers dwindling, and that is cause for alarm. No one knows exactly why, but it is clear that bees everywhere are undernourished and overworked, and that the fragile environments in which they exist are increasingly toxic. Oak Hill seemed to be a near-perfect place for bees, since no chemical pesticides are used there, but some of the neighboring ranchers are not as environmentally conscious. Oak Hill's bees could easily pick up a virus next door and bring it back to the colony. Moreover, during 2006–2007 it had not rained nearly enough in the Valley of the Moon, and climate changes were playing havoc with the flora—and thus with the bees. As the ground dries up and flowers wilt and die, pollen and nectar also disappear, and bees are deprived of their essential food supply.

Serge was worried. "If we lost the bees, it would be catastrophic," he said. "Without them, the world would be totally different. Human life itself would not be possible." But he seems to have faith in bees and their innate ability to survive, if only human beings would stop tampering with their environments and using toxic chemicals. "Honeybees are social insects," he added. "They have to live together to make it. They all depend on one another, and each individual works for the common good. They're far more advanced in terms of social living than human beings, and they've been doing what they've been doing exceedingly well for about forty-five million years. They're a very stable species, and they can go on being stable, if only we'd back away and let them do their own thing."

5

WINNOWING WITH WAYNE

ABOVE THE EARTH

By midsummer I felt that I'd been at Oak Hill too long and needed a sense of distance—and a reality check, too. I felt the need to get outside the Oak Hill bubble. So I went up above the earth in a Cessna owned by Bill Pinkus, a pilot and criminal defense lawyer who uses his plane to commute to the venues of his court cases. To really know a place, I feel, you have to fly over it and look down at it, as well as walk it and feel the ground under your feet. As an ex–New Yorker, I still had to get to know California and learn not to regard it as a foreign land or place of exile. With Bill I flew all over the state of California and peered down at mountains and coastline, valleys and ridges. I watched whales migrating south in the Pacific and flew above magnificent Buddhist temples that might have been in Thailand. When we flew over the Valley of the Moon, it was relatively easy to pick out Oak Hill, the green roof of the Red Barn Store, and the mathematically laid-out vineyards, with plants marching up and down the hills. Easy, too, to spot the big mansions at wineries, reminiscent of a feudal society with lords and serfs. Oak Hill was understated by comparison. It wasn't trying to dominate the land, unlike so many of the immense estates with gates, stone walls, and palatial homes. I noticed what looked like a toy tractor moving slowly in the fields. I knew that Paul had to be at the wheel. I saw the vegetable fields, regular and orderly. But what stood out most of all were the flowers: cosmos, zinnias, sunflowers, and amaranth. The reds, greens, purples, oranges, and yellows leapt out at me. From a thousand feet up, the colors looked as if they'd been hand-painted on the face of the earth by an Impressionist artist with a gigantic brush. Later that week, eager for yet another perspective, I walked to the top of Sonoma Mountain. I listened to the sound of the wind in the oak trees, and to the raptors as they cried out, and I peered down at the village of Glen Ellen, nestled below, peaceful and silent, a world unto itself.

A few days after flying above the Valley of the Moon with Bill, I called Sharon Grossi at Valley End and discovered that she'd gone wild with tomatoes; her Mexican crew had planted sixteen different varieties, seventy-five thousand individual plants in all. Sharon was no calmer than the last time I'd seen her. She was "under the gun," she told me, and "in a time crunch." She had fallen behind in the planting schedule, in part because she had two farms to run now and her workers had to split their time between them. In addition to tomatoes, she had planted zucchini, cucumbers, squash, beans, beets, cabbage, parsley, cilantro, onions, chard, and lettuce. She would sell almost all of it wholesale. Sharon wanted both quantity and quality. She wanted her produce to look better than anyone else's. "It's all about appearance," she said. "If your produce is more attractive than Joe Blow's produce, you have a bargaining chip with buyers. But I take one day at a time because it never comes out the way it's supposed to. It all depends on the weather, and right now the fog here is killing us."

I returned to Valley End on a day when the sun shone with a vengeance and the temperature shot up to ninety-two degrees. In the blindingly bright sun the crew harvested onions and garlic, planted tomatoes, and irrigated squash. I talked with Malu and her father, Alberto, who showed me how to weed with the pointed end of the hoe in adobe soil that had baked under the hot sun and was hard to break up. I had arranged with Sharon to work at Valley End from time to time. I wanted to be able to compare and contrast Oak Hill with another farm (after all, I taught college composition), and Valley End suited my purpose. It was much bigger, it was certified organic, and there were fewer crops. There was no one there like Paul or Jesús. But Valley End, too, had its charm.

Malu's husband, Leno, who is Sharon's foreman, was working at the farm in Yolo County, and Malu had taken the reins from him at the Sonoma farm, where she now supervised a small crew of workers that included her own father. No one seemed to mind a woman at the helm. There was work to do and money to be made. That day I helped the crew harvest bok choy, and in the packing shed we washed and packaged it. Then I sorted cherry tomatoes by color—red here, yellow there—rejecting the ones with green streaks and unattractive splotches.

During lunchtime, Malu explained that after crossing the border illegally she had worked for two years as a housecleaner in California, and that she learned English quickly while selling produce at farmers' markets in San Rafael, Sonoma, Petaluma, and Santa Rosa. She now has a Social Security number and a bank account, and she is saving money. Like the men, she gets paid every two weeks. Whether Sharon knows Malu's legal status, I did not inquire. How much she pays her workers seemed a touchy subject, too. I assume that she can't afford to pay them more than she does or she'd go broke, and then no one would make a living.

Nothing seemed to be going according to plan at Valley End that day. The transmission in one of the pickup trucks had blown up, and Sharon wasn't sure where she'd find the money to fix it. She had lost nearly all of the fennel crop. Bugs had infested much of the bok choy, and there wasn't much left to salvage. "I'm pretty broke right now," she said. Her son Clint complained, too. "This is supposed to be the year of the local farmer," he said. "But this local farm is in trouble. Everyone has the same products for sale, prices have dropped from last year, and more people are growing vegetables in their own backyards." I knew that was true all over Northern California. Almost everywhere I turned, friends were cultivating their own gardens to save money and because they enjoyed working the land. Still, it wasn't all bad news for Valley End. Big trucks from San Francisco warehouses—like Earl's Organics—arrived and carted produce back to the city. Sharon reopened her roadside stand and began to offer discounts on the farm's abundant, less-than-perfect melons.

I worked at Valley End for a few weeks. Malu and her father always fed me, and on several occasions they offered me melons, cucumbers, and tomatoes to take home. Cucumbers—with the green skins still on—low-fat yogurt, and a pinch of salt became a staple of my diet. All summer long I also dined on sliced tomatoes with balsamic vinegar, and I felt regal when I feasted on chilled melons for dessert.

WAYNE'S WORLD

At Tierra Vegetables, near the airport where Bill Pinkus housed his plane, I walked the fields with the legendary barefoot farmer Wayne James, who had been featured in the *New York Times*. Almost everywhere I went that summer, friends had insisted that I go to Tierra because it was a spectacular farm and its owners special people. Finally I had taken their suggestion. I just showed up one day and introduced myself, and after that I came back again and again. I met Wayne's sister, Lee, who didn't have a line on her smooth face; his wife, Evie, who ran the roadside stand; and their dog, Willow. Lee made delicious jams; my favorite had strawberries and chipotle chilies.

Wayne struck me from the start as a farmer whom Henry David Thoreau would have liked, not only because Wayne went barefoot everywhere and lived simply but because he had limitless energy and bounded through the fields. Of course, like Thoreau, he also grew wonderful beans. And it seemed as though nothing could daunt him, or his sister, or his wife, though they didn't make much money farming. Wayne was the first farmer I asked point-blank how much money he made farming—I was getting braver—and point-blank he told me.

"When we started out in the 1980s we grossed about seven thousand dollars a year," he said. "Nearly three decades later we're grossing about three hundred thousand dollars a year—that's before taxes, Social Security, health and other insurance. In April 2007 we incorporated and I became the CEO, but I don't get paid a CEO's salary. My net income was about twelve thousand dollars last year. You could work at Jack-in-the-Box and make more money than that. My sister also made twelve thousand dollars last year, but Evie wasn't paid at all. Every year we have to reinvest in the business about 90 percent of what we make, and we try to balance everything. We have regular subscribers who receive a weekly box of produce and who account for about 30 percent of our business. Half of those people pay up front at the start of the year. That helps tremendously in March and April, when we don't sell much at the farm stand, which is all direct cash sales and our most lucrative outlet."

Tierra was an organic farm, but it was not certified organic by the state of California. Like Thoreau, Wayne had an innate suspicion of bureaucrats and governments and wanted to stay as far away from them as possible. "I don't like someone telling me how to farm and charging me money," he said.

On one day when I visited him, he had finished harvesting many of his beans; now he had to winnow them—to separate the edible part from the vegetable matter that would go back into the ground. We passed an afternoon winnowing beans together. Cars zoomed by on River Road, which follows the Russian River to the Pacific Ocean, and customers stopped at the roadside stand. I liked to think that Thoreau might have enjoyed the winnowing and would have joined in the conversation, because he couldn't have kept away from the kind of metaphors that Wayne cultivated along with everything else.

In the 1970s Wayne grew row crops organically in Potter Valley, a rich inland agricultural area in Mendocino County. There he worked with an older farmer, a Quaker who hadn't bought into the agribusiness package. "Of course, organic farming was the norm before the green revolution introduced the chemicals that have depleted our soils," Wayne said. "Organic made a modest comeback in the 1970s. But for the most part it fizzled. There wasn't easy money in it. Some farmers sold directly to restaurants, but a lot of the restaurants went out of business before they paid the farmers what they owed, and so the farmers went out of business, too."

After Potter Valley, Wayne worked in the Peace Corps in Lesotho, trying to persuade a population of wandering tribespeople who relied largely on hunting and gathering to settle down and become farmers, as much of humanity had done thousands of years earlier. I imagined a barefoot Wayne in Africa, but I knew he was more at home in Sonoma. Occasionally he'd look back at his time in Lesotho. "As I saw it, Lesotho needed small, sustainable farms," he told me. "The people who lived there had depleted the environment. They had to have alternatives. Many of them were eager to learn about farming, but it was a challenge to get them to think six months or a year ahead, which is what you have to do to farm successfully. Sometimes I'd be frustrated, but overall it was a worthwhile experience."

In Lesotho, Wayne learned how to work with people and appreciate that people from different cultures do things in different ways. These skills came in handy when he started working with a Mexican crew. Tierra—all seventeen acres of it—perches precariously on the edge of suburbia; a housing development is visible just beyond a concrete wall. When Wayne, Evie, and Lee first

arrived in the year 1980, the soil was depleted; the previous
farmer had harvested crop after crop, year after year, without
putting anything back. This was the same old, sad story of
human abuse of the environment that I heard almost everywhere
I went. Wayne added compost and manure and grew cover crops
until the soil became fertile again. Then he began to plant with a
vengeance—everything from red onions to New Mexico chilies,
castor beans to sweet potatoes, okra to rutabaga, Egyptian flat
beets, which are ugly to look at and an eyesore, to Jerusalem artichokes, which are attractive and grow twelve feet high. On another plot of ground, near where he and Evie made their home
in a splendid nineteenth-century house with a barn, he grew
pumpkins, winter squash, and a whole acre of potatoes. "We
grow everything from asparagus to zucchini," he said, smiling.
He never gets bored. He continually grows new and different
crops—including wheat—just to experiment and for the sake of
learning. In the summer of 2007 he was on the go all day long,
bounding from field to field energetically, almost effortlessly,
and every time I saw him he seemed happy.

"This time of year it gets chaotic," he said. "Thousands of
years ago, when human beings first harvested crops, it was
probably chaotic, too. There are too many things for us to do in
a day, and we can't do all of them. We picked onions this morning, found worms, and lost 50 percent of the crop. They were
in the ground too long, but we just couldn't get to them when
we should have. Years ago, when we were less organized than
we are these days, we used to work 6 A.M. to midnight, seven
days a week. Now it's down to 7 A.M. to 7 P.M., just six days a
week." When he wasn't in the field or winnowing beans, he
was at his computer, taking care of payroll and keeping track

of what he had grown that season and how much he had made from each crop.

On the subject of local produce, Wayne could be eloquent. "When you ship produce from halfway around the world, the quality goes down," he said. "It doesn't look as good, or taste as good, or have the same nutrients. Ninety-five percent of what we sell, we picked that day." On the subject of the U.S. government and big farmers, he was impassioned. "Commercial food is cheap because it's subsidized by Washington, DC," he said. "Eating highly processed food leads to obesity, and that's expensive for the whole society. Someone has to pay the medical costs."

Thoreau would have relished Wayne's attention to detail and his love of the natural world, and he would have loved the white tailed kites that occasionally fly over Wayne's fields; the egrets that arrive because of the lush vegetation that comes with irrigation; and the tree frogs that eat the flies that would otherwise lay their eggs in chard and spinach and devastate the crop. "You can't farm and have zero impact on the environment," he said. "We have altered the wild that was originally here, but we want the wild to be part of the equation." That was Anne Teller's philosophy, too, and Warren Weber's, and Bob Cannard's.

Over the course of the afternoon we winnowed fifty pounds of beans, hardly enough to make growing and selling them for five dollars a pound worthwhile. Wayne handed me a couple of pounds and smiled. He was still in his bare feet. He was the only barefoot farmer I would meet all that summer. "Don't spill the beans," he said as I left. And then of course I did accidentally spill them in the grass outside my barn. I came to understand that collecting spilled beans is nearly as frustrating as gathering spilt milk. I would have to go back and winnow more beans with Wayne.

On the following Sunday I invited Oak Hill's Paul Wirtz and his girlfriend, Candi, for a supper I made by hand, without an electric blender or a Cuisinart. I prepared tomato soup with tomatoes I had picked myself and roasted with basil and olive oil before running them through the Foley food mill I had inherited from my mother's kitchen. I baked a whole chicken with tarragon in the Dutch oven my mother once used, along with red and yellow peppers. And I served Oak Hill corn on the cob. Paul and Candi came with wine, peaches, and melons, and we ate and drank, and watched the day slowly darken. "This was a good idea," Paul said when he and Candi were leaving. "It got us to slow down." I had slowed down, too. It was the first time all summer that I had invited guests for dinner, actually cooked a whole meal, and enjoyed doing it. Work in the fields, whether it was winnowing beans or weeding leeks, had been good for me, and eating at home felt good, too. It's all about balance.

Not long after this supper party, I returned to Tierra along with thirty or so invited guests. This time I wasn't winnowing beans but eating cooked beans, and much more from the farm, as prepared by Eric Tucker, the executive chef at the San Francisco vegetarian restaurant Millennium. A small, inspired crew helped him. Eric is down-to-earth, and he was delighted to be out of the city and at the farm. He made appetizers—these included a black bean and smoked onion torte—and for the main course a delicious ragout from Tierra's beans, along with black chanterelle mushrooms picked in Sonoma County. He also served soft polenta and chipotle-glazed beets from the fields at Tierra, and for dessert there was a pumpkin crostata with white chocolate mousse. Farmers and chefs would seem to be natural allies. But as Wayne pointed out to me, "Chefs and farmers are both very independent types, and it's difficult to get them together." Owners of Sonoma restaurants made much the same observation. In their view, farmers were ornery and standoffish. Wayne and Eric had gone out of their way to make the time and space for an event that joined not only the two of them but also their two different worlds.

Tierra and Millennium were a good pairing, and Tierra's urban fans, who bought fresh produce at the Ferry Building in the city on Saturdays, walked about the farm and met Sonomans. Most of the guests had never met one another. Tierra's produce and Eric's cooking brought us together, and, like everyone else, I went home well fed and more appreciative than ever of vegetarian cooking.

6

BLOOD AND MONEY, WINE AND WATER

DRIVING INTO THE PAST

Candi described Ted Bucklin, Anne Teller's oldest child, who had been in charge of Oak Hill for six years, as the black sheep of the family. Candi admires Ted more than anyone else at Oak Hill, apart from his mother, for his ability to inspire and lead. She is sorry he lives in New Mexico. Was Ted in exile from the family? Is he happy or unhappy to have all those miles between him and Oak Hill, where, as I had found out, no one felt neutral about him? To some he is an unsung hero; to others he is best omitted from the farm's story. To learn more about Ted, I Googled Oak Hill. The radio show *Living on Earth* had broadcast a program entitled "Family Ties" about him and the farm in 2002. Robin White, the host of the program, observed that when Ted started he "knew nothing about running the place" and that he had created a ruckus by firing longtime employees.

On the program, Anne says, "We have made a lot of mistakes. Some of the mistakes we've made together, and some of them we've made in opposition to one another. And I'm sure it's true in any family. You know, blood and money don't always mix." I could understand that she might not want me to dwell on Ted in what I would write. The only national media coverage about her farm had aired the family's dirty laundry. But that story had ended on an upbeat note. "We've really grown as a family," Anne's younger daughter, Kate, says in conclusion. I wondered, though, why, if that were true, Ted wasn't close by. Anne's younger son, Will, lived within walking distance of his mother, growing grapes and making wine. He shopped at the Red Barn for supper, and so did her daughters, Arden and Kate, when they came to visit.

"I don't know if you want me to include Ted in my book," I told Anne. We were sitting in the cab of her Toyota, and she was behind the wheel, wearing her fedora and dark glasses. The bed of the truck was filled with aromatic Gravenstein apples that had just been picked. "Of course you have to write about Ted," she said. "He knows this farm and its personalities as well as anyone. He did a lot of good things during the years he was here: rebuilt our infrastructure, improved the financial picture, and changed the farm from dysfunctional to functional. It was a very difficult time for me personally. The manager of the farm quit without notice. Otto was old and in declining health. He handed everything over to me, and I didn't know what to do. Ted came here to help, and he pulled us out of the crisis we were in. He gave it his all. But some things he did drove me crazy. He had a blustery personality, and he used swear words around the workers. I didn't think that was appropriate. Maybe, too, I regretted giving up my power and just plain wanted it back. We locked horns. Looking back, I can see I made more mistakes than he did."

We had stopped for Anne's dog, Griffey, who now sat in her lap while she drove, and she went on talking. "As you may have noticed, there are several different cultures here: Mexican, American, Irish, and French. There are adamant types and all kinds of personalities. It's not a huge place, but it has many separate segments, which makes it hard to oversee. You can get lost in the details." Then, as though to confirm that she did indeed want me to know all the ins and outs of Oak Hill, she drove around the property, pointing out buildings I had not noticed before, among them her own unpretentious home, which sits near the highest point on the property but does not dominate the land or demand to be noticed.

We parked and went inside the workers' house, where half a dozen men live. A carpenter was redoing the bathroom. The living room held a huge flat-screen TV, several radios, and the inevitable picture of the Virgin of Guadalupe. A picture of a scantily clad Yolanda Pérez—the popular singer of Spanish and Spanglish songs, whose ancestors came from Zacatecas—was taped to the refrigerator door. Inside the refrigerator were a six-pack of Corona, corn tortillas, and cheese. On this side of the property, at the northernmost boundary, stood another barn— the White Barn, which had once housed the fieldworkers and also served as Otto's office and the office of the Sonoma Land Trust. Old oak trees shaded the White Barn, which Anne now rents out for weddings to make extra money. David Lear, one of Anne's sons-in-law and a skilled carpenter, had rebuilt it, and it was beautiful to behold.

Will had married Lizanne Pastore in the White Barn in May 2007—on the house, of course. "It was a fairy-tale wedding," Lizanne said. "We were under the oaks, the buckeye tree was in bloom, and we could hear the creek. I wore a white dress, and Will wore a suit he bought for the occasion, but for the most part it was a no-frills wedding." Born into an Italian-Polish-Irish family in rural Connecticut in the mid-1960s, where she grew up with a mother who loved to cook, Lizanne first came to California as a child, and she returned when she was in high school. It didn't take long before she felt the embrace of the place. "The California seed was planted when I was young," she said. "When I was a teenager, my own stake went into the ground, and I came here after I graduated from college. Marrying Will on the property and living here now feels like coming back full circle to my own rural roots, and getting married on the property helped me feel a sense of belonging."

A physical therapist with a lively business of her own, Lizanne likes to cook when she and Will entertain guests. She keeps olives, sardines, local cheeses, and artisan breads always on hand, and her favorite dish is lamb with herbs and lentils. With Will she goes to wine tastings to educate her palate. Lizanne has also come to appreciate the land. "I never met Otto," she said. "But from what I've heard about him, it seems that Will is following in his footsteps and aiming to be a good steward. 'Deer gotta eat, too,' Otto would say when herds moved through munching on everything in sight, and Will feels much the same about them and their rights."

Anne and Lizanne have more in common than their names. They both came to Oak Hill as outsiders and sank roots down quickly. That summer day with Anne in the cab of her truck,

Anne reminisced about Otto and their courtship. "I raised bees," she said. "Otto hadn't, but he liked them. Bees were an initial connection between us. I remember I said to myself, 'There's a guy who talks my language.'" Anne showed me her fruit trees, naming each one as though they were members of her family: the pears—Bartlett, Basque, Old Comice, Seckel; the apples— Jonathan, Gala, Arkansas Black, Granny Smith, Green Pippin, Red and Golden Delicious; and the plums, prunes, peaches, nectarines, almonds, and cherries. "I have tried everything," she said. "Some things do well here, and some don't. We're in the middle of the flood of fruit now." Like almost everyone else on the farm, I was eating peaches every day: peaches with pancakes; peaches with yogurt; and peaches, hot peppers, and chicken for dinner.

Driving with Anne in her truck, peering through the windshield and listening to her, was like driving into the past, or watching a movie being narrated. That morning I saw how much the farm was a part of her life and, by the same token, how much she was an integral part of the farm. Just as the place had put its stamp on her, so she had put her stamp on it. Anne Teller and Oak Hill seemed inseparable, and listening to her I began to think of the farm as a story as well as a place—a story told by many different narrators and in many different voices. The story was still in the making, still unfinished, and no matter who was narrating, it would always return to the Red Barn, Otto Teller, and the earth itself. In the end everything sprang from that. I felt that I was now part of the story, too, and one of its tellers.

One story I would like to tell is that of the old shed at the far end of the property, the shed with the shovels, rakes, and hoes hanging outside as though on exhibit in an outdoor nursery. It

There's art at almost every turn at Oak Hill—the farm where culture has returned to agriculture.

struck me as finished as a photograph, picture perfect, and at the same time a perfect picture of the old Oak Hill. I wished that Paige Green, my original companion on the quest for the perfect farm, could have been there to take a picture for me. Anne, too, noticed the tools; it was as if she had not seen them before, or perhaps she had forgotten they were there and only now remembered them. The old tools took her into the past again.

"I should like to have seen this place before Otto arrived in the 1950s," she said. "I know that he didn't see it as something to be bought and sold but as a beautiful space to be preserved. Nowadays people like him are a dying breed; a developer would buy this place and turn it into an event center and view it only in financial terms." And then we were back at the Red Barn again. It was 11:20 A.M., and the day was in full swing. It was warm but not unpleasantly hot. Shoppers were arriving and departing with fresh produce that Miguel and the crew had just picked. Anne had a long list of things to do, but she was not entirely done with the past, and the past was not yet done with her. "Otto and I used to go to M. F. K. Fisher's house for dinner in the 1980s," she said as she parked in the shade of an immense Douglas fir. "Her idea of a good meal was champagne and oysters. She was all about seduction, an adorable woman, and liked fun and parties and what we were doing here. I remember that David Bouverie, who owed the property where she built her house, said, 'She can write the greatest prose about the merest of experiences.'"

M. F. K. FISHER'S VALLEY OF THE MOON

In the essay "Nowhere but Here," in which she recounts her life in the Valley of the Moon, Fisher wrote, "I am here because I choose to be." Mary Frances saw herself as an outsider there, but it was her lifelong fate to feel like an outsider of one sort or another, whether she was in France or in California. "I am a kind of female Elijah, fed by the kindly local ravens: fresh vegetables and fruits, all eminently meant for my table, which is seldom bare," she wrote after living in Glen Ellen for a decade. Anne and Otto were among the "local ravens" who brought her fresh

produce. Of course Mary Frances's "here" in the title of her essay reminded her of "there." When she looked out the window
of her Glen Ellen home—which I peered at whenever I went to
Oak Hill—she saw France and Italy, much as when looking out
the windows of her homes in France she had seen California.
Born in Albion, Michigan, she moved to California with her
family when she was still a child, attended the University of
California at Los Angeles, and, beginning in her early twenties,
lived in France with her first husband. For many years, France
was her home, but she never forgot her California identity;
when asked where she was from, she invariably said, "I am
from California." I thought I recognized the impulse behind
that response. When I taught American literature—Melville,
Poe, Dickinson, Kate Chopin, and Faulkner—in Belgium during the Reagan era in the late 1980s, I always said "California"
when asked where I came from, and the answer usually
brought a smile to the face of my interlocutor, despite the fact
that Reagan had been California's governor.

I liked to imagine what Mary Frances might have seen
when she looked out her window: Sonoma Highway and the
oak, madrone, bay, volcanic rock, and stone walls that give
Sonoma and Napa their distinctive look. And what would she
have seen of the valley's social strata, insiders and outsiders, old
money and new? Life in France had given her an appreciation
of social classes and class distinctions, which Americans often
ignore. Sonoma has its share of both haves and have-nots. Ob-
servers of the Sonoma scene told me that the descendants of
Mariano Vallejo and his crowd behaved as though they were
the lords of the valley. Newcomers were sometimes relegated
to the status of serfs.

If Fisher had written about Sonoma, she might have used Anne and Otto Teller for a chapter in that book, and Anne's sons and daughters might have provided grist for her imagination, for she often took facts and reinvented them. I cannot be as bold as she was. I cannot write about "invisible maps," as she called them, or write in her "invisible ink." I aimed to map the Bucklins as I saw them. And while I was still in the process of gathering information, without warning, Ted Bucklin appeared on the scene. He came to help his brother with the grape harvest, and in doing so he inadvertently helped me flesh out my portrait of the Bucklin family. If Anne might be judged by the peach, apple, and pear trees she planted, she might also be judged by her children, who are also children of Sonoma and shaped by its geography and history. Oak Hill coursed through their veins, and they adhered to its rural rhythms and traditions. All of them were engaged in farming, gardening, and protecting the environment—activities that Anne described as "ancillary" to the farm.

BUCKLIN BLOOD

What to make of Ted? He was the tallest of the clan, had excellent command of Spanish, and spoke sweetly, even rapturously, about wine, grapes, and produce. At the same time I thought I heard a tone of bitterness in his voice when I spoke to him—or maybe it was sadness and a sense of loss. "Coming to work here was like stepping into the gates of paradise," he said. "I can remember being in a melon field, picking a fresh cantaloupe, cracking it open, and the aroma filling the air. The melons were an expression of that paradise. I had the best diet ever, and on the table fresh-cut flowers of all colors and shapes. It was an embarrassment of riches. But there was also the downside—the cost in human and financial terms. You can't get far with farming, and I felt hopeless about it, except as a religious or spiritual experience." About his reasons for leaving Oak Hill, he said, "I gave more of myself than I should have—burned myself out for fleeting successes and tepid appreciation. As wonderful as the place may be, some distance feels okay. Sonoma ain't bad, but it's not New Mexico, which speaks to me in a way that even this beautiful farm does not."

Ted has fond memories of his childhood in San Francisco and Sonoma, where he and his siblings gardened, composted, rode horses, cut brush, and "learned the art of country living." After graduating with a BA and an MA in social work, he had a choice—to work in a cubicle or on the farm. He chose the farm, but he found that his social work training hadn't prepared him for farming. "There were whirlpools of trouble," he said. "Communication is a necessary thing to have in a family business, and we didn't have it."

Will, too, savors fond memories of childhood, especially of the animals—turkeys, doves, peacocks, vultures, quail, owls, and a duck named Huey—that he and his siblings raised. He has his own narrative about the farm and the family; from his point of view, the family is "a matriarchy" that began, by his reckoning, with his great-great-great-great-great- (if I counted all the greats correctly) grandmother Josefa Ortiz de Domínguez, who played a leading role in nineteenth-century Mexico as a combatant in the war for independence from Spain. With an ancestor like her, no wonder Anne and her children were so independent.

Will Bucklin, too, marched to his own drummer. After graduating from the University of California at Davis—probably *the* school to attend if you want to learn about grapes and wine—he went to France, where he did an internship at Château Lafite Rothschild. He worked his way up the ladder from cellar rat to accomplished winemaker, and today he is renowned for Zinfandels that sell for about thirty dollars a bottle. They are hard to find because he harvests only about sixty tons of grapes a year—a small drop in the Sonoma grape bucket. Will has carved out a career as a grape grower and winemaker—the *New York Times* has hailed him for his unique cultivation of grapevines—a story in itself. He lives very much in the present, but he still savors his memories of France. "When I was at Rothschild, I figured out innovative ways of doing things, and doing them faster than the French," he said. "I was told to slow down and to do everything the way it had been done. Don't get me wrong. I think the French are great. They're snobs; even the French proletarians are snobs. So am I. In France they told me not to rock the boat, in no uncertain terms. California is just the opposite; it's a rock-the-boat kind of place."

I found Will more amusing than Ted, but Ted could be more poetical. About the environment, Will is steadfast. "I'd like to be greener than grèen," he said. Of his own consumption of wine, he says with a smile, "I drink very locally." Will is a good advertisement for organic and local farming. He lives in a house surrounded by a vineyard that he doesn't spray with chemicals, and he walks the vineyard with his dog, Tanner, several times a day. He knows exactly what's going on with the grapes in the vineyard from day to day. "My eyeballs are out here," he said. "As a winemaker, I'm proud of the fact that I manage the vineyard. A

Will Bucklin, Anne Teller's younger son, with his dog in the vineyard at Old Hill, adjacent to Oak Hill, where he grows grapes.

lot of folks who grow grapes never see the wine, and a lot of winemakers never see the grapes in the vineyard."

WILL'S WINE, KATE'S RIVERS

I still hadn't met Will's and Ted's sisters, Arden and Kate, but the Old Hill grape harvest was about to begin, and I was unwilling to miss it. In fact, I wanted a ringside seat. I had watched grape harvests before. Year after year, I had gone to Iron Horse, where I had eaten sumptuous meals, drunk wonderful Pinot Noirs and Viogniers, and listened to the owners, the Sterlings, talk about *terroir,* which Barry Sterling translated as "soil," though he added that it could also mean "a sense of place." I had also witnessed the harvest at Buena Vista, which was founded in 1857 by Count Agoston Haraszthy, the Hungarian immigrant known as the father of California viticulture. My experience watching the crush at Old Hill was different from those others because here I now knew the *terroir*—the soil, climate, history, traditions, and people—better than I knew the *terroir* in any other vineyard, and *terroirists* were now my heroes. Buena Vista has a thousand or so acres of grapes; Will has only thirty certified organic acres. At his place, small is beautiful, and old is beautiful, too. Old Hill was founded in 1851, six years before Haraszthy planted his first vines, and its oldness is one of the things about Oak Hill that appeals most to me and all the Bucklins.

Half of the grapes Will cultivates are bought by the Ravenswood winery. The other half he uses to make approximately 1,800 cases a year for Bucklin, the company he and his siblings own. "I want the grape pickers to go slowly and to make careful decisions," he told me. "I want them to see a field of individual vines, not a vineyard." It sounded like a good idea; after all, Miguel and his crew saw individual zucchini, melons, and tomatoes when they harvested. They didn't pick unripe fruits and vegetables. Their eyes were educated.

The grape harvest at Old Hill began at 6:30 A.M. Sonoma's entrepreneurial wizard, Phil Coturri, was in charge of the pickers that day, though he didn't act like the boss or give orders. Everyone knew what to do. They were fast and efficient and still managed to have fun. The nineteen men, all but one of them Mexican, dashed into the vineyard at top speed and raced for several hours. When I asked Chris, the one white man, why he was there, he shrugged his shoulders and smiled broadly. "My girlfriend is Mexican, and besides, I love it out here," he said. "It's awesome." The only other white man I met doing fieldwork in the Valley of the Moon that summer was Dustin Gossett, and he, like Chris, does it because he has a passion for agriculture. Dustin did his best to fit in with the Oak Hill crew, but his full beard, straw hat, and second-generation hippie ways made him stand out, and for weeks Paul assigned him to a job picking raspberries by himself—until he demanded to be included in the crew. But Dustin didn't stick around. Young whites don't. Mexicans do.

The Mexican grape pickers at Old Hill Ranch get paid by the ton in equal shares, no matter how much or how fast they pick individually. They were a team, and they wanted to pick as many tons as quickly as possible in the few hours they were scheduled to harvest. At 6:30 A.M. it was cool, and cool was good for hard work. Ted watched from the sidelines. Will nervously paced back and forth. "I think I should have waited," he said moments after the picking began. "I should have dropped more fruit from the vines during the summer than I did. I was greedy." In fact, it turned out that he was picking at precisely the right moment; nearly every year he is anxious about the time to pick, and nearly every year his decision is proven right.

The Old Hill harvest was the speediest and most entertaining I'd ever witnessed. Miguel Santoyo, the foreman of the crew, drank coffee and shouted, "I am coffee man!" When someone said of the nineteen men on the crew, all of them from Zacatecas or Michoacán, "They're all Miguel's children—but from different wives," everyone laughed. Miguel's father, Tiburcio, who wore a white hat, a white shirt, and sunglasses, acted as the majordomo of the operation. You could see him from everywhere in the vineyard; he stood with his back to the tractor, which kept moving, and gazed with seeming indifference at the fields and the men, frequently peering down at the bin as it filled quickly with grapes. He didn't speak a word. He didn't have to. He stood there in a dignified way and provided a moving landmark for the men, who had spread out, covering a large territory. I moved as close to him as I could get, and I saw that his big hands moved rapidly, as though his brain didn't have to tell them to move. He removed grapes he didn't like, and he tossed grape leaves aside, too. They had no business there. The first bin was filled in thirty minutes, and the next in even less time. Tiburcio remained imperturbably at his post.

The men cut the grapes from the vines with sharp knives; the grapes fell into buckets, and when the buckets were full, the men lifted them and balanced them on the tops of their heads. Then they ran, breathing hard, for the tractor that was inching down the rows. Each man emptied his bucket into the big bin, then ran to harvest more grapes. At first the process looked chaotic, but I could see that it was carefully orchestrated. When I commented to Miguel on the speed of the workers, he smiled and said, "These guys like to make money." Now and then the men paused to sharpen their knives, or to drink cold water from paper cups. Occasionally, Will would stop to taste a few grapes, confer with Miguel, or whisper something to Phil Coturri, the ringmaster of this three-ring circus—minus the whip, of course. He didn't need one. The men lashed themselves.

When the harvest was over, Tiburcio smoked a cigarette, inhaling deeply. Miguel approached Will and said, "You happy; I happy." Just by looking at his face, it was hard to know if Will was happy or unhappy, but Ted clearly enjoyed the spectacle of the harvest. He could be rapturous at times. "It's a thing of beauty," he said. "The grapes are voluptuous, and I feel I'm back in the days of Dionysus and Bacchus."

With a forklift, Will loaded the grapes onto a flatbed truck while I watched and talked to the truck driver, Arcadio Santoyo, who also watched and waited. Arcadio, dressed in blue cap, blue shirt, and blue jeans, is both Miguel's uncle and Tiburcio's brother, and he is a success story—a man who owns several houses and has money in the bank. "When we first came to this vineyard it was *muy malo*," he said. "Now it's transformed into a thing of beauty." I asked him one of my standard questions: "How do you feel about chemicals?" But this time I didn't receive a standard answer. "The ground is my mother," he said. "The mother of all of us. Why would I want to kill her with chemicals?" It was one of the best answers I heard from anyone on the subject of growing organically.

Lizanne provided breakfast—coffee, melon, figs, and toast with homemade blackberry jam—and Will, Ted, and I devoured it outside on the cedar table that Will had built. "Can't beat it with a stick," someone said of the jam. We might have emptied the jar, but there was more work to be done. Will and I delivered the grapes to a winery on Eighth Street East in Sonoma, where he leased space and would make his own wine. Here, suddenly, we were in a universe far removed from the vineyard, surrounded by cement floors, stainless steel tanks, and a digital scale. The grapes were carefully unloaded, and then they were weighed. "It's the moment of truth," Will said. He had been hoping for five and a half tons. The scale read 4.4. Oh, well, the look on his face seemed to say. He could live with it.

Women were in charge here, and each had her own precise job description. Janie Mumm, the deputy weight master, who came from Omaha, Nebraska, has become a Sonoman. Michele Herald, the crush supervisor, came from New Zealand, where machines do most of the harvesting. "We're remote and it's hard to get labor," she said. It was time for me to go, and time to hear one last quip from Will to Michele. "Don't forget to add the color concentrate," he said—his idea of a joke.

In the vineyard, that very morning when we were in the midst of the harvest, Will gave me a bottle of Bucklin 2005 Old Hill Ranch Zinfandel. I drank it later with my friend Stacey Tuel, who likes to say that the two things that matter most to her (at the age of twenty-seven) are food and sex. Wine matters to her, too, and so do nature and books. We met at the Underwood Bar & Bistro in Graton, one of our favorite restaurants, owned and operated by Matthew Greenbaum and Sally Skittles. Together they have transformed the town of Graton from the dark, depressing nowheresville it had been for decades into an oasis for good food and drink and lively conversation. They also owned the Willow Wood Market and Café across the road, and it, too, was a destination for foodies. The town had a Mexican restaurant, and the Pinnacle Market, which sold only organic food. At the Underwood, Frank Dice, the jovial bartender, makes the best martinis, and he tells great stories, too, about his college days at Santa Cruz and his gritty life in San Francisco. The food at the Underwood is always exciting, and the wine list intriguing. I never do know how to use the terms that wine writers use, though I have written about wine and wineries for magazines since the 1980s. I did not know what terms to use that night, either, except to say that Will's Zinfandel was amazing. When I tasted it, I relived the experience of the harvest. Memories of the morning at Old Hill improved the wine. (Will told me that when he drinks his wine he, too, relives the harvest.) At the Underwood, Stacey and I shared all the juicy gossip we knew. Then we shared starters: stir-fried Blue Lake beans with cashews and chili flakes; a charcuterie plate with *sopressata* and salami; and a sumptuous Maine lobster and corn cake. The wine and food were a perfect match. A main course was out of the question after these rich and filling starters, but we were able to share two desserts: a chocolate layer cake and a pumpkin bread pudding. Then we walked arm in arm in the warm night air, talking about food and wine. Wendell Berry has said that "eating is an agricultural act," and it felt that way that evening at the Underwood in Graton. Of course, we eat because we must and to survive, but eating is also more than a matter of necessity. We eat for pleasure and for fun, and eating has also been a political act at least since someone said, "Let them eat cake" and someone else shouted, "Peace, bread, and land!" Food and revolution have been inextricably connected in history, and rev-

olutions in eating have been accompanied by revolutions in sex—
in 1789 and in 1968, for example. The Marquis de Sade said, and
Stacey would agree, that "sex is as important as eating or drinking, and we ought to allow the one appetite to be satisfied with as
little restraint or false modesty as the other." Indeed, eating can
also be an erogenous act, as M. F. K. Fisher knew, and as she
wrote about in books such as *Consider the Oyster* and *The Gastro-
nomical Me,* which are now a permanent part of my library.

Sibling rivalries might once have existed among Ted, Will,
Arden, and Kate, and they may at times have failed to communicate clearly with one another. But there's no doubt that they have
learned to collaborate to produce excellent wine. Old Hill Ranch
Zinfandel isn't inexpensive, and it's not easy to find, but it's rich
and complex, and it's true to the place from which it comes.

That's good news, but not all the news that summer was
cause for rejoicing. I heard that Anne's younger daughter,
Kate, had separated from her husband, David Lear, and I felt
the poignancy when Kate suggested that I meet her at the
White Barn at Oak Hill that David had rebuilt. It was David's
barn as much as anyone's at the farm. Yet at first neither of us
said a word about him.

Kate seems to me as much the daughter of her stepfather,
Otto Teller, as of her biological parents. An environmentalist
and student of nature, she followed in Otto's footsteps. Kate
loves fish as a species; she studies them partly because she re-
gards them as serving the same purpose as the canaries in coal
mines that warn of disaster. In the life-and-death sagas of the
fish populations in California, Oregon, and Montana, Kate sees
portents of disaster. She sees rivers heating up and running dry.
She sees wild fish dying off and hatchery fish taking over. She

sees aquifers drying up and water tables going down. And of course she sees global warming. Now and then, while talking, she smiled brightly, but mostly what I heard in her voice was a sense of urgency about the earth. We had better act now or it will be too late to save the planet.

Kate had been spending part of that summer in Montana, on the Bitterroot River that Otto Teller loved, and she had returned to Sonoma with dire tales of serious drought, a brutal heat wave, and "dead and dying fish that were stressed by the heat and just floating downstream." She had fond memories of Otto when he was old and sick and in the hospital. She had brought him a suitcase with his fishing gear, so that he could see it one last time, which brought tears to his eyes. Like her two brothers, Kate had strong opinions and an inclination to express them directly. She, too, expressed pride in her family and its history, and in her mother as a role model. "My mother was thirty years ahead of the time," she said. "She always took personal responsibility for whatever she did. Growing up, my siblings and I always recycled. We always had a vegetable garden, and we were in the wild, too, and that experience changed our lives forever, and for the better. Maybe that's why I worry about urbanites. They think of nature as a scary place with creepy, crawly things. They'd rather go shopping in the mall than go for a walk in the woods. Moreover, they often resort to technological solutions to complex problems. That's a depressing way to fix problems, and it makes me think something is wrong with our whole modern mind-set."

We had been sitting under the oaks. It was time to go inside the White Barn. "My husband remodeled this building," Kate said, finally acknowledging David and his role at Oak Hill. "He ripped out rotten wood, poured new concrete floors, and rewired the place." She pointed: "This was the kitchen. Over there was a bedroom with a dirt floor for the workers, and Otto had his office upstairs." Then we were in the open air again. The fog had lifted, and the morning chill had gone. "You know, when my mother came here, it wasn't just for Otto," Kate said. "She fell in love with this place, too, and its beauty."

THE GAUZE THROUGH WHICH WE SEE THE WORLD

The Bucklins, as I learned in talking to Kate and her siblings, didn't always directly say what they wanted to say. Ironically, they sometimes communicated more than they intended, but, especially where nature was involved, they said what needed to be said. That also proved to be true of Arden Bucklin-Sporer, who lives in San Francisco and works for the school district. Arden—the name suggests the Forest of Arden and the word "garden" with the letter "g" lopped off—started and now nurtures the gardens-in-the-schools program in San Francisco, where kids grow vegetables and fruits and learn to weed and harvest, much as she and her siblings had done in rural Sonoma when they were young. "Arden's life project is a continuation of what we do here at Oak Hill," Anne said. Indeed, Arden brings the best of the farm to the city, to the urban kids who often don't know where vegetables and fruits come from.

Born in the 1960s and raised in San Francisco, and a gardener from an early age, Arden struck me as the perfect citizen to guide the city's gardens-in-the-schools program. She took it from nothing to a patchwork quilt of tiny but fertile agricultural parcels that link communities in a city bulging with ethnic diversity. In the mid-1990s, Arden broke ground for a garden at Alice Fong Yu Elementary School in the Sunset District, where her own inquisitive kids were learning to read, write, add, subtract, and speak Chinese, a required subject at Fong Yu. (When Arden's children attended the school most of the other students were of Chinese origin, but there were also students from Latino, Filipino, African American, and white families.)

When I visited the Alice Fong Yu garden, I saw that the sign outside is in both English and Chinese. "The students garden in Chinese," Arden told me. "They use the Mandarin words for crops like pumpkin and lettuce; they take the words home with them, and they teach their parents about gardening." Did she and the teachers in the schools talk about the importance of the local, I asked. They did not, Arden said. To do so, she felt, would be overtly political and something that would rankle the school board. I thought how strange that the innocuous-sounding word "local" had become so charged, even controversial.

Arden guided me through the garden, pointing out a slug here, chard gone to seed over there, and the aging sunflowers. "No two gardens are the same," she said. "Every garden is its own universe." In this garden, on a hillside once covered with weeds, was an outdoor classroom with bales of hay that served as makeshift seats, a small pond that provided habitat for insects and frogs, a tiny space for native plants, and two holes where kids could dig in the ground. There were also raised beds to grow fruits, vegetables, and herbs, everything from pineapples to radicchio, lavender, and radishes.

"Human beings are hardwired to appreciate growing and harvesting," Arden said. "Deep in us, as a species, and especially in boys, there's the love to dig, and here they can dig to their heart's content. We tell their parents not to send them to school in their best clothes. They have permission to work in muddy soil and get dirty. And they get very dirty here. Even kids who are unhappy in the rest of the school find happiness here in the garden digging and just having quiet time with the earth."

Throughout the school year, the program entails that the teacher responsible for the garden set up a wok and prepare meals with fresh food. "It's amazing what kids will eat when they grow it themselves," Arden said. "They can't get enough kale, garlic, and bok choy. Even my own kids, who were veggiephobes, would sit down and eat the vegetables they grew here."

Arden was ecologically aware and aimed to leave as light a footprint on the planet as possible. On the day I met her at the school, she arrived on a bicycle, wearing sandals, white pants, a blue and green scarf, and sunglasses. She locked her bike to the chain link fence and climbed into the front seat of my Volvo, and after a pit stop for coffee and a scone at Arizmendi's Bakery, we visited one San Francisco neighborhood after another. At the Mission District's César Chávez Elementary School, where Susan Cervantes painted, with lots of community help, a mural of Chávez, farmworkers, and Martin Luther King Jr., the students were growing lavender, basil, amaranth, oregano, and zucchini. In Hunter's Point, at the Willie Brown Academy, named after San Francisco's charismatic former mayor, we meandered through a small apple orchard that bore a sign reading "Pesticide Free Zone." Here there was a new greenhouse and a rich compost pile. Beans wrapped themselves around corn stalks in one field, and berries, grapevines, tomatoes, chard,

squash, peppers, and *mashua*—a root crop from the Andes—
nestled closely together, vying for the warm morning sun. At
Sherman Elementary, the asphalt playground had just been
broken up and removed to make way for both a garden and a
stream. At the entrance to Tule Elk, a preschool, there was a
sign with a quotation from Wallace Stegner, whose work I had
discovered through my mother, who adored *Angle of Repose,*
The Big Rock Candy Mountain, and *The Spectator Bird,* as well as
Stegner himself because he had a vast reservoir of hope about
the West and the possibilities for human growth. The words
on the sign—"Whatever landscape a child is exposed to early on,
that will be the sort of gauze through which he or she will see
all the world"—were too far from the ground for the young
students to see, let alone read. The quotation must have been
aimed at parents and teachers. The words took me back to my
childhood on Long Island, before the coming of suburbia, when
potato farms stretched as far as the eye could see and there were
real woods and lakes and miles of undeveloped property right
on the water. That landscape was the gauze through which I
saw the world. Arden had her own gauze, too, and the Stegner
quotation reminded her of it.

"I have a distinct memory of the dappled light on a creek, the
sun on my back, the heavy, water-soaked legs of my corduroy
overalls," she said. "My brother Ted and I were catching frogs.
We were small—maybe four and five, and we played happily
for hours. Someone must have come for us, fed us dinner, and
put us to bed. But the freedom from parental watchfulness, the
chance to make our own decisions, was marvelous."

Inside the garden at Tule Elk there were gooseberries, corn,
lavender, native plants, and manzanita, the shrub with green

leaves, distinctive red bark, and branches that twist as though shaped by a sculptor. Arden had grown up smelling manzanita, which covers California hillsides and gives the terrain some of its character. "In this garden, kids will grow up smelling manzanita," Arden said. "They'll learn to recognize it and appreciate it their whole lives. That's what Stegner meant, I think, when he talked about landscape and the gauze of childhood."

"It's not the people who make the difference but the place," Anne had said to me that day in her truck. "People just pass through here; the place is the important thing." For the first time in my life I could appreciate that perspective in which place, not people, comes first. Alexandra Bergson, the central figure in Willa Cather's *O Pioneers!*—perhaps *the* great American novel about farming and farms—says much the same thing, and I remembered her words now. "We come and go, but the land is always here," she says. "And the people who love it and understand it are the people who own it—for a little while."

SÍ, SE PUEDE

With Anne's and Willa's words in mind, I returned to César Chávez Elementary School, this time to look more closely at the mural together with Susan Cervantes, the artist who had designed it. For all its realism, the mural, entitled *Sí, Se Puede* (Yes, we can), also includes magic and symbols. And for all its protest, it also proclaims a sense of love and reverence. I saw the distinct, bright colors: reds, blues, oranges, and greens. I saw details: grapevines growing out of the earth; eagles soaring overhead; children marching with Chávez; big teardrops falling to the earth to water the crops; and the banner with the words "You are responsible for yourself, and that's how you become free."

In Susan's mural, Chávez was a visionary with wisdom born of struggle, a secular saint with a halo around his head. Dolores Huerta, too, a cofounder of the United Farm Workers, occupied a prominent place in the mural, and when *Sí, Se Puede* was dedicated in 1995, she appeared at the ceremony. Not surprisingly, it occupied a special place in Huerta's heart—and in Cervantes's, too, though she has painted more than one hundred murals in San Francisco, many of them similarly about farming, farmworkers, and food.

Born in Dallas, Texas, Susan Cervantes began to paint as a teenager; she studied at the San Francisco Art Institute at a time when abstract expressionism was all the rage and art with social commentary was regarded as passé. With Luis Cervantes, her husband, who had grown up in a family of farmworkers, she went to Mexico to see Diego Rivera's murals. In the 1970s she founded Precita Eyes, a community organization in the Mission dedicated to the creation and preservation of murals.

"I like murals because they're art by, for, and about the people," Susan explained that damp afternoon. She wore a beret and carried an umbrella. "I've learned to see that murals are a way for us to reclaim our environment, give voice to the community, and regain a sense of ownership. This isn't really my mural. It belongs to the people. I'm the conductor. I help everyone express their own inner light—the same kind of light that emanated from César Chávez."

7

RUDOLF STEINER AND SONS

TOP SECRET

Except for the family wedding he and Candi attended in Wisconsin one weekend, Paul had not enjoyed a single idle day that summer. He plowed, planted, cultivated, harvested, watered, and seemed able to keep the whole farm and all its many fields in his head, which was overflowing with vital information that summer of abundance. When it was over, he would look back at it and wonder how he could have managed to do it all. The near-constant activity enabled me to appreciate farming and farmers in a new way. Planting doesn't take place only in the spring, and harvesting doesn't take place only in the fall. Both take place all year round, though some times of the year are busier than others. July and August are especially intense because, in addition to the summer crops being harvested, Paul was also planting broccoli, cauliflower, Brussels sprouts, and chard for the winter and spring. In July part of his head was already in March. Jesús's schedule for planting flowers was much the same. In March he planted for June; in November, for February. The farmer needs always to be a step or two ahead of the season at hand.

In addition to keeping records in his head, Paul kept a log of the crops he planted, where and when he planted them, and the yields from each field. He referred to his log in much the same way that a football coach for the Green Bay Packers, his favorite team, might refer to the playbook. On the cover of Paul's black notebook were the words TOP SECRET in big letters—his idea of a joke, though I didn't get it at first. I would spy the book on a table in the packing shed where vegetables were stored, and I didn't dare open it. But eventually I had to look, and I wasn't scolded. Its hundreds of pages went back several years. They detailed an exhaustive agricultural history of the farm and showed that to succeed in this line of work you had to be organized, efficient, and intelligent. Paul translated for me, since much of it was in code: H-1, H-2, H-3, for example, and D-1, D-2, D-3. "H" stood for "horse," he told me, and "D" for "deer." Fields H 1–3 were near the horse barn, while fields D 1–3 were closest to the forest, the home of the deer. There was also the "Chicken Field," which was near the hen house, and the "Arroyo Fields," which were near the stream. Jesús had names for his fields, too—"Pomegranate," "Red Barn," and, after one of the former owners of the property, "Johnson Beds." Paul listed the name of each field, what he had planted there, and how many rows of each crop. He also kept a record of the compost he added to the soil, and about compost he spoke rapturously. From the way he described its texture, color, smell, and weight, you might think compost was the food of the gods. I happened to be at Oak Hill on an afternoon when the compost arrived from Jepson Organics, and the event was treated like a major occasion. Of course, it was.

Nearly everything that is harvested goes into the packing shed on Arnold Drive. From there it goes out to stores and markets. Occasionally a distributor, like Sonoma County Growers Exchange, picks up produce. Nothing stays in the shed for long; turnover is rapid, and the constant ebb and flow of produce depends on the season. There isn't anything fancy or elaborate about the place, and no sign, either, to identify what goes on here. Paul has a cave-like office in the back, where he keeps his essential tools. Here, too, are seeders and spreaders, which he has welded himself. "Welding is essential on a farm," he told me, and, indeed, on every decent-sized farm I found someone who could weld.

There was a walk-in cooler—necessary during hot weather—to keep the most perishable produce: a large room with a cement floor, a low ceiling, and a fan where onions are stored. In the small kitchen, Paul, Miguel, and the crew had lunch: leftover chicken or steak for Paul, and homemade tamales and jalapeños for Miguel and the crew. In the office there was a computer, a fax machine, and several expensive scales to weigh fruit and vegetables. In the shop at the back were wrenches, welders, and all kinds of farm tools. Paul locked the shop whenever he left for the day. The tools were too valuable to lose to thieves. On one wall was an R. Crumb poster of Mr. Natural on a tractor. The tractor had been humanized; it had eyes and teeth and looked lovable. I knew that some farmers felt as close to their tractors as they did to living human beings. At Tierra, Wayne James wore a T-shirt that read "A farmer and his tractor . . . It's a beautiful thing." The farmers I saw on Petaluma Hill Road and elsewhere in Sonoma County certainly spent hours on their machines, going over their fields again and again, enclosed in the noise and in a world that I thought of as tractor heaven. Paul, too, loved tractors, but he loved people far more, and when he found someone who could operate a tractor safely, he relinquished sole responsibility for plowing the fields.

Smack in the middle of the summer Paul nearly had a meltdown. An Oak Hill delivery truck blew a tire, and when he brought the vehicle to a Big O store for repairs, the mechanic took one look at the treads and said that the truck would need four new tires. Paul shook his head and wrote a check. Later the same day the cooler broke, and Paul had to repair it as quickly as he could, for by now it was eighty-eight degrees in the sun, and the produce had to be chilled or it would perish. When I saw him the next day the truck sported new tires and the cooler was running properly at forty-two degrees. The produce had been saved, and Paul was relieved. "I thought I was running out of gas yesterday," he said. "I hate to take it so seriously, but I don't like to lose produce that we've worked so hard to harvest. I also have a work ethic that my father must have drilled into me; I'm always aiming for efficiency."

Paul had a spiritual side, and one hot summer afternoon, when we found ourselves together in the coolness afforded by the packing shed, he allowed himself to unwind and express his deepest feelings about farming. He may have been drawn to German science and efficiency, but he was also drawn to German romanticism and mysticism. No one else was close by that day, and nothing tugged immediately at Paul's elbow or seemed to haunt him. He was entirely present with me over a cup of chai tea that he brewed. It was the kind of interlude I had hoped for ever since I'd met him in the spring, and after that interlude I saw Paul in a new light. That afternoon, I also felt a sense of kinship with him. I had started out by searching for the perfect or near-perfect farm, where I might feel at home, and in the process I had discovered a farmer whom I had grown to like and admire.

"I have a lot of respect for the unknowns of farming—for what's happening in the earth itself, and for the mystery of it," Paul said. "We're often caught up in planting schedules and the science of things, and respect for the unknown can get lost. But then you'll be out in the field, and the moon comes up, and something special happens. It's magical, like when you see the force with which a bean comes out of the ground—ka-boom!—or when a plot of bare ground suddenly becomes a field full of tomatoes.

"I also have selfish reasons for farming. It provides a lot of independence—and a sense of gambling. You use your intuition; you play your hunches; and when you hit it right, it feels good. A farm is a swirling mass of energy; sometimes it can feel like it's spinning out of control, and it can also feel perfectly wonderful."

FARMING THE SPIRIT

If I wanted to learn more about the spiritual side of farming, I ought to read Rudolf Steiner, Paul suggested. It was not the first time I had heard the name, and now I felt that I could no longer brush him or his controversial ideas aside. He was the founder of Waldorf education, which offers innovative ways for children to learn, and teachers, students, and their parents at the Sebastopol Waldorf School described him glowingly. Paul lent me his own copy of Steiner's *Spiritual Foundations for the Renewal of Agriculture,* which was originally published in Germany in 1924 and translated and published in English in 1993 in the edition I took home with me. "Why don't you read this and tell me what you think," Paul said. Back in my kitchen, I cooked and ate, standing up, three ears of freshly picked corn with butter and black pepper and sliced tomatoes with vinegar and DaVero olive oil, cucumbers, and yogurt. With so many vegetables on hand, I'd become a part-time vegetarian. I was eating more slowly than at any other time of my life. I stopped and looked at the ear of corn in my hands. I thought of where it was grown; I remembered the day it was picked, and then I took another bite and chewed slowly. It was delicious.

Then I sat down and read Steiner. Some of his ideas seemed crazy. He recommended, for example, filling a cow horn with manure and burying it in the soil. Then in the spring one was supposed to dig it up, remove the contents of the horn, dilute them in water, and spray the solution over plowed fields. All that for better crops! I was unlikely to adopt that method, and I wasn't sure I would seek out the produce of a farmer who employed such a method. But I enjoyed many of Steiner's ideas. "In nature, and actually throughout the universe, everything is in mutual interaction with everything else," he wrote. Bravo, I thought. I also liked Steiner's love of vegetables; he was a paragon of the Vegetable Man. "We can all describe a beet, and say whether it is hard or easy to slice, what color it is, or whether it has these or those constituents," he wrote. "But with this we are still very far from any understanding of the beet, and even further from any understanding of how the beet interacts with the soil, and with the season when it is ready to harvest." What I admired most about the book was his enjoyment of the company of rural folk and outdoor life, despite his having been a bookish intellectual. Perhaps his fellow Europeans—Freud, Einstein, and Thomas Mann—would have shared his enthusiasm for the agricultural life, but they seem to have been much more comfortable in bourgeois circles, laboratories, and lecture halls than in fields close to the earth. "I have always found what farmers and peasants thought about things much more intelligent than what scientists thought," he wrote. "I would much rather listen to the experiences of people who work directly on the fields, than to all the ahrimanic statistics we get from science."

I knew what Steiner meant. I had similar ideas and feelings. I, too, prefer being with farmers to hearing facts about farming, or even to being with farm advisers. But in the interests of research and scholarship, I knew I had to talk to a farm adviser and see agriculture from that perspective. When I visited Paul Vossen—the farm adviser for Sonoma and Marin—in his Santa Rosa office at the University of California Extension, I found him dry. He sat behind his desk and delivered an uninspired spiel. But he was thorough. Vossen had facts and figures about crops at his fingertips, and he was realistic and practical. He saw it as his job to protect farmers from charlatans, and I couldn't fault him for that. "There are horticultural snake oil salesman," he said. "My job is to expose these people." On occasion Vossen manages to get into the fields. He still grows his own vegetables, and he is enthusiastic about locally grown olives and locally produced olive oils—like DaVero, which is as good as any made in the United States or Italy. But Vossen struck me as a man who has spent too much time inside an office as part of a state institution and not enough time on farms. (Anne Teller, on the other hand, who thinks highly of him, told me that he comes to Oak Hill whenever she needs help with pests or crops.) Vossen himself seemed to feel that he is missing out on the present resurgence of organic farming, small farms, and fresh produce. But it's probably too late for him to leave his office and join the burgeoning movement. Then, too, he sees all the things that can go wrong on a farm, and that's hardly encouraging. "It's the rare individual who can stay a farmer," he cautioned. "And what happens when you're old and can't bend over?"

I had interviewed Vossen's Mendocino County counterpart more than twenty-five years earlier, during the heyday of marijuana cultivation. He had spoken to me only after I promised him anonymity. "We're in a difficult position," he had said. "We're connected with the University of California, and officially we don't encourage people to grow marijuana, but marijuana is a plant, and if a farmer wants advice on pest control or investment of profits, we provide it." That adviser, forever anonymous, delighted me with his candor on the subject of marijuana, and I think he would have delighted Steiner. Then, as now, candor is hard to come by. "Marijuana has revived this whole area," the Mendocino County adviser had said. "The growers are good capitalists. They grow marijuana better than the big corporations will ever be able to, and they do far more than grow marijuana. They raise organic beef, organic turkeys, raise sheep, and weave beautiful things with the wool. At Christmas they come into town with rolls of bills that would choke a horse. The merchants love it." That was the truth of the matter. But almost no one else would come out and say it.

ALICE WATERS'S FARMER

Bob Cannard, Paul Wirtz's teacher and mentor—and the teacher and mentor of hundreds, if not thousands, of California farmers, gardeners, and orchardists—taught agriculture for more than twenty years at Santa Rosa Junior College. "I wouldn't be farming now if it weren't for Bob," Paul said one day. "He was so idealistic. 'Don't be afraid, just do it'—that's the message I heard in his classroom. I grew up with tractors and knew all about machinery. But I didn't know anything about soils until I studied with Bob."

Sonoma is a small town, the Cannards are one of its leading families, and everyone in town knows something about Bob. One day a book will be written about him, and it will probably be as long as Tom Whitworth's biography about Bob's father, in which the senior Cannard says, "I may be a link to the past, but Bob is the link to the future." That biography will draw on conversations with Bob's wife, Carlene, who once cooked at Chez Panisse, Alice Waters herself, Bob's brothers and sons—one of whom farms with him—and many others, too. What I have written here are my immediate observations and impressions about him. I've gathered stories from a variety of sources in Sonoma, among them chefs, farmers, and reporters. Bob isn't exactly secretive, but he isn't out there for all to see, either. For a farmer who's a local celebrity, he's also private.

Cannard had been employed by Santa Rosa Junior College. But no one is less academic or bureaucratic than he. And no one is more legendary in the world of organic farms than he, not only because he lets weeds grow side by side with crops but also because he supplies Alice Waters with mountains of fresh produce for Chez Panisse. Together, Bob and Alice have changed the world of food and farming, where they are a power couple and complement one another superbly: he grows the fresh organic crops; she prepares the delectable dishes and acknowledges small indispensable farmers like him. Chez Panisse is the best imaginable advertisement for California's new aesthetic of organic, local, and fresh, which is being disseminated by an army of mostly young, eager, idealistic men and women who choose to cultivate their fields by hand, without chemicals and pesticides, often with love and devotion, and inspired by the mystical ideas of Rudolf Steiner. And the advertising at Chez Panisse is free.

Born in Pennsylvania in 1953 and raised in Santa Rosa, Bob Cannard is a hard man to pin down; he is always on the go, from sunup to sundown, and when I finally did catch up with him at his home in the hills above the Valley of the Moon, he said that he had twelve agricultural operations going at the same time. How he could be in twelve different places and wear so many different hats, I didn't know, and it made him seem more than human, a superfarmer. I spent an afternoon with him while he repaired the steps in an old turkey shed. He was going to host a party for the extended Chez Panisse family, and because his house, where he had lived since the mid-1970s, wouldn't be big enough, he was preparing additional spaces. To make the turkey shed usable, he needed to install a new sturdy

No farmer could be closer to the ground or more down-to-earth than Sonoma's Bob Cannard, a longtime organic farmer and teacher of agriculture who has supplied Alice Waters at Chez Panisse with fresh vegetables since the 1970s.

flight of stairs for the many feet that would climb them, some possibly unsteady after food and drink. Bob worked the whole time I was there.

I watched while he took apart the old flight of stairs and began to build the new one. After several hours of labor, he had to attend to another job (or perhaps it was pleasure that took him away, though I suspected that he wouldn't readily admit that he takes great pleasure in anything specific or mundane other than the great adventure of life itself). I watched him take measurements, cut wood with his power saw, use a level, drill holes, add screws, and assemble the risers and steps. I did not see the finished product, and one might say that everything with Bob was a work in progress. I sat in the bright sun on a chair he'd set out for me, with his two dogs, Mac and Zoe, close by, and I lobbed pitches into his strike zone, hoping he would hit home runs like the Yankees' Alex Rodriguez, who happened to be hitting home runs fast and furiously that summer.

Bob didn't like to be set up any more than he liked to be pinned down, and he wriggled uncomfortably in his responses to my questions, the expressions on his protean face changing from moment to moment as he smiled, grinned, smirked, frowned, and looked surprised or dubious. I did my best to stroke his ego, but he didn't want to be stroked. Later that week, when I described our encounter to his friends and acquaintances, they all said, "Yup, that's Bob."

Everyone loves Bob Cannard or looks up to him, though he often feels uncomfortable with so much adoration showered on his head. Bee, an energetic Asian woman who sells much of the produce he grows at Green String, the organic farm he co-owns with the winemaker Fred Cline, told me that Bob had far less money than Fred, but that Bob was richer in his heart. He was lovable and ruggedly handsome in a kind of Hollywood way, and he looked as if he might have been a matinee idol and played romantic lead roles, the solitary hero on a farm, maybe—though not on a tractor. Because it turned out that Bob doesn't like tractors. He almost spit when he said the name "John Deere." The only machine he really endorses is the human body, which he said can do anything and everything and is the most renewable of resources on the face of the earth.

Looking back now and rereading my questions and his answers, it strikes me that it is as if we had been on a kind of open-air TV talk show, though surrounded not by cameras or a live audience but just by wind, mountains, and blue sky.

"I'm not a farmer," he had begun, as though to clear up any misconceptions I may have had and despite all evidence to the contrary, including the crops right there in front of my eyes. "I don't work," he continued. "I can't do actual work, which means a repetitive motion for prolonged periods of time. I like to cultivate short attention spans. I grow foods for humans and for nature. Everyone must have lunch—people and the soil. These weeds here improve the soil."

Was the Valley of the Moon special?

"I find beauty in every part of the planet, and don't want to raise one piece of it over the other pieces for fear of perpetuating the injustices of locality," he said. "Sonoma Valley, Sonoma County, Northern California are blessed places, but not as blessed as when the indigenous people lived here."

What about Alice Waters?

"We have a kind of marriage," he said. "We've been at it for in excess of twenty years. We've both grown together, and that's the truth."

How did he feel about Carlo Petrini, the founder of the Slow Food movement?

"We shared a platform together at the Sonoma Community Center, and he struck me as a sincere man trying to forge better conditions," he said.

What about the company of others?

"I like the company of the structure of nature," he said. "I spent many years living alone, and I was perfectly content."

On American farmers: "The farmer in our society is at the bottom of the ladder, below the teacher, nurse, and caregiver in a nursing home."

On ownership and property: "I don't own anything. I don't desire to be encumbered by ownership. I don't own this place or any of the places where I work. Ownership is a manifestation of insecurity, and I do my best not to contribute to that."

About the future he could be as dark, pessimistic, and apocalyptic as Kate Bucklin. "Nature is collapsing, and the planet is depleted," he said. "We're in a global crisis. We created the Sahara and the Gobi deserts, and we'll create a desert in Sonoma County if we're not careful. If we don't change our agricultural practices soon, we won't be able to grow anything, much less grapes. That's the story of America: abuse and degrade the land, and move west, young man. But we are at the end of the continent and have been for a long time."

I don't know if Bob meant to make me feel uncomfortable, but the longer I sat there, the more I felt I had to do something to save the planet. I had been optimistic all summer. I'd had the summer of my life out in the open air, working in the fields with Paul, Jesús, and the crew; eating fresh produce; and listening to Anne Teller's stories and meeting her children. The wine had been good, too. I was intoxicated with the beauty of the Valley of the Moon. And now Bob brought me down to earth, reminding me of the precarious state of humanity. No one I had met that summer was more intense than Bob, and no one had spoken about life from a more deeply seated feeling of urgency. He was as candid as anyone I met in the Valley of the Moon, and he spoke of unpleasant realities, too. I was certain that he would have enjoyed the company of Rudolf Steiner, and that Steiner would have enjoyed his. They struck me as being on the same wavelength: though one was European and the other American, both of them were spokesmen for nature and the natural. Both of them aimed for the harmony and health of the whole planet. "In nature there is no such thing as a pest," Bob said. "Bugs are agents of mercy. Anyone who tells you that farming is unnatural isn't telling the truth. The farming practices that we have inherited from the past were unnatural, but the farming that I do here is nature-friendly farming.

"I'm off," he said abruptly. "Call me on your cell when you want to talk again. The other phone's no good at all." On the way to my car I noticed a big vat containing a thick, gooey mass. "What's that?" I asked. "Fermenting figs," Bob said. "I'm going to add them to the vinegar I'm making." No, sir, Bob Cannard doesn't work, but for a man who doesn't work, he manages to get an awful lot done. I felt I'd just met a modern Hercules who could do half a dozen jobs at the same time and never get tired. He could even get the jobs to do themselves, or so he might tell himself. He struck me as a superlative storyteller and myth-maker.

8

FOLLOW THE VEGETABLES

THE EYE OF THE LAW

By the end of summer I'd been to Oak Hill so often that I began to think my Volvo could get there on its own. Down Petaluma Hill Road, turn left at Crane Canyon, and zoom past Sheila Smith's horse stables, past their locked gates, high walls, pond, old barn, and sleek horses in the pasture. As the car climbed the twisty hill, I gazed at the grapes, at the old abandoned orchards, at yet another old weather-beaten barn, and at the herd of goats bleating in the cold. At the summit I looked down into the valley on the other side, at grapes as far as the eye could see, and beyond them at oak and eucalyptus and Bennett Valley Grange Hall No. 16, where local ranchers and farmers gather. A national fraternal order founded in the 1860s to help farmers get back on their feet after the ravages of the Civil War, the Grange has, over its long history, defended property rights, patriotism, and family values. Grange Halls are scattered about Sonoma, and a new generation aims to bring them into the age of organic farming, locavores, and the Slow Food movement. Here now, on the wide stretch of road, were Matanzas Creek Winery, founded by Sandra and Bill MacIver, the Bennett Valley Fire Station, and a series of small houses. Then came a narrow stretch of shoulderless road that gave one the feeling of driving a gauntlet. Grapes spread out to the right of the road, and a steep hillside with rocks and dry grass rose on the left. At Warm Springs Road the car crossed the bridge, and I admired the new green barn there. From Sonoma Highway I gazed at M. F. K. Fisher's house and admired its stunning picture window, noticed the early-morning hikers in Sonoma Valley Regional Park, and acknowledged the Glen Ellen Fire Station, invaluable in a region where fires are feared as much as drought and flooding.

Now, suddenly, there were not-unfounded fears of another sort. Citizens in the Valley of the Moon worried that men and women on all sorts of jobs would be rounded up and sent back to Mexico. Indeed, authorities often raid businesses and stores in the little towns and cities of the county, arresting and deporting workers who can't produce green cards or genuine identification papers. Rumors of impending raids can spread like wildfire. The government is going to crack down, one man says, and another man repeats what he said, and soon it sounds like the truth. Newspapers announced that employers were required to fire any worker whose Social Security numbers could not be verified, and workers with more than one number would be in trouble. Apparently I had worked that summer with men who fell into those categories. It all seemed nebulous, nefarious, and murky. Kafka would have understood this surreal situation.

At Oak Hill, Anne called an outdoor meeting near the White Barn to apprise the workers of the situation. She had received official letters from the government, she said, but that was about all she said. I looked at them—Jesús, Miguel, Valde, Silvano, Servano, and Juan—and I couldn't tell if they really were as cool, calm, and collected as they seemed or were worried but not showing it. They seemed to wear masks. Surely, I thought, they had been here before; some may have been deported and come back. Paul told them that neither he nor Anne were the police. It wasn't their job to enforce the law or to act as criminal investigators, he said. Later that day, one employer of nearly one hundred Mexican men who harvested grapes for him told me, "If the immigration law were to be enforced here, the whole economy would go belly-up. I think about the situation every day, and I have to consciously stop myself from thinking about it every day, because it makes me crazy. Everyone who comes to work presents me with 'papers.' From my perspective, they're all legal."

When I consulted with my friend Uriel, he wasn't surprised by my news. Local Spanish-language radio stations were broadcasting announcements about immigration raids, he said, and about the businesses that had been hardest hit and the precautions that people might take to avoid arrest and deportation. Los Tigres del Norte, the popular Mexican band, turned headlines about immigration into their songs, and Uriel had a host of stories to tell once again about his experiences.

"We all have movies in our heads about the ways we've crossed the border," he said. "I do. We've all been over the mountains, and across the deserts. When I got here, I worked in the fields, picking prunes and apples. I would do the same work again, but now they would have to pay me a lot more money. If Mexicans weren't here, the California farm would go out of existence, and if Mexicans in California didn't send their money back to Mexico, the Mexican economy would falter." Meanwhile, Mexican workers obviously were here, at Oak Hill and elsewhere, working hard and sending their hard-earned dollars across the border.

To the relief of everyone I knew in California, Charles R. Breyer, a level-headed federal judge in San Francisco, ordered an immediate delay of the Bush administration's law and chastised the Department of Homeland Security, the chief law-enforcement agency that had crafted the new requirements. Homeland Security had failed to provide a sound legal argument for the law about farmworkers' Social Security numbers, Judge Breyer said, and officials hadn't taken into consideration the economic impact on businesses. I don't know if Miguel and the crew read the papers or listened to news on the radio, and I didn't buttonhole them about their legal or illegal status. I wasn't the police, either, but they all seemed less anxious now, and they worked harder than they had worked all summer. There was more work to do, too, more vegetables to pick and bring to market. More mouths to feed, and more demand for organic. The rhythms of the farm in summer sped up, and they were contagious. I certainly worked harder, faster, and at the end of each day, I could look back and say that we'd all accomplished a lot together: we'd planted, hoed, and harvested, and we'd come together as a crew. We were invincible.

LEEKS, ONIONS, AND EL REY DEL ROCK

One day, which at first didn't seem any different from any other day, I felt that the workers regarded me as one of them rather than as a gringo *maestro,* a writer from another world.

But perhaps I was only indulging a personal whim. Perhaps, like Tolstoy's Levin in *Anna Karenina,* and like Tolstoy himself, I romanticized men of the earth; perhaps I was a romantic. But before you judge, here's what happened. It wasn't one single thing all by itself but a series of events building organically one on the next. All that eventful week we had worked like hell from early morning until the end of the day, and we had taken pride in our work. We were on a roll, a roll with an unmistakable rhythm to it; once it caught us up, there was no stopping us. And on the morning we planted six thousand King Richard leeks, we felt like kings ourselves. It was in a field where broccoli had been harvested and that was still so rich and fertile that it didn't need added nutrients. It had been fallow for six weeks, and Paul had prepared it for us with the Kabota tractor.

We walked through the field gently dropping baby leeks that Paul had sprouted in the greenhouse. We dropped them in groups of three every eighteen inches or so, row after row. Then, on hands and knees, we went down each row, digging holes, planting leeks, covering them, and scooting on down the row. I had never worked so fast or accurately. No one had told us to work quickly, but we all did. All I could see was the ground in front of me. No one spoke; there was nothing to say. No one had assigned individual tasks, but each of us assumed a responsibility and took turns doing what had to be done. By now I had also lost a good deal of my self-consciousness and awkwardness. The field was my home now, and I knew instinctively what to do. I loved the earth, and it belonged to me.

There was also something about wearing work gloves that made me feel special. They were made in Santa Rosa, and they cost just two dollars apiece. We went through dozens of them that season. Miguel wore them, and so did everyone else, and putting them on made me feel initiated into a tribe: the tribe of fieldworkers. Even with armor I couldn't have felt more knightly. We planted leeks, washed our hands thoroughly, and then harvested raspberries—*frambuesas*—tossing aside every imperfect berry and stashing boxes in the cooler. Next we took a break and ate corn on the cob steamed in its husks, peeling the husks and biting into the soft kernels. Then we harvested melons. It took me a while before I could tell which ones were ripe just by looking. Miguel knew. Ripe melons have darkened on the outside. We picked and picked, and I kept hoping we'd stop and eat one. At last Miguel took out his knife and cut a melon open. I heard the sharp blade slice through the rind and the fruit. I smelled the ripeness instantly. We stood in the field in the sun and ate one melon after another—devoured them ravenously— and left the rinds there to rot. Then, while we harvested frisée, I broke the silence and began a conversation with Valde, who told me that he made seventy dollars a day and lived rent-free in the workers' house at Oak Hill. Of course he sent most of his money home to his family. In Mexico, doing the same labor, he would have earned only ten dollars a day. This was the first time I connected with Valde, and I felt I had broken a barrier.

Soon after that long day, we spent a day planting cauliflower and cabbage, while kestrels, black birds, and hawks flew overhead in a darkening sky. For the first time I used a wheel hoe, a simple cultivating implement to level the ground—the playing field, as I liked to call it—and Miguel looked at my work and said, "Muy bueno, maestro." It was the first time he had complimented me, and I felt proud. We took a break, and Paul brewed coffee, talking about his boyhood days in Wisconsin, how he hadn't wanted to follow in his father's footsteps, growing cran-berries, and how he became a vegetarian. "I had some conflicts with my dad about using herbicides," he said. "He could see I wasn't going his way. When we go back there, I always bring my parents organic vegetables. My mother likes them and re-spects what I do. Dad just doesn't seem to be impressed with small-scale agriculture that doesn't pay top dollar. His own fa-ther did what I do, and he may feel I'm going backward, not forward. He worries I'll be an old farmer with no money, no future—nothing."

We went into the field again, and Paul climbed into the Ka-bota and plowed some more. The crew, of which I now felt a part, filled up cartons with thousands of onions, and our hands took on the color and aroma of onions. I must have been feeling weary from the toil and repetition, because without being aware of it I let out a loud cry with a musical lilt to it, as though trying to sing. Miguel laughed and said, "Pavarotti." I responded with a broad smile, "No! Elvis!" whereupon Servando chimed in with, "El Rey del Rock." Without thinking, I began to sing, "Love me tender, / Love me true," and everyone stopped packing onions and roared with laugher. What possessed him, I don't know, but Miguel took what was at hand and gave us his best imperson-ation of a woman. He grabbed two onions, placed them on his chest, squeezed them, and at the same time puckered his lips and rolled his eyes. He was perfect. "Guapo," I said, which brought more laughter. Even Dustin Gossett, the hippie wanna-be farmer, laughed, and he, too, became part of the crew that af-ternoon.

The next day I was up at 5 A.M. and arrived at Oak Hill at 6:30 to pick flowers with Jesús, Juan, Horacio, and the other

The farmworkers labor long, arduous days and have to think on the job; they do much of the weighing and packaging of vegetables right in the fields on kitchen scales like this one.

men who made up the crew. Again I had to learn new skills; flowers weren't like vegetables. We cut cosmos, zinnias, and, best of all, sunflowers that towered above our heads; when I walked through them, I felt as if I were in a forest. Juan, who was probably the oldest farmworker at Oak Hill, taught me how to cut each flower individually and how many would make a bunch. What mattered wasn't the numerical count but the feel

Juan Castanon has worked at Oak Hill for decades and loves the beauty and fragrance of the flowers and gathers and handles them with a sense of pride.

of the flowers in your fist. He also taught me to place each bunch in the shade so they would not wilt. The flowers would have to look and smell as though they had just been picked.

Later that morning, I worked side by side with Jesús, who added to my education and explained that there was an Oak Hill method of cutting flowers and that each new recruit needed to learn it. "But we tell everyone that if he has a better way, then he can do it *that* way," he said. And he added, "We have a saying in

Mexico: 'Every master has his own book.'" I replied, "It's an art," and Jesús said, "No, it's a matter of practice. It's a matter of learning to eyeball, learning hand-eye coordination." So I learned to see with my hands and feel with my eyes. Counting didn't matter. The actual number of flowers wasn't crucial. I learned to know what made a bouquet by touch and a sense of beauty beyond calculation. I carried the cut flowers to the truck and laid them down gently. I watched the men as they did the same work I was doing, and I noticed that they were more dignified than I, and more stately, as though they were carrying flowers in a funeral procession. Again I had the feeling of being in a picture; here, again, was an aesthetic experience of the kind I wanted. Diego Rivera, who loved to paint flowers, might have captured these sunflowers in tropical colors on one of his canvases. The dusty old truck now overflowed with flowers. In its new incarnation, it might have served as a hearse on the way to a cemetery. With grace, Horacio took a handful of small, delicate sunflowers and placed them on the windshield of the truck and on the roof of the cab. The dusty old truck was transformed into a thing of beauty. I have rarely seen men so enamored of flowers and so festive about them. One of the men drove the truck slowly through the field, while we silently walked alongside. We brought all the flowers to the Red Barn and placed them in buckets filled with water. Then Horacio and Jesús listed the flowers and their prices on an invoice. This was a totally different kind of work from what we'd done in the fields. Now it was a matter of numbers and dollar signs. Eyeballing, rounding off, and hand-eye coordination had no role now. "I don't like the paperwork," Jesús said. "It's my least favorite thing to do." But paperwork was essential if the farm was to prosper. He knew it, and so he did the work.

THE PARTY GOES ON

The flowers we cut were destined for Oak Hill's store in San Francisco's Ferry Building. I visited the store and met Bob Berman, the manager, who wore a green apron and a beard and took a break from selling to talk to me. He had graduated from the University of California at Berkeley with a degree in English in 1968 or 1969—he wasn't sure exactly when, and after all this time it didn't matter. (As the comedian Robin Williams has said, if you can remember the sixties, you weren't really there.) "We have flowers from March to November, and wreaths all year long," Bob told me. "The Ferry Building was meant to showcase local artisan products and attract local people, but it has gotten away from that. The shoppers here are largely tourists. They're largely unaware of what the words 'organic,' 'local,' and 'sustainable' mean, and we have to explain. It comes with the territory. Green is 'in' this year more than ever before, probably because of Al Gore's movie *An Inconvenient Truth* and Michael Pollan's book *The Omnivore's Dilemma*. Pollan came to Book Passage, which is in the Ferry Building, and his appearance and reading prompted people to buy organic and local."

I felt that I had been down on the farm too long and that, with the end of summer approaching, it was time for a weekend of riotous city living in "Baghdad by the Bay." That's what famed *San Francisco Chronicle* columnist Herb Caen called San Francisco to capture in a phrase the city's mix of exotic, polyglot neighborhoods. But with the United States at war in Baghdad and all across Iraq, and with American troops waging a seemingly endless war against terrorism around the globe, the phrase no longer seemed appropriate.

A member of the crew that picks flowers, which are trucked all year round to the Ferry Building on the Embarcadero in San Francisco, where farmers and rural ways meet city dwellers and urban life.

The country was at war! Or was it? In San Francisco, a city that by and large opposed the war from the beginning, it seemed hard to believe, especially with so much carousing, drinking, and eating with abandon. I recalled that there was an ongoing party in San Francisco during the war in Vietnam, when the city offered rock concerts, drugs of all sorts, and a revolution in sexuality, and the Haight-Ashbury provided a haven for runaway teenagers from around the country. The wild life of the city has come down a notch or two from its 1960s pinnacle. Yet it is still very much a party town full of party animals, including Mayor Gavin Newsom. Are these the last days of the American empire? Is the movement—for it is a movement as much as it is an economic trend—toward the small farm, toward organic, natural, and local, part of a larger rebellion against globalism and globalization? Is it all part of an effort, whether deliberate or not, to move away from the decadence of mall artificiality and a decaying empire? Is the movement toward the local something new? I thought that the answer to all those questions is "Yes," though in the 1960s I had not had an easy time distinguishing the last throes of a death culture from the new cries of a life culture. Today, farm fields, farmers' markets, and the locavore movement look like a real alternative to a dying empire with its mercenaries and global corporations that disdain real food.

After my visit to the Oak Hill store at the Ferry Building, I arranged to meet my brother, Adam, and his family—his Mexican-born wife, Adelina, her sister, Ellie, and their mother, Victoria—as well as my nephew, Ismael, and Katherine, a trusted family friend, at Mamacita, a gourmet Californian-Mexican restaurant in San Francisco's Marina District. We ordered more food than we should have, but we ate it all and enjoyed every bit of it—from the guacamole to the *gorditas de picadillo* and desserts. Victoria loved it because it reminded her of Mexico and because the beans were *perfecto*—perhaps the ultimate compliment from a Mexican woman who has cooked beans all her life. As is true almost every night of the week, at least two-thirds of the produce that went into the dishes that night—like grilled *calabaza,* salmon *enchipotletado,* and *almejas villa*—came from Oak Hill, and the menu spelled out in black letters the farm-to-kitchen connection in descriptions like "Oak

Hill's mixed heirloom tomatoes with queso fresco" and "grilled chipotle-glazed Oak Hill zucchini." Here we could see the country in the city.

The Watergate reporters Bob Woodward and Carl Bernstein followed the money to see where the trail led. I chose to follow the vegetables, and I was pleasantly surprised. Sam Josi, the owner of Mamacita, was one of Oak Hill's biggest fans. Born in 1978, he was also one of the youngest members of the extended Oak Hill family. His grandfather Norman Scott was Anne Teller's third husband, and Norman's death from cancer had been difficult for everyone in the family. Sam knew all about the profitability of the Red Barn Store—"It's the cash cow of the operation," he said. He was as familiar with the farm's debts and credits as he was with his own revenues at Mamacita, and he was about to open an upscale deli, also in the Marina District, that he called the Blue Barn in a tip of the hat to Oak Hill's Red Barn and White Barn. Sam kept a close watch on the number of crops Paul grew, the wreaths Jesús made, and how many ears of corn were sold in the store. He had help from Beth, the bookkeeper, and from Lynn, the office manager, who kept track of orders for fruits and vegetables from restaurants such as Mamacita.

In 2003 Anne Teller commissioned Sam to write a business plan for Oak Hill. Ever since, he has been involved as friend, financial consultant, and purchaser of Oak Hill's farm-fresh produce. I went to him because of the good food at Mamacita, but also because I wanted to know if small, local farms like Oak Hill were or could be profitable. Sam seemed like one of the most reliable, as well as accessible, sources of information on the subject of sustainability. He knew about business and profit and loss.

"If you're writing a book about the realities of small farming, you have to talk about profitability," he said. A graduate of Tufts, where he majored in both banking and international relations, he had worked for years in the volatile field of global finance, living in Lebanon, Spain, and Japan. He had made money—he seemed to have a knack for that—and then he returned to California and enrolled in the Tante Marie Cooking School. He had a knack for food, too. He seemed pleased to be out of banking and in the restaurant business. "There are just as many hours," he said. "But I like what I do a whole lot better." He also felt good about his connection to Oak Hill. "I was coming from a world of order and system to a world of chaos," he said. "At the farm they didn't know what was doing well and what was doing poorly. After I arrived we implemented mechanisms to collect data that I could analyze, and we have been acting accordingly. Lynn Thomas keeps track of everything. I think at first they looked at me as the evil corporate raider and didn't trust me. But over the last year or so, we've worked out a balance. We have rhyme now, as before, and we also have reason."

When I suggested that Oak Hill seemed like a twenty-first-century business, Sam laughed and said that Oak Hill had barely made it into the twentieth century. "The sheer scope of what Oak Hill does is special when you look at industrial farming, where the focus is often on one or two products, like iceberg lettuce or strawberries," he said. "It's counter to the whole homogenization thing, and from a business point of view, the diversity of crops is inefficient. It's not easy to sustain a farm that grows so many different things, but Oak Hill is a thing of beauty. People there are close to each piece of fruit and each vegetable, and that is rare in the twenty-first century."

"Is Oak Hill profitable?" I asked.

"It's true that Anne has long subsidized the farm," he said. "But they're all doing a phenomenal job, and they have achieved profitability—except at the Ferry Building, where the rent is high and sales have not been what we were led to believe they would be. Oak Hill can do it. It's an uphill battle in a good way. Yes, it is profitable."

If Oak Hill was to be the hero of my book, I asked, who might the villain be? "Make modern agriculture the villain," Sam said. "It's an easy villain. Look at the industrialization of the cattle industry! Look at the wealthiest farmers and ranchers in America, who want to expand their profits and don't care about flavor, nutrition, the environment, or anything but making money! Make our whole society, which supports corporate America, the villain. We're going to have to find a different way to consume. We'll need to think about the environment, and our long-term ride on the earth for future generations." Coming from Sam Josi, the global financier turned chef, these words about consumption and the environment meant more to me than if they'd come from a fiery environmental activist or one of the many San Francisco anarchists who denounce corporations and globalization.

On the other side of San Francisco, in the sunny Mission District, Craig Stoll has made a mark for himself by cooking Italian cuisine with California flair at Delfina, the restaurant he owns with his wife, Anne. He is the executive chef and buys much of his produce—including frisée, chicory, arugula, and chard—from Warren Weber, who grumbled to me that he often can't get a table at the restaurant he supplies. To Stoll it's a point of pride to use local produce from small organic outfits like Weber's Star Route and to cook with lamb from Bellwether in Sonoma, which some say tastes like "the Lamb of God." Craig cooks with the freshest of ingredients and uses only those that are in season—though, when it comes to Parmesan cheese, he buys the imported Italian variety. Not until July does he begin to add vine-ripened tomatoes to the menu, because he wants the tastiest locally grown tomatoes, not tomatoes shipped from Mexico or the Central Valley. Though he sometimes hankers for asparagus in September, he waits until early spring, when local asparagus becomes available. He talks like a San Francisco native, but he grew up in the 1970s in Westchester County, just north of New York City. When he was still a boy, his "foodie" parents, as he calls them, took him to Manhattan restaurants at all hours of the day and night, and to Zabar's to shop for cheeses, olives, and herbs. The food bug bit him early, but he didn't have a food "epiphany" until the 1990s, when he lived in Tuscany and worked there in acclaimed restaurants. "I learned that there's a lot to be said for *terroir*," he explained on a quiet Friday afternoon when the kitchen workers were intently shelling fava beans and chopping parsley for that night's dinner. "Northern California has come a long way in terms of produce, but some things just taste better in Italy. Our *terroir* isn't superior to Tuscany's."

In person, Craig doesn't look quite as young as he does in his picture on the Delfina web site, and he isn't as clean-shaven either. Unlike Sam Josi at Mamacita, he does not shout his allegiance to local farms and sustainable farming methods. Nowhere on the Delfina menu did the name of Star Route or any other organic farm that supplies the vegetables appear. "We walk the walk, but we're not on a mission to convert anyone, and we don't feel that we have to talk the talk," he said. However, Craig does influence what farmers grow and how they grow it. Though he does not actually plant seeds in the ground himself, he plants the seeds of ideas in the minds of farmers, and they in turn plant the seeds that take root and produce the kinds of artichokes and chicory, for example, that he wants to serve in his restaurant.

Authenticity is what he aims for, but he isn't a purist about it. "We take classic Italian dishes, like osso buco or risotto milanese, and we tweak them to give them a California touch," he said. "We don't nail it every time, but we do a good job." Indeed, at both his restaurant and his pizzeria next door, I felt—to borrow the line from an old advertisement—that I might close my eyes and think I was eating in Italy. Italian and French tourists to San Francisco have that impression, too. "If they don't have a huge chip on their shoulders, they're blown away by the food," Craig said. "But there are always Europeans who think, 'Hey, this is America and you guys don't have a thing to teach us.'"

To many Europeans, America is the chief culinary culprit in the world—not at all a Jolly Green Giant like the one who converted me to green peas when I was a kid. Europeans like to point out that the United States is the birthplace of the global fast food industry, the specter of which prompted the Italian activist Carlo Petrini to start the Slow Food movement. Slow Food has spread from country to country. It has taken hold across our own nation, too, even in California, the birthplace— in San Bernardino—of McDonald's in the 1940s. More and more, thanks to such chefs as Alice Waters and Craig Stoll and such writers as Eric Schlosser, the author of *Fast Food Nation,* Americans are beginning to regard fast food and agribusiness as the villains in the struggle between corporations and health-conscious consumers.

THE GRAPES OF WRATH REVISITED

In California, agribusiness has been cast as the bad guy almost as long as there has been agriculture in the state, but especially since 1939, near the height of the Depression, when millions were out of work and hungry. It was also the year when scientists discovered that DDT was effective as a pesticide. That same ominous year, two books about agriculture appeared on the scene and became classics almost overnight. In *Factories in the Field,* Carey McWilliams went so far as to denounce "the rise of farm fascism," as he called it, in California. Basing his opinions on his own observations of the horrendous labor conditions in the San Joaquin Valley in 1935 and on extensive library research, he called for the abolition of "the wasteful, vicious, undemocratic and thoroughly antisocial system of agricultural ownership in California." He even argued for "the substitution of collective agriculture." Remember this was a time when, if Americans looked abroad, they saw the imminent threat of fascism in Germany and Italy. To such liberals as McWilliams, the Soviet Union's collective agriculture looked like it might be the dawning of a new day for humanity.

In *The Grapes of Wrath,* John Steinbeck depicted much the same social problems. In several chapters, which read more like meditations on history and economics than plot- and character-driven narrative, he stepped out of his role as omnipotent author and addressed his audience directly to describe the dire picture. He saw clearly what had happened to farming in California: "The businessmen had the farms, and the farms grew larger, but there were fewer of them." And he saw what would increasingly happen. He was prescient. The corporate trend toward monoculture that he observed in the 1930s continued all through the twentieth century. "They raise one thing—cotton, say, or peaches or lettuce," one of Steinbeck's characters observes of the farms he has seen. Elsewhere in *The Grapes of Wrath,* Steinbeck invited readers to "taste the wine" and to notice that it had "no grape flavor at all, just sulfur and tannic acid and alcohol." What had happened to the grapes and the wine happened to every other crop grown with chemicals and machinery on immense farms where the mentality that prevailed was, if not fascist, then certainly feudal.

I wasn't sure what McWilliams and Steinbeck would have made of Oak Hill or the other organic farms I visited. While neither cared for pesticides and herbicides, the word "organic" wasn't part of their vocabulary, and "small" and "sustainable" weren't readily available concepts at the time. McWilliams and Steinbeck both saw big, implacable forces driving people, and, being products of the Depression and the Roosevelt era, they looked to government for a solution to problems. If they could have returned to California and revisited the places they had known in the 1930s, they would have shaken their heads disapprovingly. The problems they depicted have not vanished. My Sonoma County neighbor and former colleague Gerald Haslam—who was born in Oildale and raised in Bakersfield, and who knows as much as anyone about the history and economics of the Great Central Valley—sees much the same disregard for the land and those who work it that Carey McWilliams and Steinbeck had seen. All that year that I worked in the fields, I visited Haslam to talk about labor and economics. He reminded me that agribusiness still holds sway and still runs roughshod over people. Even big corporate farms that switched to organic, because organic is profitable, can be brutal taskmasters.

The many books that have been written about food and agriculture in the past seventy-five years would surprise McWilliams and Steinbeck. Neither one of them wrote much about meals, cooking, or eating. There's nothing about the diet of farmworkers in *Factories in the Field*. Steinbeck's novel is in part about hunger, but it's the absence, not the presence, of food that's noticeable about *The Grapes of Wrath*. The single most important food in the novel is the breast milk—and the metaphorical milk of human kindness—that Rose of Sharon feeds the dying man, in a passage that shocked many readers. Puritans might still be offended today. Now and then the members of the Joad family—Ma, Pa, Tom, and Rose—sit down to a meal of pork, potatoes, and biscuits, but their meals are few and far between. Steinbeck does, however, describe in remarkable detail, and with great prescience, the processed industrial lunch that an Oklahoma tractor driver eats: "white bread, pickle, cheese, Spam, a piece of pie branded like an engine part." It's a vivid and telling detail, and the image of a branded slice of pie evokes something off the assembly line—like a Henry Ford automobile.

ALWAYS ON TOP OF THE BOTTOM LINE

Organic, it seemed to me, after nearly a year as a farm reporter and sometime farmworker, would clearly grow one way or another, either on a big, industrial farm or on a small farm with intensive labor. Statistics from California Certified Organic Farmers, the organization that monitors changes in the field, show that certified organic acreage in the state increased from 170,071 acres in 2004 to 218,322 acres in 2005 and 351,887 acres in 2006; there were significant increases in Sonoma, Napa, and Marin, as well as in Monterey and Santa Cruz. (Oak Hill didn't figure in the statistics, as it's not certified organic.) Big farmers tend to sneer at small farms, and some of the staff at the Farm Bureau with whom I spoke weren't taking small seriously, but those experts didn't change my thinking. I *wanted* to believe that small would grow, that there would be more small farms with small landholdings all over the state and the country. Bob Cannard thinks so, too, and that's the kind of thinking that makes me optimistic.

If I wanted evidence of the pattern that I hoped would take hold, I had only to go to Other Avenues, a food store at the end of Judah Street, a few blocks from the Pacific Ocean in San Francisco. Other Avenues is small and intimate; it has been in existence for decades, and it evolved in fits and starts.

Only in the spring of 2007—relatively late in the game—had the employees who owned and ran the store made a pledge to carry produce from small, local, organic farms. After that they lost no time in implementing their pledge. On an afternoon visit, I saw produce from small and medium-sized farms all over California; I recognized some of the names, like Quetzal, but most of them were new and unfamiliar to me: Stone Free, Pure Pacific, Route One, Twin Girls, Happy Boy. These farms were in towns, villages, and small cities off and on the beaten track: Hollister, Freedom, Frazier, Carpinteria, Dinuba, Linden, Marysville, Oxnard, Santa Cruz, Corning, Monterey, Watsonville, Willow Creek, Madera, Goleta, Guinda, Fremont, Santa Rosa, and Steinbeck's hometown, Salinas. The array of produce was stunning.

I wrote down most of what I saw, and it made a long list. There were tomatoes, avocados, shallots, pomegranates, peaches, plums, kale, dandelion greens, kadota figs, cilantro, iceberg lettuce, Brussels sprouts, rutabaga, radishes, okra, sweet peppers, cayenne peppers, habaneros, purple peppers, lemon cukes, calliope eggplants, and the most beautiful vegetable of all, purple cauliflower, which looked psychedelic.

Shanta Rimbark Sacharoff, who was born in India to a Brahmin family that raised peanuts, and who had worked at Other Avenues since its inception, disabused me of any notion I may have had that it was a hippie store and a relic from another age—though she could sound New Agey. "We all have a farm connection in our psyche," she said and went on to explain that Other Avenues was on a solid business footing and that, as she put it, "we're always on top of the bottom line."

"We have people who shopped here in the 1970s, when they were in their twenties and thirties," she said. "Now they're in their fifties and sixties, and they're still shopping here. They get a senior discount. They're grandparents, and their grandchildren shop here." Shanta is a cookbook author; her *Flavors of India* offers vegetarian recipes, and she also writes for Other Avenues' quarterly newsletter, providing recipes for dishes like guacamole, *chilaquiles*—which she makes with tofu, not beef— and baba ghanoush made with Japanese eggplants.

J. B. Rumburg—a key team leader at Other Avenues— echoed Sacharoff's sentiments. He grew up in Marin County, started to eat organic food in the 1990s, when he was a high school student, and hasn't stopped. "We're a sustainable business," he said. "We've found a niche on this end of town. Go a few blocks further west, and there's the Pacific Ocean, and after that you have to go all the way to Hawaii to shop. This is *the* place to shop in this part of San Francisco."

J. B., as everyone calls him, didn't pull any punches. "One third of the stuff here is corporate," he said. "'Natural' is corporate now, though we stay away from the largest corporations. It's hard not to play any part of the corporate game." Other Avenues plays the game cleanly. They are a worker-owned cooperative. The workers share in the take, and they don't mind saying a kind word about economic and political equality. J. B., Shanta, and the other workers at OA, as they call the store, walked right into the mouth of the "gnarly beast"—Paul Wirtz's phrase for the gigantic food/farming business—and they walked out unscathed. And if they could do it, surely small stores elsewhere can do the same.

Veritable Vegetable, too, aims to conduct business cleanly, and, as one of its slogans proclaims, to "put nature back in natural." A twenty-five-thousand-square-foot warehouse in San Francisco with more than a hundred employees, Veritable continually moves tons of produce around California, and its two dozen or so trucks are rarely empty. Bu Nygrens, an ex–New Yorker, gave me a tour of the facility, where I saw boxes of California fruits and vegetables, as well as fruits and vegetables from around the world. There was both organic and conventional produce: bananas, carrots, yams, pineapples, mushrooms, limes, eggs, and milk. "If people shopped and then cooked and ate at home with their own families, Veritable would always be in business and not have to worry about market fluctuations," Nygrens said. "They'd all be better off eating fresh food at home."

On the subject of Northern California as an exception to national patterns of farming and eating, she observed, "I don't mean to be chauvinistic. Much of what we see here in terms of organic and sustainable is also in Boston, Austin, and Minneapolis, but the San Francisco Bay Area has been in advance of much of the country." Nygrens knows, too, that San Francisco citizens within a small radius of Veritable Vegetable don't all benefit from the locavore movement and the "delicious revolution." "Right in this city kids go to bed hungry at night," she said. "There's something very wrong about that, and hungry kids put the debate about local versus organic in perspective. Here at Veritable we believe that in addition to organic produce we have to have social justice, protection for farm laborers, ecological energy use, and packaging that's good for the environment. We're just at the start of the movement to make the world a greener place."

9

OLDIES AND GOODIES

FROM THE BRONX TO STONE EDGE

Fall swept through the valley and altered the landscape. A chilly
wind blew leaves from the trees, and the leaves swirled in kalei-
doscopic colors. During the day, temperatures rose steadily, so it
went from cold to hot, foggy to crystal clear. At sundown, temperatures dropped sharply. The vineyards changed from green
to orange and red, and grape harvests went on and on. Apples
ripened in abundance, and all the other fall fruits tumbled
down, too: pomegranates, persimmons, and pears, all of which I
ate profusely, with Café Fanny Granola, or with blue cheese
from the Cowgirl Creamery, or all by themselves.

At the full moon I raced the moon in the Valley of the
Moon, behind the wheel of my Volvo, along Sonoma Highway,
and discovered (no surprise, really) that no matter how fast I
traveled—well above the speed limit—the moon receded faster
and remained out of reach. The Valley of the Moon, in the light

of the full moon, was a ghostly place, and I could see why Jack London had been seduced by it and why he'd written such stories as "Moon-Face," which is about men driven mad in the spectral moonlit valley. I slowed down and cruised through the little towns clustered along Sonoma Highway. Slow is good for driving as well as for eating.

Autumn rain came early and hard; the hot, dry ground soaked up the cool water, and the dust that had built up over the summer months vanished. The earth was reborn. Fields became muddy; vegetables were muddy, too, and in the shed one afternoon, I found Paul wiping mud from squash to make them look more attractive. Though it rained, he also continued to irrigate—beans and carrots had recently been planted. Silvano and Servando, at a considerable distance from each other in the field, harvested herbs: tarragon, thyme, and parsley. And crows cawed and circled overhead.

Days and nights rushed by in a silent roar. I went back to my job at the university and tried not to allow it to interfere with my work on the farm and my writing about farming and food. When I asked Kevin, one of the campus gardeners, if fall had really arrived, as I seemed to think it had, he said, "Yup, we're in it right now." Tom, one of his coworkers, agreed. "There's a bite in the air," he said. The students in my classes hadn't noticed any difference when I asked them whether fall had arrived. We're still in summer, they said in chorus. They clutched their cell phones, peered at their computer screens, listened to music on their iPods, and I thought that their preoccupation with technology and instant text messaging might have served as the springboard for a sermon about the ways in which Americans have lost touch with the seasons, nature, and the earth itself. But some students were buying organic produce at Oliver's, the supermarket near the college, and cooking nutritious meals. Some have broken their addictions to Burger King, Taco Bell, and McDonald's, and that is cause for hope. Moreover, some students were also working as interns at Valley End and learning from Sharon Grossi how to run a farm.

Paul called fall "a funny time" because this was the time when he had a small window of opportunity for planting cover crops. "I have to stay on the ball," he said. "If it goes on raining, it will never dry out, and we won't be able to get into the fields." But he didn't think the plants were confused, as I thought they might be, by the combination of hot days and cold nights, rain and sun, wind and autumn afternoon stillness. They were smart enough to know the season, and they responded accordingly, he explained. They would go on putting down roots, absorbing sunlight, taking nutrients from the soil, and growing as they had for millennia.

To Lena Hahn-Schuman, a master gardener and mistress of heirloom plants and shrubs, we were in an "in-between season"—a kind of fourth season that some also call "Indian summer." That phrase brought back my own boyhood memories of September and October on the East Coast, when the water in Long Island Sound was still warm enough for swimming, the bluefish ran off Montauk Point, and my dad and I would buy apple juice in the barn where it had been hand-pressed by the farmer himself. All year long Lena worked on a farm not far from Bob Cannard Jr.'s place. Before I visited, I had to give her my word that I would not mention the names of the owners of the farm where she works. Stone Edge is the name of the farm, but you will not find the names of the owners at the entrance, which has an iron gate and thick walls made from the stones unearthed on the farm. The couple who own the farm, which is maintained by an efficient crew of Mexicans, don't want to advertise themselves or see their names in print. They do not need to sell the produce that Lena grows, but they sell vegetables to Café La Haye, a small, superlative restaurant just off the plaza in Sonoma, and to Gaige House, a charming bed-and-breakfast in Glen Ellen—both places to which Oak Hill also sells.

Stone Edge's cook, Moselle Beaty, makes delicious food with the fruits and vegetables she picks from the gardens, which allow her to give free rein to her culinary imagination. Born in Sonoma in 1960, Beaty grew up in a family of eight brothers and sisters. Her Swedish mother kept house and raised the children, and her Finnish father worked in the Bay Area's shipyards. Swedish, Finnish, and English were spoken at home, but it was the language of food that brought the family together and kept it together—all ten family members sitting down to share meals.

Beaty learned to cook from her mother, who rarely used recipes. "We didn't have measuring cups," she said. "My mother would eyeball all the ingredients; a pinch of this, a handful of that." Beaty, too, rarely, if ever, uses recipes; she never attended a cooking school and has never submitted a résumé to get a job. But she has earned a living as a cook all her adult life. She makes her own pasta, fires up the outdoor oven at Stone Edge to bake pizzas, picks vegetables from the garden for broccoli and pumpkin soup with Gruyère cheese, and cooks salmon on a cedar plank with herbs from the garden. "When I was hired I said, 'You'll never know what's going to show up on your plate for dinner until you see it there.' They didn't have a problem with that. They have real respect for how food is grown, how it's prepared, and how it's a part of the world in which we live. I wish more people realized that there's an art to gardening and cooking, and that they weren't so eager to throw something into a microwave and eat on the run."

At Stone Edge, Beaty works not far from where she grew up. But Lena Hahn-Schuman is working clear across the country from her starting place. Her zigzag journey—from the Bronx, where she was born, to Stone Edge, where she is officially known as the "potager"—took her to Vietnam before it took her to California. In the 1960s, after attending Bronx High School of Science and majoring in biology at the City College of New York, she married a U.S. army psychologist and traveled to Saigon, where he served in the military. There she shopped at the open-air markets that thrived despite the war; she bought fruits and vegetables, even if they seemed strange to her, as well as live chickens and rabbits from the farmers who had raised them. During this time she turned her talents to cooking. In 1967, in the midst of the Summer of Love, she settled in San Francisco and began to conduct research for the National Institute of Mental Health (NIMH) on the effects of marijuana on laboratory mice. She found that "stoned" mice had fewer offspring than mice who were "straight"—conclusions that the NIMH didn't want to hear. They had hoped for more damning evidence about the harmful effects of marijuana.

In 1972, about the same time that my parents took up organic farming, Lena and Herschel, her second husband, moved to Sonoma County. They started growing peas and tomatoes, which they sold for twenty-five cents per pound—dirt cheap— to neighbors and friends who came from Berkeley seeking produce without pesticides. She started a wholesale organic plant business that she called "Oldies and Goodies," and by the 1980s it was booming. Though she had never grown much more than geraniums on her fire escape in the Bronx, she discovered that she had a green thumb, and that she loved growing a wide range of crops in all the seasons of the year.

"One of the main problems with agribusiness is that it creates huge quantities without quality," she said one brisk morning. We were walking freely about Stone Edge because the owners were away at their home in the city. I felt like the plain country mouse at liberty in the absence of the lavish city mice, a tale my father had told me when I was a boy and that had encouraged me to appreciate rural folks. "Agribusiness depletes the soil, and the food is depleted, too," Lena continued. "Big corporate farms choose varieties of corn and tomatoes on the basis of productivity and shipability rather than on the tenderness of the kernels or the juicy flavor."

We gazed at a hornbeam tree that had dropped all of its leaves at the same time, leaving a beautiful pattern on the ground—all the more reason not to rake them up. I admired the purple verbena, Iceland poppies, purple basil, and Italian heirloom peppers like *corno de toro*. Listening to Lena, I sensed that the young woman who had graduated from Bronx High School of Science still knew her sciences, and that she knew her political science, too. "Agribusiness makes us dependent on imported energy sources like oil," she told me. "Chemical fertilizers, which we don't use here, are made from oil, and it takes oil, too, to truck all those poor, depleted vegetables from big farms in the Central Valley to distant cities all over the country. When you think about it, it's hard not to conclude that America is crazy for the way that agriculture works—or doesn't work—for most people."

Stone Edge isn't a real working farm like Oak Hill, Lena wanted me to know. "This is a farm for people who have the means and a moral conscience—and an aesthetic sense, too," she said. Indeed, Stone Edge struck me as both a work of art and a meditative place, a retreat from the crowd. The stonework by Pedro Castillo, the Mexican mason, was magnificent, and the lush, vibrant gardens were pleasing to the eye. For the most part, Lena didn't plant anything in a straight line; almost everything was either in a semicircle or in the shape of a crescent moon, and vegetables and flowers grew side by side in raised beds made of stone—the highest raised beds I had ever seen. Strawberries grew big, plump, and tasty. The Pequin peppers, particularly prized by the Mexican workers at Stone Edge, were hotter than hot. In winter the Belgian endives were transplanted inside and cultivated in the warmth and darkness of the greenhouse, where they turned white.

The garden also contained an old, rare medlar tree—which I would find in Shakespeare, Lena informed me—daisies, and pumpkins, that ubiquitous fall vegetable. In this in-between season she had just planted fava beans, arugula, and rainbow chard, all of them popular with chefs, and Stone Edge would sell a lot of these vegetables. Lena also grows garnishes for restaurants; I saw trays filled with tiny growing plants, pea shoots, curly cress, fennel, and chervil, all of which, she explained, "add a burst of flavor." I suddenly remembered that my friend Matthew Greenbaum, the executive chef at the Underwood Bar and Bistro in Graton, had told me that he goes to sleep at night thinking of garnishes, and that he sometimes dreams of them. The art and craft of cultivation and cooking are all about the little details on the farm and in the kitchen—and about mindfulness. I could see that focusing on details helps to grow beautiful garnishes and tasty dishes. It's important to pay attention to your own locality, listen to what gardens and fields say, and respect them. In the autumn Lena saves seeds from the vegetables, fruits, and ornamentals she has grown, and she plants them in the spring; local seeds are adapted to the particular place, far more so than seeds from faraway places, and they turn into healthier plants.

Lena led me through a grove of cedar trees—deodara and incense—and, surrounded by their perfume, I felt that I was in a magical place and Lena was a magician who kept rare plants, trees, and shrubs alive. She returned to the subject of agribusiness, which is nearly everything that Stone Edge is not. "Commercial agriculture has robbed people of a sense of seasons," she said. "Seasons are good. They make people feel whole and integrated and a part of the earth, not lords and masters of the earth. We can all learn to appreciate the unique and satisfying tastes of winter produce and fruits in season."

Grapes and olives were cultivated at Stone Edge, and though the grapes had already been picked by the time I arrived, I watched a labor-intensive olive harvest that took all day. Later the olives would be pressed at the Olive Press in the town of Sonoma, made into extra-virgin olive oil, and sold in beautiful jars in such markets as Whole Foods. The label on the front read "Stone Edge," and the one on the back read "Organically farmed olives from the Manzanillo tree are hand picked and meticulously separated from stems and leaves to avoid any bitter flavor." The day I was there, the jovial all-Mexican crew spread tarps on the ground and pulled the olives from the trees with little rakes. Then they gathered up the fruits and carried them to a big vat, where they removed leaves and stems. I tasted olives from a tree and found them to be bitter; they would have to be brined, Lena explained, to make them edible.

PHIL COTURRI'S OPERA

Phil Coturri, the burly man with the beard and the ponytail who was in charge of both the olive and the grape harvests at Stone Edge, was the main manager of organic vineyards in the Valley of the Moon and the Mayacamas Mountains. No one was more familiar with the valley's viticulture, unless it was perhaps his older brother, Tony, who takes his organic Petite Syrah, Zinfandel, Pinot Noir, and Merlot wines to Texas, Tennessee, and Massachusetts. Tony adds no chemicals—no sulfites, either—so his wines are fragile and perishable. Tony, a baby boomer with a full beard and a deep love of learning and literature, likes to pour wine at his home in the hills, then sip and talk about winemaking in Sonoma. On a late afternoon in fall I sipped wine with him and listened to his tales. The thirteen original wineries from the 1970s had grown to more than a hundred by the start of the twenty-first century. The price of land had risen from about ten thousand dollars per acre to as much as three hundred thousand. "My wines are earthy," Tony said. "They taste like the place they come from, and they tell the story of their place as all good wines should."

The day I observed the olive harvest at Stone Edge, Phil bounded about energetically. He sang his own praises and made jokes about himself that his work crew enjoyed. "I'm not a hippie anymore, and that's why I wear my hair in a ponytail," he said, but no one quite believed him. He looked and sounded like a hippie. If Phil had wanted a public relations man, he wouldn't have had to look far. Rob Schultz, one of Phil's field managers, who carried out his orders and conveyed them to others, had short black hair and black-rimmed glasses, and he spoke Spanish nearly as well as he spoke English. He knew Phil's virtues as a master of the vines, and he was determined to learn as much as he could, as quickly as he could, by following Phil from vineyard to vineyard, olive grove to olive grove.

Born and raised in Iowa, his heart set on farming, Rob fled the cornfields and threw himself into the world of grapes—healthier than corn, he claimed. Rob didn't care for Iowa corn; he didn't like to eat it, and he didn't like what it had done to the state of Iowa, either. "When I left, I was sick of looking at corn," he said. "I don't mind if I never see another cornfield. Corn takes a heavy toll on human beings and on the environment. You can't swim in Iowa's lakes, rivers, and ponds anymore because of the toxic runoff from the chemicals that are used in agriculture. Iowa soil is dead. Once upon a time, there was prairie, but it's gone, along with birdsong and birds. If I'd go for a walk in the cornfields, I'd break out in a rash and itch all day." Rachel Carson's warnings had come true.

Sonoma might have been superior to Iowa in many ways, but it isn't perfect. In Rob's eyes, Sonoma has a caste system, with the biggest landowners—some of them descendants of the ranchers who had been given land grants by Mariano Vallejo in the nineteenth century—at the top. Then come the Sonoma-born rednecks who have the good jobs in construction. And at the bottom of the ladder are the "guys like me," he said, "along with the men from Michoacán." Rob's sociological observations were spot on. The Valley of the Moon has impoverished laborers and prosperous landowners. Of course, some of the men who arrived penniless and worked hard made enough money to buy not one but several homes. Sonoma could be a land of rags to riches, and I've met more than one poor boy who has made his fortune.

One poor boy who made it big is Preston Dishman, the chef at the General's Daughter restaurant in Sonoma, who came from Boone, North Carolina—"a little tobacco growers' town that turned into a poverty-stricken area." At his first job he scooped ice cream, then he learned to cook in Florida and New York, and when he came to California, he joined the farm-to-table movement, growing vegetables on the thin strip of land around the restaurant he started—in a house originally built in 1864 by General Vallejo for his daughter Natalia and his son-in-law Attila Haraszthy. Preston also grows vegetables at nearby Benzinger Winery, which adheres to biodynamic farming methods. "Growing up, it was a rarity to go to a restaurant," Preston said. "Sometimes we'd go out for a meal after church. Mostly, food was prepared by someone with my own last name, and with a name like Dishman I'd have to say that cooking chose me." In 2007, *Gourmet* magazine included his restaurant, the General's Daughter, on its list of the one hundred best farm-to-table restaurants in America.

In Sonoma—which sees itself in competition with Napa as a premier grape-growing and winemaking region of the world—Phil Coturri is probably the leading apostle for the organic cultivation of grapes. Organic accounts for only about 10 percent of the crop, and Phil doesn't hesitate to say that organic cultivation is more expensive than conventional—four hundred to five hundred dollars more per acre, by his estimate—but he also claims that wine made organically is as good as if not better than wine made conventionally. Coturri organic wines are excellent, and so are Bucklin's organic wines. Most important, Phil likes to point out, if you grow grapes organically, you don't live or work in a toxic dump.

If he had been born in another era, he might have become a priest and poured wine at mass at Saint Francis Solano Church in the town of Sonoma, where Anglos and Latinos, Italians and Mexicans, worship side by side. But Phil came of age in the 1960s, when the church had lost much of its appeal for young Catholic boys like him and his brother. Moreover, both of their grandfathers were Italian-Swiss immigrants who worked in the wine industry. Their grandfather Enrico, who, so family legend has it, came to America with ten dollars in his pocket, made wine barrels, and he taught his son, Harry "Red" Coturri, who in turn passed the lore on to his sons. By the time Phil was thirteen, he was growing grapes and making wine with his father and his father's business partner, a parish priest. Knowing that priests were making wine seemed more than enough of a blessing for Phil and Tony to do the same. Phil seems well within his rights when he says, "I never made a conscious decision to do this. It's in my blood."

In the 1960s, marijuana called to him. He may have smoked a little pot and inhaled, too. He may even have grown a marijuana plant for the sheer joy of it. But he never became what he calls a "career criminal," one of those who made marijuana into their cash crop and then could not stop growing it when it started selling for four thousand dollars per pound. The plant that had been dismissed as a weed became the "greed weed," and a hefty proportion of the back-to-the-land generation was sidetracked into growing marijuana for profit instead of fun or recreation. I had seen examples of this kind of marijuana growing in the mountains of California, and so had Phil, and while neither of us thought these growers were evil incarnate, we weren't about to applaud them as the cultural heroes many of them thought they were.

At St. Mary's and then at Sonoma State University, Phil wrote verse and studied poetry, especially the works of Gary Snyder, Philip Whalen, and Lew Welch, the Beat poet who wandered into the wilderness near Snyder's house with a rifle and never came back. Poetry penetrated deeply into Phil's soul. During our conversation, he recited a line or two from Matsuo Bashō, the seventeenth-century Japanese poet who wrote "At a Hermitage," which seemed contemporary to me:

A cool fall night—
getting dinner, we peeled
eggplants, cucumbers.

Phil knew personally many writers, artists, and musicians—among them Jerry Garcia of the Grateful Dead—who were brought down by their addiction to drugs, and he was determined to be a survivor, a living, not dead, Dead Head. It helped that he enjoys a keen sense of humor and that, like his friend and contemporary Bob Cannard Jr., he has a way of making work seem like play. While working in vineyards and olive groves he is part jester, part prankster —and he still gets the job done.

For Phil there are two seasons, not four: the first is from November through March, which he considers the calm time; the second is April through October, the crazy time. I saw him in both seasons and noticed the differences in his demeanor. At Will Bucklin's vineyard during the crush, he spoke rapidly on his cell phone; he had one eye on the grapes, kept another on the crew, and seemed to have yet a third eye for watching the sun in the sky. I also rode with him in his Ford pickup truck on a lazy autumn day; then he leaned his arm out the window and re-laxed, and we cruised slowly through the valley, climbed into the mountains on the way to Moon Mountain Vineyards, wound this way and that over rough roads and through vineyards planted on steep inclines.

During that calm time Phil stopped halfway to the top of the mountain, pulled the brake, and got out of the truck without warning. I had no idea what he was up to. Before I knew it, he had ambled into the vineyard, scooped up two handfuls of earth, and placed them under my nose. "Smell that," he commanded. I had smelled the earth all summer, up close at Oak Hill. I knew the smell of good earth. Phil didn't have to tell me that "this earth is alive" for me to know it. We stopped at the top of the ridge—halfway to the moon—and peered down on San Fran-cisco, which was blanketed in a thick white fog that made the place look like the snowy Himalayas, or like a landscape in outer space.

Phil had taken me here for a reason. He wanted me to see the spectacular view, but, more important, he wanted me to under-stand that everything in nature is connected. I half expected him to break into an aria from an Italian opera. He sounded operatic when he said, "The rain that lands at the top of this mountain range finds its way into the bay. And if I pee up here it will find its way down there. As the manager of this vineyard, and as a steward of the land, it's my responsibility to make sure that chemicals don't end up in San Francisco Bay."

He peered at the sun, gazed at San Francisco, and smiled a beatific smile. "I have learned everything I know about the environment from poetry," he said. "And especially from Gary Snyder's poetry. Poetry taught me the interconnectedness of life, and that everything is political. In the old days all the poets embraced politics; you had to be political to be a poet in the first place.

"I look down at the Valley of the Moon, and I see that the organic movement, which started as a hippie pipe dream decades ago, has succeeded far beyond what anyone ever imagined," he said. "Organic has been accepted by the bourgeoisie; they're paying for it now." There is a certain irony here, and perhaps also a kind of poetic justice. What the bourgeoisie once dismissed as hippie nonsense, they now embrace for themselves. The vineyard owners for whom Phil works may think that he is too far out when he says that he has learned everything from Snyder's poetry; but if so, he wouldn't care one bit. He is living his life according to his own principles, and that's what matters to him.

WHOLE FOODS COMES TO TOWN

Phil was right. Organic has certainly been taken up by the bourgeoisie at Stone Edge, and by the forward-looking members of the bourgeoisie who own vineyards, olive groves, and mansions across the length and breadth of the valley. Then, too, both the philosophy and the business of organic have been adopted by

Whole Foods Market, one of the quintessential bourgeois bohemian, or bobo, institutions in Sonoma and all across the country. Whole Foods Market had already conquered much of the food business in Santa Rosa, Sebastopol, and Petaluma—as well as San Francisco—before it came knocking at the gates of the town of Sonoma, expecting that it would be welcomed wholeheartedly by the citizens. What happened surprised everyone.

When the store—number 196 in Whole Foods' transcontinental empire of markets—opened a few blocks from the main plaza in June 2007, it was with as much fanfare as if it had been a historic event on the order of the legendary Bear Flag Revolt of 1846, when insurgent Americans, led by Captain John C. Fremont—acting, possibly, on orders from President James Polk—seized control of Sonoma, created the California Republic, and three weeks later joined the United States. There were no guns in evidence at the grand opening of Whole Foods, and no one was taken prisoner, but Mariano Vallejo—or at least his able impersonator George Webber, a local actor known for inhabiting the roles of historical personages—made an appearance. George Webber gave a "trippy" performance, to borrow a hippie expression that seemed appropriate to his theatrical personality.

Like Rob Schultz, George, too, is a fugitive from Iowa. Born in 1954, he came to California in 1971, worked at the Pacific Stock Exchange, and, after falling in love with the history of Sonoma, turned to acting to bring history alive. He reminded me that Kit Carson, Ulysses S. Grant, and William Tecumseh Sherman once prowled the streets of Sonoma and went hunting for grizzly bear, which probably explains why grizzly bears are no longer around. With Carson, Grant, and Sherman armed and firing at will, they wouldn't have had a fighting chance. Promoting himself as

"Sonoma's Professional Multiple Personality Artiste," Webber has created several archetypal characters, including "Professor Vine" and "Luigi, the Singing Italian Waiter." He has also "done" Mark Twain and General Vallejo, though he has not done Jack London. "At first people thought I was crazy. Now they know I'm not," Webber said. I thought he was zany in an endearing way. You have to be zany to walk about town in costume, as Webber did; you have to be zany to approach Whole Foods before the store opened in Sonoma and ask to be part of the ceremony. Whole Foods didn't leap at the opportunity to include him, but he didn't let that stop him. He donned his General Vallejo costume and wandered through the crowd of five hundred people who had shown up for the opening.

Whole Foods won a significant battle when it broke into Sonoma—there was fierce opposition—but it might have lost the war for the hearts, minds, and pocketbooks of the local shoppers. The *Sonoma Index-Tribune,* which had sent a reporter to cover the event, placed the story on the front page with a photo of the store and Dana Leavitt, the manager. Arms were decidedly not in evidence at the grand opening. But the strong hand of a well-conceived public relations manager was obvious in the photos of nineteenth-century Sonomans, discovered at the Depot Museum, that the store's marketers posted in the front windows. They seemed to say, "We love you dearly. Please love us." A shopper could not miss the words "local," "organic," and "green" outside and inside the store. Whole Foods was presenting a face to Sonoma, and that face was Sonoma itself.

The year before the new store opened in Sonoma had been challenging for the megacompany. Granted, a number of new stores opened that year from coast to coast, including in New

York, and they all did well. I visited Whole Foods in Union Square in Manhattan several times, and it was always thronged with shoppers; there were long lines at the checkout counters, and the place felt like an assembly line. In Sonoma, by comparison, the story was very different; whenever I visited that Whole Foods, it seemed cavernous and was largely empty of shoppers. Employees smiled and offered greetings, but they stood around waiting for something to happen, and it rarely did.

Whole Foods had a challenging year in 2006–2007 not because of a downturn in the economy or competition from Safeway but because of a best-selling book that did more to shake up consumers of food products than any book since Upton Sinclair's *The Jungle* took on the meatpacking industry in Chicago exactly one hundred years earlier. In *The Omnivore's Dilemma,* Michael Pollan—perhaps the most provocative and intelligent American author on the subject of food in our time—took Whole Foods to task for its failure, as he perceives it, to live up to its image as savior of that holy trinity: organic, local, and sustainable. With intellectual panache, Pollan accused Whole Foods of marketing "supermarket pastoral"—a kind of glamorous fiction that encourages consumers to believe that shopping at the store will put them in direct, intimate contact with the earth and all its purity. "While the posters still depict family farmers and their philosophies, the produce on sale below them comes primarily from two big corporate growers in California, Earthbound Farms and Grimmway Farms, which together dominate the market for organic fresh produce in America," Pollan wrote in the chapter entitled "Big Organic." A bit further on he observed, "To participate in a local food economy requires considerably more effort than shopping at the

Whole Foods." Executives at Whole Foods felt that Pollan had insulted the company, and they immediately went on a counteroffensive to repair the company image. They mounted an aggressive public relations campaign to undermine Pollan's claims and demonstrate the company's goodness, wholesomeness, and community values.

The town of Sonoma accepted Pollan's critique of Whole Foods. Why shop there, citizens told me, when they could go to the Red Barn or the farmers' market, or grow vegetables in their own backyard? Many were personally offended by Whole Foods. One friend described the company as Goliath and the town as David, and of course they identified with little David and not the giant, Goliath. I saw their point. The more I thought about it, the more I thought that Whole Foods in Sonoma was an example of corporate hubris. The town and the store weren't a good fit. Oak Hill and the farmers' markets had come to represent the best of Sonoma, whereas Whole Foods seemed to represent the worst. The store was too big in this place of small; it was global instead of local; and perhaps it was not even sustainable. But I wanted to be fair to Whole Foods. In fact, for years I had shopped happily at their store in Sebastopol. I loved that store in large part because it remained true to Food for Thought, the organic market that Whole Foods had taken over, gobbling it up as it gobbled up food stores all across the country. Ernie Shelton and his brother Jim had started Food for Thought in Sebastopol in 1990, when there was no farmers' market in town, and no organic food store, either, even though Sebastopol was inundated with hippies and yuppies.

By providing quality produce and creating a seductive store ambience, the Shelton brothers wooed the town away from rival supermarkets, though people also complained about their high prices and called the store "Food for Gold." Ernie had been a pioneering organic farmer and a trendsetter in the natural food industry, and over the course of several decades, with persistence and honesty, he helped to bring innovation into the mainstream. In Santa Barbara in the 1970s, on some of the richest land in the state, he belonged to a community that called itself the Brotherhood of the Sun, which raised and sold organic food. He worked hard, prayed hard, meditated twice a day with like-minded spiritualists, and worked for a series of health and natural food stores all over the West that changed the ways people ate and thought about food. When he and Jim sold Food for Thought to Whole Foods, they made enough money to retire for the rest of their lives. Today Ernie still gardens in his backyard, and he still believes in growing organically. "The best fertilizer is the farmer's footsteps," he said on a summer day when we picked apples from one of his trees. "Human interaction with the crops is essential; it helps to walk, talk, and interact with what you're growing; and these days farmers raise great food using biodynamic methods."

I knew the people who worked at Whole Foods in Sebastopol; they were often locals, and they shopped there with everyone else in town. I also knew the local residents, many of them still hippies, who make Whole Foods their stomping ground and meeting place. I could always find what I wanted at Whole Foods in Sebastopol, whether it was smoked salmon, freshly baked bagels, or any one of an array of organic products: goat cheese, broccoli rabe, kale, cabbage, soy milk, figs, polenta, butter, and olive oil. The store seemed to read my mind and know what I wanted. Moreover, everything was easy to find because the store was small—less than half the size of the thirty-five-thousand-square-foot Whole Foods in Sonoma or the monstrous fifty-thousand-square-foot store in Napa; the Napa store was an instant success story and packed with customers singing its praises. The fact that Whole Foods failed to capture a sizable portion of the market for groceries in Sonoma and succeeded in Napa is emblematic of the social and cultural differences between the two towns, and the two valleys in which they are situated. Sonoma is a down-to-the-ground kind of place that prides itself on small and local. Napa is loftier, grander, with big houses, big wineries, and big stores. Sonoma has Readers' Books, owned by locals. Napa boasts a Borders.

I began a serious campaign to find out about the Sonoma Whole Foods Market. Walking around and observing while shopping at the store was no problem, of course, and I did this. Early in my research for this book, while I was visiting Dean & Deluca in Manhattan, a vigilant employee asked me to leave because I was writing down my observations in a notebook in the midst of the produce section. Apparently this was not allowed. I learned from that experience to simulate shopping—to slowly fill a shopping cart and take notes at the same time. This was easy at the front of the Sonoma Whole Foods; where it got hard was at the back. I knew I had to have permission from a manager to see what went on behind the scenes; I preferred not to risk an embarrassing ejection from the store, or perhaps an arrest. That seemed excessive. After all, this was not a story about torture or terrorism, where going undercover might have been appropriate.

I started at the bottom of the Whole Foods food chain, working my way up the ladder as high as I could, and I found that I liked the people who worked there, especially at the bottom. At the same time I disliked the company. Whole Foods management seemed to squelch the creativity of the staff, or at least it did not facilitate their expressing creativity unless it conformed with company policy. As I saw it, the demands of the corporation outweighed the needs of the individuals. I also learned that I couldn't rely on seeing any one employee on subsequent visits; Whole Foods Market retains the right to transfer its employees. In fact, one major player at the Sonoma store was transferred because it wasn't doing well financially.

Almost all of the Sonoma Whole Foods employees had read Michael Pollan's *The Omnivore's Dilemma;* it seemed to be required reading. Many told me that Pollan's criticisms are fair and accurate, though they also said that they felt he hadn't given the company credit for what it had done to promote and popularize organic, local, and sustainable. They all felt that Whole Foods had reformed its ways, and that it was on the right track now—thanks to Pollan. I wanted to see if the store had really changed for the better. It took persistence on my part to find out; I had to call and call and call again. Getting into the Red Barn had been easier. On the day I met Rachal Cyphers, the store marketing and community relations representative, she had scheduled a tour of the store, but no one had shown up. "I was born and raised in Sonoma," she said. "My mother was a hippie and cooked brown rice and vegetables. We had a garden when I was growing up." Rachal knew exactly what to say and what she had to accomplish, and she knew, too, that she had an uphill fight on her hands. "I want to get away from the 'whole paycheck' image that has been attached to the store," she said. "We're competitively priced; we always have great buys, and we're open 365 days a year. We encourage local production of food, and local people like Bob Cannard Sr. pick up compost here for their chickens." (What she conveniently neglected to say, and that I heard from Bob Cannard Sr. himself, was that he didn't actually shop at Whole Foods.) Dana Leavitt, the store's manager, plugged Whole Foods and its CEO, John Mackay. Only by repeated calls and persistent pleas did I get to speak to him. "Socially conscious is John's thing," Dana said. "Whole Foods is an incredible place to work. The store here is community driven, and we want it to be a place to meet friends and hang out—to get a cappuccino and converse. I plan on being here until I die." Unfortunately, things didn't work out for Dana at Whole Foods in Sonoma. He was transferred and would have to retire from another branch.

At the regional headquarters in Emeryville, California, Jonathan Packman—the regional coordinator for all Whole Foods bakeries—met me in a conference room that boasted color photos of carrots, blackberries, asparagus, and blueberries that looked good enough to eat. Born in Brooklyn and raised on Long Island, Jonathan had grown up with traditional Jewish food like stuffed cabbage and potato kugel. Before coming to Whole Foods, he had attended Cornell and worked at the Ithaca Farmers' Market and the Finger Lakes Organic Growers Cooperative in upstate New York. He had organic credentials.

"The 'whole paycheck' thing has been an albatross around our neck," he said. "We offer the same quality produce or better than our competitors do, and you can spend the same or less money at Whole Foods as at Safeway or Trader Joe's for the same or similar products." On the subject of Michael Pollan's *The Omnivore's Dilemma,* he said, "He tried to put us in a pigeonhole and claimed we weren't doing a good-enough job. We really do want to create an authentic experience at Whole Foods. We want to support local communities; we want to anticipate future trends in the industry and meet the needs of customers."

I now had permission to talk to employees at Whole Foods in Sonoma, though I was explicitly told not to go into the kitchen. When I persisted, I was told it was off-limits not because there was something to hide but because it was "chaotic" and "for your own good." There were other disappointments. Tim Walker, one of the bakers, wanted to make a rye bread and sell it at the store, but before he could do so he had to submit the recipe to headquarters; bakers higher than he on the corporate ladder would make the bread and decide whether or not to approve it. Tim loved bread; he was a born baker, could work with both hands equally well, and was itching to make good bread. He did his best to love Whole Foods, but Whole Foods didn't seem to love or appreciate him.

"I was born in 1953, the year of *Playboy* and the Corvette—a great year," he said without stopping his work, kneading the dough for two loaves of bread at the same time and never becoming distracted. "At that time, bread was mostly atrocious; whole-wheat bread was unfashionable, and white bread was the desired entity. Ed Brown's *The Tassajara Bread Book* got me started on real bread in the 1970s, and I haven't stopped since then. I got the ultimate compliment about my Pugliese not long ago from a woman who said, 'I'm Italian and every time I eat this loaf, it takes me home.' You don't know how good it felt inside to hear her say that."

Greg Grabow was a natural for making coffee quickly; Maggie Brady, who had come to the Sonoma store from Whole

Foods in Palm Beach, called him "Boomdiggety," and he was that and more. "If there's one thing you don't want to wait for, it's coffee," he said while making a vanilla lavender latte for a customer and pouring me a cup of French roast. "It's not in the psyche of American consumers to wait for coffee. They want it, and they want it fast. I do it fast and always have done; I grew up with Yuban—my mother said it was the best she could offer—and I didn't become aware of coffee with real flavor until the 1990s."

On the other side of the store, Ron Romano in produce looked as if he had time on his hands. Before he came to Whole Foods he had worked as a stock option trader on the floor of the San Francisco Stock Exchange, and he took a cut in pay to become a greengrocer. "I'm happier here than I was on the trading floor," he said. "It was fast paced, intense, and anxiety producing. You stand next to people you think are your friends, and you discover that they'll take your money in a heartbeat."

Greg, Maggie, Tim, Ron, Rachal, and Dana seemed to like one another, and they treated one another as friends. I liked them, too, but I had the feeling that Whole Foods in Sonoma could use a jolt of energy from the Red Barn or the farmers' market. Something or someone was needed to wake the place up. But maybe it would sit there, shelves packed with products for sale, and no one would come into the store to buy them. Perhaps a Whole Foods store in a place that had citizens like Anne Teller, Paul Wirtz, Jesús Soto, and George Webber just wouldn't be able to win over local customers.

I failed to get into the kitchen, but I had gotten nearly everything else I wanted: a glimpse into the lives of the people who worked there. Now I was hungry. I looked around the store—well lit and immaculately clean—and I thought about shopping for supper. Then I thought again. I didn't know what precisely I'd do about dinner, but I knew I didn't want to buy the fixings at Whole Foods. I got into my car and drove toward home. Around the bend and before the straightaway on Sonoma Highway, I saw the sign for Oak Hill and slowed down. Here I would shop. It felt absolutely right. Gael was still in the Red Barn. Quickly I picked out three ears of corn, a couple of ripe melons, and two cucumbers. At the counter I took out my wallet and thought about the delicious dinner ahead of me. Then I was on my way home at last.

10

A PLACE FOR THINGS TO HAPPEN

SONOMA PLAZA

After the early rain, the fields suddenly turned green, and the earth looked as if it were springtime again. In the Red Barn Store, plump cherry tomatoes were available again, along with a variety of autumn squashes: delicata, sunshine, acorn, butternut, and spaghetti. In the sun it was hot, in the shade it was chilly: T-shirt and sweater weather at the same time. Jimmy Reed's voice filled the barn, and Priscilla Coe, a loyal customer and locavore, was gathering all the vegetables she'd need for the next few days. "My favorite part of the week is when I come here to shop," she said. "I shape what I eat around what they grow here; it's so delicious." When she didn't get to the Red Barn, she'd shop at the Tuesday night farmers' market in the plaza at the heart of the town of Sonoma, a festive occasion not only for buying and selling fresh produce in the open air but for eating, drinking, meeting friends, and listening to live music, especially country-and-western. Priscilla is not alone in being loyal to Oak Hill; I met others like her when at the end of summer I started working at the farmers' market, which begins in spring and ends in fall.

I had never worked in retail sales. After overcoming my initial nervousness about weighing accurately on the old-fashioned scales and getting the prices right, I enjoyed selling produce. This was the way it had been, I told myself, when villagers came to market towns to sell what they had made at home, buy what they needed, and exchange gossip. Sonoma comes alive on Tuesday nights, and then it feels like a community with a strong sense of identity. I liked waiting on customers, especially on the women who asked me to pick out a few ripe apples or select flowers to grace a dining room table.

On warm nights in August and September, the arms and shoulders of the women were bare, and I was reminded of sensuous nights in Provence and the feeling of the Mediterranean. The most beautiful women in the world shop at the Tuesday night market. It seemed so easy—far easier than I had imagined—to make a woman (or a man, for that matter) happy with the beauty and abundance of the produce—and with the price, as well. Shoppers smiled and radiated a sense of joy. I had seen similar looks of delight on the faces at the Union Square farmers' market in New York. Here, as there, people know that organic produce is good. Here was a connection that felt warmer than the fast financial transactions at checkout lines in Safeway, Whole Foods, or Sonoma Market. Here there was no long-distance trucking, no middleman. From Oak Hill to the plaza was a matter of minutes, and it was a drive I enjoyed in a truck full of flowers, fruits, and vegetables.

The Sonoma plaza is the perfect place for a farmers' market. Not only is it at the center of the town, it's also the town's centerpiece: a spectacular showcase of past and present, with history embedded in its very shape and size, and in the stories connected with it. General Mariano Vallejo had overseen the construction of the plaza in the nineteenth century. He had worked, more or less faithfully, from a 1573 design by King Philip II of Spain that was intended for the towns to be built in New Spain during the rush for gold and empire. All over South and Central America, plazas were built according to Philip's plan and imperial vision. Other towns across California have plazas, but according to my reliable source John Woodbridge, the only plaza in California to be built to King Philip's specifications is the one in the town of Sonoma.

Woodbridge, an architect, urban planner, and author of nearly half a dozen books, as well as a resident of Sonoma, showed me copies of the relevant historical documents from Spain, including the plan for Sonoma, which is laid out on a grid, with all the streets emanating from the plaza. (*Spanish City Planning in North America* tells some of this story.) Woodbridge, who is married to the Pulitzer Prize–winning poet Carolyn Kizer, knows a lot about the splendid architecture of Sonoma, as well as the history of his own house, built in 1872 and modeled after the bungalows that the British built in India to beat the heat.

"Vallejo was a great city planner; you have only to look at the plaza to appreciate his greatness," he said. "The plaza is a place that was made for things to happen, and things have a way of happening there. In the mid-nineteenth century, Sonoma was the largest town in California north of Monterey. It was also the western command post for the U.S. military until it was by-passed by Napa, Petaluma, and Santa Rosa. Later, it showed signs of becoming a backwater, and when Carolyn and I came here after she won the Pulitzer, it was a place to get away from it all."

Kizer was listening to him tell the story, and now she joined the conversation. "Sonoma is a special place," she said. "When we first arrived it seemed urban and sophisticated, rural and re-laxed, all at the same time. It hasn't changed much since we first came here, and every time I come back here after being away it feels as though I'm seeing it for the first time." Then, as though to give me a parting gift I might take home, she read aloud from "Running Away from Home," her long, delicious poem about Spokane, Washington, where she was raised, which includes the line "I know your secrets." She read beautifully, perfectly. I left Carolyn Kizer and John Woodbridge in their home, feeling that I now knew some of the secrets of Sonoma as well as of Spokane, and indeed, Sonoma seemed a good place to run away to and live under the radar of fame.

In the plaza at night, under the stars and the crescent moon, with the massive stones of City Hall illuminated by electric lights, I felt the presence of the past, and I felt a part of the old tradition of marketing without bar codes and computerized cash registers. On Tuesday nights all transactions are in cash—no checks or credit cards—and after a while I could add quickly and accurately in my head. I liked the feel of the money as it changed hands, and I liked watching the till as the fives, tens, and twenties piled up. In two or three hours, we might make as much as twenty-five hundred dollars—not bad for selling onions, sunflowers, kale, and frisée while chatting about the weather or explaining how to cook celery root—in a stew, for example, or sliced thin in a salad.

Plaza shopping isn't slow. From 5:30 P.M. precisely, when the Tuesday night market starts with the blast from a horn, until 7:30 P.M. or so, the tempo can be frenetic. I liked the rush, but I could understand why Miguel found the spectacle sobering, if not depressing. The boxes that he, Valde, Jesús, and the others had filled so carefully with vegetables and with such intensive labor were emptied in no time. The produce was dispersed all over Sonoma, and the crew would have little if any time to take a breather. The men needed to go back to work almost immediately, to fill the boxes all over again, so they might be emptied all over again, and so on, around and around, from farm to market in a furious tempo from July to October.

One of my customers, a man of Middle Eastern descent with whom I got into conversation, bought pounds of kale and juiced them every morning for his health and well-being. I became a convert to kale and cooked it and ate it daily. A Mexican family—husband, wife, and tiny baby wrapped in a blanket, all of them recent arrivals to Sonoma—wanted garlic; they had U.S. government food stamps intended specifically for purchases at farmers' markets. I sold them two handfuls of garlic and noticed that there were others like them, newcomers to America who shopped in the plaza. It seemed that the circle for organic produce had widened and that customers weren't only white and middle-class. In Santa Rosa a new community garden had been built in a Mexican neighborhood. Families there grew vegetables and created a sense of community; there were fiestas with music and tacos. Kids, especially, liked everything about it.

In Sonoma, shoppers could be extravagant or parsimonious, as they chose; one man bought six pounds of eggplant and six pounds of tomatoes, while a woman bought four tiny carrots, one onion, and one tomato. There was Priscilla Coe, whom I had first met at the Red Barn. "You see," she said proudly. "My favorite part of the week *is* to buy from Oak Hill, either here or at the farm itself." There was the big, beefy fellow who, puffing and chewing on a cigar, asked me to drop the price I had asked for corn from $2.50 to $2.25. Not a problem. I handed him the change he wanted. I almost always undercharged rather than overcharging, and if I did overcharge by even as little as twenty-five cents, the look on the face was enough to wound me. A couple of times I gave too much change and was pleasantly surprised when it was returned to me.

All the shoppers seemed to calculate the total of the items they had picked out; if my total didn't match theirs, they were unhappy, and that meant that you risked losing a customer to one of the other farm stands. There was competition, and not much fraternization, between the rival farms—farms including the Patch, Arrowsmith, Mt. Moriah, and Ortiz Brothers. I was proud that Oak Hill had the largest stand and the best produce.

Behind the stand we were a boisterous crew. Candi Edmondson, who was in charge of sales for the farm, gave out recipes and explained fruits and vegetables that were unfamiliar to shoppers. "The Rosa Bianca eggplant is creamy and good for baba ghanoush," she explained one evening. Like others at Oak Hill, Candi, too, was an artist—she was a photographer and a landscape painter—and she brought to the market an eye for the color and shape of things; she always arranged the produce artistically. Once a week, for a whole year, she had set up her

*A painter, photographer, and creative cook, Candice Edmondson works at the lo-
cally owned Sonoma Market, which carries Oak Hill produce, and at both the
Tuesday night and Friday morning farmers' markets in Sonoma, where citizens
shop, exchange news, and gossip about events far and wide.*

camera at several locations on the farm and took photos that
captured the changes in the seasons. I got the impression that
the images were in her head and that she could project them on
her own private screen almost any time she wanted to. She also
painted images of the farm in brilliant colors and exhibited her
work in the Red Barn. When she talked about the landscape, it
was with the eye of a painter. "I love the brown hills and the

blotchy oak trees," she said. "Of course it's pretty when it's green, but green does not say 'California' like the brown hills." On Tuesday nights, she darted about and shouted—she was a ball of energy but didn't pressure anyone to buy anything. "I'm not a hawker," she said. "The product speaks for itself and sells itself." But she believed passionately in organic farming, and she was as passionate about the produce as about her art. "There is nothing more important than growing food for people," she said. "And I enjoy cooking and eating almost everything that comes out of the fields."

Jesús Soto and Seth Dolinsky—Seth sometimes wearing his "Woodstock 1994" T-shirt—worked effortlessly on market nights; they were masters of the market. Seth is an investment adviser and makes a good living; he, too, believes in the goodness of local organic produce, and he wanted to help Oak Hill. Seth's seventy-seven-year-old father, George, who worked in Manhattan much of his life, brought fast-paced New York style to our stand. The king of kibitzers, he handed out cocoa nibs and goji berries, which he claimed would increase life expectancy, and he told one and all in a raspy voice, "You are your own messiah." Vanessa Wardwell, who was born in the town of Sonoma and raised in Glen Ellen, was, at the age of twenty-one, the youngest and perhaps the perkiest of our crew. Wearing orange Crocs, she was happy to be there. "If Mario Batali can wear Crocs when he's on the Food Network, so can I," she said. "I love Mario, and I love food TV." The plaza on Tuesday night was a haven for young people like Vanessa, and though they mostly ate fast food, they gave the scene a youthful flavor.

When I wanted a break, I wandered through the plaza, listening to the live music, buying and eating pork tacos, and

*Born and raised in Sonoma County, twenty-something student Vanessa Wardwell—
a recent convert to good food—works at the Tuesday night farmers' market in the
plaza in the town of Sonoma, when everyone shows up for fresh produce, live music,
and community spirit.*

drinking beer. I ran into friends from the past: Rose and Larry
Murphy, who have owned Murphy's Irish Pub for years; and
Tony and Judith Marciante, who grow grapes on the edge of
town and make their own wine, which allows Tony to feel re-
connected to his Italian roots. He tried to work at Whole Foods
in Sonoma, but he lasted only a month in the fish department
and didn't like the insistence on "customer service, customer

service, customer service." It broke his heart to see the waste—
the seafood that went unsold and was thrown into the dumpster
behind the store at the end of the day.

Hilda Swartz, the founder and manager of the Sonoma farmers' market, sells her color photographs of vegetables at the stand
right next to Oak Hill's. "The market helps keep our area green,"
she said. "It's a place where people can buy food that's safe,
healthy, and fresh, and the money goes right to the farmers themselves. The plaza is a special place, and on market day, Sonoma
people feel the plaza belongs to *them,* and that it's *their* market."

With a little coaxing, Hilda will recount stories of the ranch
in Riverside County where she grew up. "My father specialized
in tree-ripened peaches," she said. "He delivered peaches door
to door—to Newport Beach and Huntington Beach—and han-
dled them like eggs because they bruise easily. As a girl I picked
peaches and made ten dollars a day, which seemed like a lot of
money in the 1940s. Then I went to college, and after gradua-
tion I taught high school home economics in Los Angeles and
then at Grossmont College in San Diego. A lot of people don't
want to farm anymore. It's one of the hardest jobs there is, but
there are new farmers coming along now. You know, I've enjoyed this year's peach season tremendously. I never tire of eating a good peach."

Paula Downing, Hilda's counterpart at the year-round farmers' market in Santa Rosa, turned to mass marketing to bring in
customers. She advertised on local radio stations, and now shoppers recognize her voice when she opens her mouth to speak.
Santa Rosa has a population of 150,000; Paula's goal was to persuade 1 percent of them to shop at the farmers' market on
Wednesdays and Saturdays. "Farmers' markets are the 'in'

thing," she told me and then asked a rhetorical question she answered herself. "Where do you matter in this world? Not a lot of places. At the farmers' market you feel like a human being. The food is amazing, and it's fun. What's not to like?" But her market has had its share of troubles; organic farming doesn't always make for good citizenship, and Paula has had to intercede to stop backbiting, petty jealousies, and infighting. "I told them, sell your food and be nice to one another," she said. "It's a privilege to be here, and if you're not going to behave, you can go. It's a small community. I'm the parish priest, and that's the way it has to be."

THE ELASTICITY OF LOCAL

I was fortunate to live close to several first-class restaurants and open-air markets. There was the Parkside Café, owned by Mark Dierkhising, who came from a Minnesota family that had had both a farm and a restaurant and who lived the farm-to-table life before it became a movement. Once a month Mark prepares a gourmet prix fixe meal that features Sonoma County fruits, vegetables, meats, mushrooms, and chicken. Mark Malicki is another successful Santa Rosa chef who shops at the market Paula Downing manages. He buys in bulk and receives substantial discounts. "I like farmers' markets because you don't have to go through big distributors," he said. Mark Malicki shops almost everywhere every day of the week; he shops all over the Bay Area—at Monterey Market and Berkeley Bowl in Berkeley, at 99 Ranch Market in El Cerrito, and at Mexican and Asian markets close to his Café St. Rose. Mark believes in buying local and cooking with local produce, but he also defines the banana leaves that he uses for cooking as "local" because he found them around the corner in the store that sells imported Asian products. He also orders foie gras from the Hudson Valley in upstate New York because he says it's better than the local product.

The gospel of local bugs him. "The biggest question that waiters get asked in Café St. Rose is 'Where is this grown?'" he explained on a quiet Wednesday morning while cooking a pig's head from Black Sheep Farm in California in a cauldron of boiling water. "The whole local thing can get ridiculous," he added. "A woman yesterday wanted to know where the leeks on her plate were from. The waitress told her, 'They're illegitimate leeks.' It drives me nuts. In France, when you order porcini mushrooms you don't know exactly where they're from. In California we go overboard." Mark could afford to be elastic with his definition of "local." Whatever he cooks, his customers will be sure to eat; people come to eat at Café St. Rose from all over the United States.

I first met him in the 1980s, when he was the chef at Truffles, the best restaurant the town of Sebastopol has ever had. By then he had already made a name for himself in New York by cooking for celebrities, including the singer-songwriter James Taylor, the charismatic lawyer William Kunstler, and the versatile actor Christopher Walken. He also cooked for photographers—among them Steven Meisel, Norman Parkinson, Bruce Weber, and Horst P. Horst—and for dozens of supermodels—including Janice Dickinson, Iman, and Andie MacDowell. In those days in New York, when he was twenty-something, he didn't take much interest in the origin of produce. "I knew about farms in New Jersey," he said. "But mostly I associated vegetables with the trucks that pulled up at the back of the restaurant." After New York and Sebastopol, he went to work for Iron Horse Vineyards in Forestville, where the owners, the Sterlings, cultivate a five-acre vegetable garden and an eight-acre orchard. Mark could pick what he wanted, then bake, fry, roast, or barbecue to his heart's content.

By his own reckoning he'd been discovered as a great new chef and then cast off at least four times. "Apparently I'm a rising star again," he said. "Better than being a setting star, and if you calculate by Andy Warhol's fifteen minutes of fame, I figure I've gotten an hour to date." He still has a certain New York sass about him. He will say almost anything that's on his mind at any time, and then again he won't say anything at all. "At Iron Horse once, we were tasting Cabernet Sauvignons, and someone was there from the *Wine Spectator.* They asked me what it tasted like, and what came to me was shoelaces; that's what I said. Wine and food does that to you. Some foods, like stew, I don't want to eat because they make me sad. I hate stew. When I was a kid my mother made a stew, mostly of potatoes, the whole time my father was on strike and not working and not bringing home a paycheck. Stew reminds me of that sad, sad time."

One night, after working at Oak Hill and feeling exhausted, I ate dinner at Mark's. There was a duck entrée and a candied apple for dessert, but what I enjoyed most of all was the curried soup of sliced butternut squash and coconut milk. After that evening I made it regularly. I didn't have a recipe. I experimented until I liked the taste, and it reminded me of Mark, his restaurant, and Oak Hill. The coconut milk was imported, and so was the curry powder, but the butternut squash was from

Oak Hill, picked by my own hands. One afternoon, between 2:30 and 4:30, Valde, Miguel, Jesús, and I had picked two and a half tons of it while Paul pulled the tractor through the fields. We had been on a roll. The yield was far greater than Paul had expected, and squash was everywhere. Harvesting it felt like gathering money to put in the bank. With its thick skin, the squash would last for months, and in the midst of winter it would bring back memories of summer.

Earlier that day, Paul had said I could drive the tractor, and I had looked forward to that moment; it would be like sitting on a throne. I sat down in the driver's seat as Paul began to explain the workings of clutch and brake. But then he had said, abruptly, "It's not going to work." I didn't argue with him. I could see that he had made up his mind. I had come that close to driving the tractor and becoming, at least for an afternoon, a tractor king. Perhaps it was good that I hadn't driven it; the fields were muddy following a rain, and the tractor pulled a rig in back that held half a ton of squash at a time. I wouldn't have wanted to turn the rig over and injure Miguel, Valde, and Jesús. Safety had to come first.

But, as a kind of consolation, I was allowed to drive the Oak Hill flatbed truck at the 110th annual Valley of the Moon Vintage Festival Parade. I had arrived at the meeting place expecting to ride in the back of the truck, which was decorated with peppers, pumpkins, marigolds, sunflowers, and ears of corn and looked like a veritable cornucopia on wheels. But when I arrived, Candi explained that I was to drive; she, Lynn Thomas, and Jesús—who wore a Mexican hat and a belt with a big buckle—would ride in the back. The truck had automatic transmission, so driving wasn't a problem. I had only to take my foot off the brake and press down gently on the gas pedal to move at the snail's pace required. We went down Second Street and around the plaza slowly; this was only the second parade of my life, and I enjoyed it tremendously. "Oh, how beautiful" and "It's so pretty" I heard spectators say of the festooned truck. But we didn't win an award from the judges at the reviewing stand.

Paul drove the tractor behind me, and Candi smiled and called him "Farmer" when we started out. He was first and foremost Paul Wirtz, of course, but by then—four months after first meeting him—I, too, could see him as the archetypal farmer with his machine. I had met other farmers—Wayne James at Tierra, Kevin McEnnis at Quetzal, and Bob Cannard Jr.—and I knew that no two farmers are the same, much as no two farms are the same. But at that moment I allowed myself to see Paul as a representative of all the farmers in America. I imagined, too, that he represented all farmers to the crowds gathered in the plaza. He was young, looked healthy and happy, and though not grandstanding or jumping up and down for joy—that wasn't Paul's way—he seemed delighted to be acknowledged by the town that he helped to feed all year long, though his labors in the field mostly went unseen. At the annual parade, Paul had his day in the sun—there in the plaza that, as John Woodbridge had explained, "was a place that was made for things to happen."

FULL BELLIES, HOES DOWN

All over California it was time to celebrate and time for farmers to meet the men, women, and children who bought their produce, thereby making it possible for the farms to go on season after season. Perhaps no farm was better at telling stories about itself, and about the revolution in organic farming that was gaining momentum, than Full Belly in Capay Valley in Yolo County. Every fall for decades, Full Belly had held a huge party, a combination of county fair, picnic, and hoedown, that the farmers called a "Hoes Down" because no one on the farm worked that day and all tools, from hoes to pitchforks, were at rest.

I drove to the party with Paul, Candi, and Candi's son, Quenten, to hear what the farmers at Full Belly had to say about the state of agriculture in California. By the time we arrived in the afternoon, the twentieth annual Hoes Down was rocking. The previous summer, five thousand people had shown up, and this year they were expecting more. Thousands had arrived by noon, and they were eating barbecued chicken, drinking beer, taking tours of the farm, watching the Pomo Nation Tribal Dancers perform, and much more. The whole farm was one vast stage of many smaller stages; the Hoes Down was a live happening.

Full Belly, which started in the 1980s, grew little by little and then by leaps and bounds. At first the farm's founding members rented 250 acres from a widow who thought the place had too many rattlesnakes to make it good for anything. In 1990 the four partners began to buy portions of the property, and by 2000 they owned it free and clear. By 2007 those same four partners, fifteen full-time employees—in the summer the number jumped to sixty—and six or so interns grew a hundred different crops and five hundred different varieties of crops. By the summer of 2007 they had 1,500 subscribers, from Capay Valley to Berkeley and beyond, who received fresh produce all year round.

The farm has a large herd of sheep that do the kind of work often allocated to tractors. But sheep are better than tractors; they add fertilizer to the soil as they chew and mow down the cover crops. They also provide lamb, wool, and yarn. Someone said that the sheep are the farm's secret weapon, and it's not the only secret weapon. The farm is also a home for bumblebees, which play a part in pollination; bats, which eat pests; raptors, which help control the rodent problem; and dogs, which keep deer away from the crops and hunt out insidious gophers. And the barns provide homes for useful owls. "We stack things up here," one of the farmers said. "And we harvest energy." Make no mistake about it, industrious men and women keep Full Belly going 365 days of the year with hard work, but those same men and women put nature to work for them as much as possible, and nature puts them ahead of the game. The whole farm is an intricate system of interconnected parts that feed one another, underground as well as aboveground, and Full Belly made me think of an M. C. Escher painting in which up is down and down is up. The point, of course, is to keep the farm going, enrich the soil, and feed, if not the whole world, then at least as much of the world as 250 intensely cultivated acres can manage. The partners are as adept at marketing as at farming, and Full Belly struck me as a combination of holy crusade and successful business enterprise.

Andrew Braitt, a serious-looking young man with glasses and a beard, took Paul, Candi, me, and a small group of people at the Hoes Down into a peach orchard planted in 1994. "We had the best year ever for peaches," he said. "Of course there were zero peaches the year before, but it's usually feast or famine with fruit." Andrew had a lot to say and not much time to say it in. He had a lot of ground to cover, too, and we moved from the peach orchard to the walnut orchard, then to a block of broccoli planted from seeds, and finally to a field with cover crops—Sudan grass, buckwheat, and cowpeas—that towered above him. Sheep would be useless here; the cover crop was so tall and jungle-like that only a tractor would do.

Andrew expressed thankfulness for the end of harvest. It would soon be the dormant time of the year, when he could recharge his batteries, and he was eager to thank the visitors to Full Belly. "If you weren't eatin' what we're growin', this ground would be covered with houses and paved over with cement," he said. It was a grim thought, and it had a visible effect on the faces in the crowd of people who had come to celebrate at Full Belly. "We wouldn't be here without you," Andrew continued. "It used to be we all knew someone who lived or worked on a farm. But in the last half century people have moved from the country to the city, and so we all know fewer and fewer farmers. Now farm families are less than 2 percent of the population."

Was there a father of the movement to which he and Full Belly belonged, someone asked. "There's no one person," he said. "What you see here is the culmination of thirty years of hardworking, tenacious folk driven by passion."

Paul Muller was one of the pioneers at Full Belly, and he had the same answer to that question. He looked to no one single teacher. Dressed in sneakers, jeans, and tinted glasses, he said, "It's a community thing. It's about people putting together different pieces to make a whole." Muller, who grew up on a dairy in San Jose, had attended the University of California at Berkeley, but he was not enthusiastic about his college education. "At Berkeley they told us that it was essential to move people off the land and replace them with capital and machinery," he said. "That didn't make sense. We were also taught that Americans could get their food from someplace else on the planet, but that wasn't true then, and it still isn't true. We have got to grow our own food and not import it or we will end up like all the failed empires of the past: dependent on distant lands."

Muller showed us a field that had had garlic and now was planted with artichokes and strawberries. He reached down and scooped up a handful of soil and explained with fervor, "Beneath your feet, there's a universe of billions of microorganisms that are digesting and liberating the nutrients and making them available to the plants."

Perhaps more so than anyone else at Full Belly, Muller is a shameless proselytizer and proud to admit it. Like Andrew Braitt, he offered sober thoughts, but he also pumped us up with his vision of a bright farming future. "We invited you here to celebrate, but we also want you to become advocates of change and to pressure Congress on the Farm Bill," he said. "We came here in the 1980s, rather than to the Great Central Valley, because we could afford to buy land here and because we rejected the paradigm for traditional agriculture that still operates there for the most part. We felt that agriculture had to change and that we needed to think about the ethics of farming—and about growing the best-quality food. The point is to have more farmers, not fewer, and, in fact, we *grow* farmers here. Our interns learn by doing, and they go out into the world and become farmers committed to taking care of the land for future generations and growing nutritionally complete foods."

On that day Full Belly lived up to its name and reputation. We feasted, drank beer, sat in the sun, and talked about the future of

Oak Hill. Full Belly might make anyone stop and think; it seemed to make Paul, especially, conscious of his role as a farmer. At Full Belly there were four equal partners and a full complement of assistants. Paul likes teamwork and collaboration; at Oak Hill he is often alone, on his tractor or turning the pages of his "Top Secret" notebook, planning what to plant next. If only Oak Hill could mechanize more, he said, and grow fewer crops, then work might be less demanding and he might feel less driven. Anne Teller is committed to growing diverse crops; Oak Hill cultivates more than two hundred varieties for commercial purposes on approximately forty acres, and that kind of diversity on the relatively small scale of Oak Hill means hard work year round. In diversity lies its salvation—or at least sustainability—but sustainability isn't easy for any farm. At Full Belly, where nearly everything exists on more than one plane, and metaphor seems to grow out of the earth itself, there was ample food for thought. I fed my head until it was crammed full of ideas, then drove home in the darkness, through fields I could not see, silent and alone with my own thoughts.

11

DAYS OF THE DEAD

RURAL GESTALT

Fred Euphrat gazes at Sonoma and sees it turning into Provence.
It is a future he doesn't like, and he doesn't mind saying so. Fred
has a quick wit and a disarming sense of humor that makes him
well liked in his community. He speaks out on almost all the environmental issues of our day—on the radio, at town hall meetings, in a delightful book entitled *Sonoma Mandala,* and any time
people will listen. Fred has facts at his fingertips and a way with
words. A graduate of UC Berkeley—with a BA in physical geography and a PhD in watershed management—he is a licensed
forester; when he walks through a forest, he can read its history
in the flora and fauna. As a boy, he, like Ted Bucklin, attended
Town School, a private academy in San Francisco, and he has
known Anne as "Mrs. Teller" ever since third grade. Years later,
when she asked him to manage the forest at Oak Hill, he leapt at
the opportunity. In one week he and his crew thinned the trees,

thereby decreasing the chance of a destructive fire. He also found a marijuana plantation in the thick of the woods and let Mrs. Teller know.

For decades Fred has studied soils and soil erosion, and he is now a paid consultant to the California State Legislature's Joint Committee on Fisheries and Aquaculture. He knows a lot of local history—his own ancestors arrived in Sonoma in the 1850s and rolled cigars from tobacco grown along the Russian River. His understanding of human history, and the history of the soil, enables him to take a long view of a subject that many citizens are shortsighted about. Not surprisingly, he offers dire predictions.

"Don't get me wrong. I love wine," he said over an early-morning breakfast in Healdsburg, where he lives with his family and runs a business called Forest, Soil & Water, Incorporated. Nothing is more important to Fred than forest, soil, and water; if they are healthy, then animals, plants, and human beings will be healthy, too. "We seem to be turning into France," he continued. I wasn't sure whether that was a compliment or a criticism; I soon found out. "We're becoming a patchwork of villages, vineyards, and copses of woods. That might be nice for some of us, but if you're a forest-dependent species, it might spell your end. If you're a watershed, it wouldn't be good, and if you're a salmon in one of our streams, it would be very bad news."

Fred sees the world through his own eyes, but he also has the remarkable ability to put himself—in an instant—into the body of a fish and look at the world through the fish's eyes. "If I were a fish in Sonoma County now, I would say, 'Where is the cold water that used to be here? Where are all my friends, and how do they expect us to survive when they pull us out of oceans and rivers in great numbers?'" Back in his identity as an environmentally conscious human being, he puts together the pieces of the near-apocalyptic jigsaw puzzle he sees. He tossed out an idea I heard for the first time. "Forests grow fish that reach out to the ocean to bring back nutrients. Salmon are important as a totem, and I want people to think of them as the most important part of the equation. Their change has always reflected the advance of Western civilization. The indigenous people depended on salmon, and when the salmon came up rivers and streams to lay their eggs, it was a party for everyone. Indians ate the salmon; bears ate the salmon and shat in the woods, and that put nutrients into the soil, which is the essential element that connects everything else, including farming, the food we eat, and the environment."

Fred argues that ever since the arrival of Europeans in Sonoma, human beings have engaged in a wanton assault on the environment. They sterilized the soil to eliminate nematodes so that the land could be farmed efficiently and profitably. They depleted groundwater and destroyed watersheds, forests, and streams. Fred is afraid that in the race to promote and market its unique qualities, Sonoma will lose its identity and become another outpost of American homogeneity. In his eyes, the *terroir* of the place would vanish, rural life would disappear, and the local would be swallowed up by the global. "If I have one single message, it's that we have to be post-pioneers," he said. "We have to be restorationists. We will all be in 'slurbia' if we don't watch out. To maintain our rural gestalt, and to hold on to that sense of the wild that is slipping through our fingers, will take time, money, and work. It's the price we have to pay to live in the country."

Yannick Ponte—the only Frenchwoman I know who lives in Glen Ellen—argues that the wild and the rural have already vanished in the valley. A native of Bordeaux, with a bourgeois father and a communist grandmother, she feels more akin to her grandmother than her father, and she feels like an alien in Sonoma. "The wealthy are taking over the valley," she said on an afternoon when she served me olives, cheeses, cold meats, dark bread, and red wine. It's part of her DNA to serve food and wine. "It's a zombie world here and in France, because the French are copying the worst of America," she said. Her husband, Don Ponte, who is an accomplished artist, agrees with her. Raised in San Francisco in a large Italian family—which gave him the feeling of living in Europe—he attended the Art Institute, befriended Richard Brautigan, the author of *Trout Fishing in America,* met City Lights bookstore's Lawrence Ferlinghetti, and worked for Henri Lenoir, the Old World bohemian who owned the legendary literary haunt Vesuvio's. Don arrived in Sonoma in the 1970s and never left.

"I thought I was in the middle of nowhere," he said. "It felt like the 1930s, and there was something magical about the fact that Jack London had lived here. Then people started moving in because they liked the rural life and the trees, and they built houses and cut down the trees. I'm an idealist, and I'm disappointed with the way things have turned out." In his art Ponte recreates the world that has vanished, the world that he misses; in a poster for the Glen Ellen Village Fair, he turned back the clock and depicted, in the manner of Thomas Hart Benton, Jack London on a buckboard driving a team of horses on the town's main street. The poster showed no cars and no crowds, and the landscape in the background showed no houses, mansions, or vineyards, just valley and mountain.

Listening to Yannick and Don complain about the decline in the quality of life in the valley reminded me of Friedrich Engels's observation about so-called progress in *The Origin of the Family: Private Property and the State,* which first appeared in 1884. "The more civilization advances, the more it is compelled to cover the evils it necessarily creates with the cloak of love, to excuse them, or to deny their existence; in short, to introduce conventional hypocrisy," he wrote. Of course, it is no longer merely a question of rich and poor, haves and have-nots. Everyone who lives on the earth breathes the same air, drinks more or less the same water, and suffers from environmental degradation. Granted, some cities are more polluted than others. Granted, too, some people might drink bottled water, but the supply of water is finite, and the globe is finite, too. The rich may export toxins and have better medical care than the poor, but they can't export their own cancer or dispatch to another planet the ravages of war and social injustice. They don't have a separate highway system, and they live in the same cancerous cities as everyone else. The world seems as hypocritical a place as when Engels wrote in the 1880s. Civilization still conceals its evils as best it can, and often under "the cloak of love." The fast food industry and agribusiness have polluted and perverted, and in their ads they insist that they do it all for us, their consumers, in the name of love. Ads tell us to love burgers, beauty products, and computers.

Europeans and Yankees have been coming to Sonoma for more than one hundred and fifty years, and they have done their best—or worst—to turn it into an extension of Europe, to tame it, control it for cash, and feel comfortable in its rough environment. When Robert Louis Stevenson, the Scottish-born author of *Treasure Island* and *The Strange Case of Dr. Jekyll and Mr. Hyde,* came to California in the 1870s he saw it as a place with a split personality—a Dr. Jekyll and Mr. Hyde landscape. On the one hand it seemed primitive and backward—"like England a hundred years ago"—but on the other hand it seemed more advanced and more "civilized" than the Old World. Stevenson used a telephone for the first time in his life while he was visiting California—an experience he describes with delight in *The Silverado Squatters,* a narrative about his California sojourn. "So it goes in these young countries: telephones, and telegraphs, and newspapers, and advertisements running far ahead among the Indians and the grizzly bears," he wrote. Though he explored vineyards in California and drank California wine, he noted that California's vineyards—which he called "outposts in the wilderness"—were unlike European vineyards. "There is nothing here to remind you of the Rhine or Rhône, of the low Côte d'Or, or the infamous and scabby deserts of Champagne; but all is green, solitary, covert," he wrote.

JE T'AIME

Stevenson explained that it was "difficult for a European to imagine" the place because it was new and of "such an accidental pattern." The place he was speaking about was the town of Calistoga. Had he observed the town of Sonoma, with its European-style plaza laid out by Mariano Vallejo, he might have told a different story. Sonoma seemed to want to be like Europe.

There are streets—like Place des Pyrenees—and stores—like Chateau Sonoma and Être—with French names. Close to the plaza there is even a street named France, and French movies like *Je t'aime,* not by coincidence, have often enjoyed long runs in the Sebastiani Theatre.

Sondra Bernstein describes herself as an unabashed Francophile. She owns the Fig Pantry, which provides food to go, and two gourmet restaurants, the Girl and the Fig and the Fig Café. Her mission is to marry French food and French culture to a certain kind of California abundance epitomized by the fig; the word "fig" appears in nearly every aspect of her business. She is fig crazy.

Born and raised in Philadelphia, Bernstein attended Arizona State University. At the restaurant chain TGI Friday, she learned "the really big lessons: how a big organization works, and corporate rules and systems." She brought some of the TGI Friday experience with her to Sonoma, where she fell in love with the place at first sight and started a small business that grew rapidly. "I have a fig fetish," she explained in her office at the Fig Pantry on the outskirts of Sonoma. "Figs are a symbol of our beauty and bounty. They're erotic, delicate, luscious, and biblical." Bernstein wants locals and tourists who eat at the Girl and the Fig to feel they are in France, savoring "the French experience," as she has come to know it herself. Her wine list offers only Rhône-style wines, and she makes sure her employees provide "French tableside service."

Francophiles have crawled all over Northern California; for years a popular billboard read, "Don't Leave Sonoma Without Visiting France," as though Sonoma were the New France and heir to the tradition of French winemaking. You can see and taste the French tradition at Hanzell Winery, where the Pinot Noir vines are among the oldest in California. Their 2005 Pinot Noir sold for one hundred dollars a bottle. That was more than I could afford, but I bought one. And I learned the history of the winery from Robert Sessions, who has worked at Hanzell for decades, and from his son, Ben, who grew up with grapes and wine. James Zellerbach, of the Crown-Zellerbach Corporation and once a U.S. ambassador to Italy, created the winery in the 1950s. He modeled the main building after an old structure at Clos de Vougeot, a historic winery in Burgundy, and aimed to turn Hanzell into a copy of that legendary grape-growing and winemaking region. The experiment didn't work. Sonoma wasn't Burgundy, and the public wasn't ready for American Burgundies. Still, Hanzell imported French oak barrels to age the wines, and American wineries adopted the practice. When Zellerbach died in 1963, the estate was sold to Douglas and Mary Day, and then to the French aristocrats Barbara and Jacques de Brye. Their son, Alexander de Brye, inherited the property and kept the French legacy alive. Jean Sessions, who plays a role in Sonoma's social scene, wants to import such Italian traditions as the idea of *la passeggiata,* a stroll through the main streets of a town to the plaza. Sonoma's plaza was made for *la passeggiata,* and Jean encourages friends, old and new, to join her and her husband at sunset on market days at the plaza.

THE MEXICAN CONNECTION

Oak Hill, with its emphasis on crops that, like tomatoes and corn, are native to the New World, and with its Red Barn and

White Barn set against an overarching blue sky, strikes me as embracing the Americas wholeheartedly. Of course, the Mexican influence is always apparent in the prevailing sounds of Spanish and in the outdoor altar to the Virgin of Guadalupe that stands outside the fieldworkers' house and is always decorated with fresh flowers. Jesús, Miguel, and the other men who work in the fields have brought their culture to Oak Hill; at lunch they're more likely to be eating tamales than sandwiches, and they listen to Mexican music on the radio. The wreaths they make on the third floor of the Red Barn are inspired by Mexican traditions; one of the wreaths is named "the Peyote" because it uses the bright colors of the Huichol Indians and because, if you look at it long and hard enough—or sometimes even after just a glance—you might think you are under the influence of peyote. Jesús also makes decorative *mogotes,* as he calls them—they're little teepee-like structures—by tying dried cornstalks together tightly at the top, leaving them more open at the bottom. (In Mexico, larger *mogotes* are used in the fields to store ears of corn and keep them dry in the rainy season.)

At Oak Hill the farmworkers celebrate Cinco de Mayo, the date in 1862 when Mexican farmers and workers defeated the French army at Puebla. At the celebration I attended, they had barbecued beef and chicken, made salsas and guacamole, and invited all the Anglos from the farm to join them. Jesús made a speech in English and in Spanish in which he said that Cinco de Mayo symbolized the coming together of two races and two nations.

Anne Teller, who feels a connection to her Mexican and Guatemalan ancestors, has deliberately chosen not to turn the place into an outpost of Provence. The day Oak Hill celebrated the Day of the Dead—El Día de los Muertos—the traditional Mexican festival to honor the lives of friends and family members who have died, I joined the celebration; I had been looking forward to it for weeks. For the first time that autumn I drove to Glen Ellen at dusk, not at dawn, and when I arrived the Red Barn was illuminated in the darkness and awash in a sea of Mexican music. Inside, an altar had been set up with photos, flowers, candles, and poems, and Mexican food, prepared by the local chef and caterer Isa Jacoby, was spread out on big tables. The *carta del día,* the menu, decorated with black-and-white skeletons by the nineteenth-century Mexican folk artist Posada, listed the dishes:

Sopa de Calabaza con Sangre de Betabel
Tamalitos del Jardín
Tortillas de Harina o Maíz
Salsa Cruda y Asada
Guacamole y Verdura Cruda Tostadas
Pan de Muertos
Dulce de Leche con Manzanas
Galletas
Bebida de Chocolate Caliente

I have been eating Mexican food ever since 1975, the year I lived in Mexico. Almost every year I return to Mexico to visit my friends Dianne Romain and Sterling Bennett, two former colleagues from Sonoma State University. They built a house in Guanajuato and grew their own organic vegetables in their garden. Digging in the earth, planting, and harvesting made them feel at home there, and having their own produce allowed them to have a far healthier and more diverse diet than they otherwise would have had. From my experience in Mexico and California, I knew that some of the chefs who make the best Mexican food are gringos and gringas like Isa Jacoby; her food is gourmet.

Along with John McReynolds, Sheana Davis, Dana Jaffe, and the many chefs in restaurants around the plaza in Sonoma, Isa has helped to make the Valley of the Moon a paradise for locavores. She lives in the Mayacamas Mountains above Oak Hill, and she often walks to the Red Barn to shop for produce. Born and raised on Long Island, she attended Beloit College and worked at John Peterson's family farm. This farm is the subject of *The Real Dirt on Farmer John,* a bittersweet film in which Isa has a part as Peterson's ex-girlfriend and everybody's favorite hippie. Some of her recipes are in *Farmer John's Cookbook,* though she usually doesn't use that or any other cookbook— whether she makes food for two or for two hundred. Food is part of Isa's heritage. Her grandfather was a baker, and she began to bake bread when she was a teenager in high school on Long Island. In the 1970s she joined the back-to-the-land movement and took part in the "renaissance in American farming"; like others in Oak Hill's extended family, she has rejected factory farming and industrial cooking. She worked at Zabar's, the famous food store in Manhattan, and she ate and cooked her way around the world—Europe, South America, and Asia—before she settled in Sonoma. Though she has been a cook and caterer for much of her life, she knows that we do not live by food alone. "Our stories are what nourish us," she told me on a morning she made a spectacular breakfast of homemade breads and spreads, and we looked down at the Valley of the Moon. "When I came to California I came for the food, because it comes right from the earth and the sea. I came to Sonoma for the elements: the fresh air, the spring-fed water, and the fiery spirit. I stay for the community, the connection to the earth, and the groundedness. We're privileged to be able to live here. We can walk around, pick and eat walnuts, persimmons, and pomegranates. Just grazing, you can find enough to feed yourself, and I love going to the farms and the farmers' markets. I like seeing the piles of vegetables and the aesthetic arrangements."

The Mexican food she made for the Day of the Dead celebration was displayed aesthetically in the Red Barn, and the entire celebration, too, was an aesthetic experience. The Mexicans, old and young, were dressed elegantly and colorfully, some of them in traditional Mexican shirts and hats. Miguel Barrios introduced me to his wife, who was dignified, almost regal, in a white dress. For the first time, Miguel called me "Jonas"—the Spanish version of Jonah—so as far as names went, we were on an equal footing at last. Anne Teller was there, and all of her children except Ted. There was Arden, Will, Lizanne, and Kate, who introduced me to her new beau, Tom. Kate's estranged husband, David Lear, was nowhere in sight, though Anne had invited him and still considered him part of the family. I had met David when he was designing the set for a Santa Rosa production of John Steinbeck's *The Grapes of Wrath,* and naturally our conversation had turned to the barns at Oak Hill that represented the two bookends of the farm. They carried a great deal of symbolic weight for David. "The white barn is feminine, and the red barn is masculine," he said. "The red barn is the king, and the white barn is the queen. There is a quiet majesty in a barn, and barns are living things that convey the force of life itself, and contain a wealth of history." At the Day of the Dead celebration, I would have been inclined to say that the Red Barn seemed both masculine and feminine, both king and queen, because it brought everything and everyone together. That night I felt a part of the whole, a member of the extended family, and I was moved when Kate said, "It looks like you've been adopted by Oak Hill." I managed to say, "It's mutual." I was happy that the observation came from Kate, who is, perhaps of all the siblings, the most attuned to the spirit of the place.

The whole community turned out to celebrate the Day of the Dead, and I would like to say that it was the event of the season, but I had not attended all the many social events of the season, which would make anyone's head spin. Ted Eliot, a former U.S. ambassador to Afghanistan and for many years now a resident of Sonoma, was there with his wife, Pat, who had first come to the Valley of the Moon as a teenager in the 1940s; in those years, she kept her horse in Jack London's stable. For decades Ted's work in the diplomatic service had demanded that the Eliots live all around the world, unable to stay for long in any one place or feel part of a community. Now Sonoma gave them what they had sorely lacked. The had become good friends of Anne Teller's and were now as much a part of the valley as she was. Ted was from Boston and a graduate of Harvard. There was still something Bostonian about him, but he'd become a Californian. Now he and Pat participated in keeping Sonoma green, preserving forests and watersheds, and preventing ostentatious houses from spoiling the landscape. They and their neighbors fought to keep Sonoma Mountain, the great sacred space of the Valley of the Moon, free of commercial development. In Sri Lanka and the former Soviet Union, they'd witnessed the destruction of the environment, and they were determined not to let it happen in their own backyard.

Much the same impulse to preserve motivates David Bolling, the editor of *The Sonoma Index-Tribune,* the town's oldest newspaper, which he is aiming to modernize without offending older, more traditional readers. Throughout the Day of the Dead celebration, Bolling did what the editor of every local paper ought to do. He talked to readers face to face and fielded questions on controversial topics, among them the new hospital and the recent murder of a young man of Mexican ancestry that had cast a dark shadow across the community.

Despite that tragedy, hundreds of people ate, drank, talked, and danced for hours. I watched Paul dancing with Candi, thinking what a well-suited couple they seemed. I danced with Gael, and with Anne, who looked younger than ever. I met Anne's sister and many of the regular Oak Hill customers, who shopped every week at the Red Barn or at the plaza. The Day of the Dead celebration was a way for Oak Hill to thank the customers and the fieldworkers and their families.

All the while the live music, mostly *norteño,* kept playing. Jesús, wearing a wide-brimmed Mexican hat, sang with his brother, José Guadalupe, as musicians on accordion, *bajo sexto*—a big twelve-string guitar—and drums accompanied them. I knew that Jesús always advised newly arrived immigrants from Mexico to learn English and integrate into American society. He had done that himself, but he had not forgotten his Spanish, and, as his songs made abundantly clear, he had not lost touch with Mexico. In one ballad, entitled "El Cabrito," which he has recorded—it's available on CD—he describes the exploits of a proud Mexican bandit. El Cabrito gets into a dispute with a *federale* when he's high on *perico,* cocaine. He pulls out his .38, scares the lawman nearly to death, and lives to tell the tale. "There is some truth and some make-believe in the song," Jesús explained. "I took the exploits of a real person and inflated them." In another song, entitled "El Patrón," he tells the story of Juan Barron, a big-hearted Mexican and the polar opposite of El Cabrito—as good a man as the other man is bad. Barron goes to the United States and succeeds as a businessman without being spoiled by success. After he achieves the American Dream, he returns to Mexico and shares his wealth with friends and family, the church and the school. I didn't need Jesús to say, as he did, "I have put some of me in the song." Juan Barron was Jesús Soto's ideal self and his own best role model.

OLD FARMERS

The celebration of the Day of the Dead at Oak Hill prompted me to think about the death of my father in the fall of 1977, and to remember his life as a gardener and farmer in Huntington and Sebastopol. If he were still alive, Samuel Robert Raskin would be ninety-seven now, probably too old to be farming, but perhaps not. Farmers live long lives in Sonoma—and in the state of Zacatecas, too, where Jesús was born and raised, and where his grandfather Benigno, who lived to a ripe old age, had been a farmer and doctor of sorts who helped to heal the wounded during the Mexican Revolution of 1910–1920. My father had been my closest friend. I had worked with him in much the same way that Valde and his son Jesús worked together. We planted and harvested crops, made compost and tilled the soil together. I missed his company, and I felt in need of a fatherly farmer, or perhaps just an older male figure with at least one foot on the ground and in the fields. My older brother, Fred, who died in November 2005, had grown his own fruits and vegetables on Fire Island—not a hospitable place for farming and gardening. He'd added tons of compost to the place, bringing it in plastic garbage bags by car and by ferry, and he'd built up rich soil on those sandy shores.

Fred was really only a cousin, but I felt as if he were my older brother. His own father had died when he was a boy, whereupon my father had taken him under his wing, and he'd grown up with us in Huntington. Fred learned about farming from my father and carried on his tradition of growing organically. If Fred could farm on Fire Island, one might farm almost anywhere on the face of the earth. The summer I visited him and his girlfriend, Charlotte, a Dutch doctor, I worked in the garden—weeding, watering, and harvesting tomatoes, peppers, and broccoli rabe, which Fred cooked for dinner along with barbecued fish.

At eighty-four, Chester Aaron was the oldest farmer I knew, and I knew that he planned to go on farming until he died, though he confessed to me, "It's harder to push a wheelbarrow across a field now than before." He was still growing garlic in his garden near Occidental, California, and he was still one of the best-known gourmet garlic growers in the United States and around the world, in part because he wrote enthusiastically about garlic as an aphrodisiac, as a cure-all for cuts, scrapes, and the common cold, and as an important ingredient for cooking. Carlo Petrini, the Italian founder of the Slow Food movement, has sung Chester's praises. Chester's *The Great Garlic Book: A Guide with Recipes,* which has become a classic on the subject, has made him friends everywhere. In 2001, *Newsweek* magazine published a two-page spread about him as one of the quintessential garlic growers in America and included a big color photo of him in a cowboy hat that pleased him tremendously.

Chester was born in Pennsylvania to a Jewish family. During World War II he served in the U.S. Army as a machine gunner. The seminal experience in his life took place in 1945, when he was twenty-two years old and a member of the Seventieth Armored Infantry Division, which helped to liberate the German concentration camp Dachau. On the day I came to chat with him about garlic, he showed me the photos he had recently unearthed of himself with emaciated prisoners, as well as a red and black piece of cloth with a swastika, which he'd brought home from the a war as a souvenir. He isn't a morbid fellow or in a mental rut, and yet he has never gotten over the experience of seeing Dachau and its prisoners as a young man.

"Dachau was the epitome of death," he said. "Growing garlic is the epitome of life, but as I approach death, Dachau is the only thing I really would like to write about." Once upon a time, he was married. For years he taught creative writing at St. Mary's College, and he'd written both fiction and nonfiction for adults and children. When he retired to Occidental, the Italian families in town embraced him as one of their own, and that pleased him more than academic accolades. The subject of old age and farming interested me greatly, and since I was in the presence of an old farmer, I asked for his perspective. "Old factory workers become all twisted up and unable to work when they're old," he said. "But I have never met an old farmer around here so bent he couldn't work. Most of them work until the end, and they enjoy it."

Chester is a good example of the ways in which local meets global. Garlic is grown all over the world, from the tropics to

Siberia, China to Transylvania, and there is a network of garlic growers spanning the earth. They communicate with one another over the Internet and by e-mail, and they exchange garlic bulbs by mail. "Unlike academics, farmers don't forget you," Chester said. "I've traveled around the country, and everywhere there are garlic growers; they take me in and make me feel at home." Every year he plants garlic in September and October and harvests a ton and a half in May and June. "I make money from my books *about* garlic, but not *from* growing garlic," he said. "It doesn't pay for itself." At the time I visited him, he was at war with the wild turkeys that were descending on his garlic beds and nearly completely destroying them. He was just about at his wits' end, but he kept on, much as he kept coming back to the subject of Dachau that morning under the redwood trees. "I remember approaching Dachau, and the smoke in the sky, and the smell of burning flesh," he said. "When we arrived, prisoners emerged, stumbling and staggering. I wondered how in the hell did these few people manage to survive? I realized that it was more than the food they put into their bodies. It was a state of mind, and it's only recently that I've realized that what keeps me alive is working here, growing garlic and being connected to people around the world who love garlic as much as if not more than I do."

Whereas Chester cultivates one crop, Bob Cannard Sr. cultivates many crops in his garden in Sonoma. He has a huge barn, perhaps the largest barn I have ever seen, which he built together with his sons. Like Chester, Bob intends to farm until the end of his life. "I'll grow vegetables for as long as I'm alive," he said as he sat in the sun, wearing a cap, short pants, and a short-sleeved shirt. "When I can't grow them, I won't be alive." Like his son Bob Jr. had done when I met with him, Bob Sr. worked the whole time I talked to him, slicing mushrooms that he would dry and distribute to "older people who can no longer fend for themselves." At eighty-one he is a big, tall man, with a face red from the sun, and he can still do a hard day's work. As a young man he must have been as strong as the proverbial bull or ox. He grows flowers—aster, foxglove, delphinium—and vegetables and fruits, including the tomato plants that, at eight feet, were the tallest I had ever seen, as well as melons, beans, celery, zucchini, chard, beets, endive, parsley, cucumbers, guava, plums, peaches, apricots, and cherries. For years he had grown pineapples; then his wife stopped eating them, and so he stopped growing them. "There isn't a thing that can't be grown in Sonoma," he said, and I believed him. "Sonoma, not Santa Rosa, is the chosen spot of all the world as far as nature is concerned. We have a tropical climate. You could grow coffee, but it wouldn't be very good quality. You need to be at least six hundred feet above sea level, and we're only fifty feet. You can grow commercial bananas; two of my sons do. And you can grow commercial avocados, too."

Bob Sr. knew the history of Sonoma County from the time of the Indians to the present day, and he knew the history of its agriculture from grapes to dairy farms to peaches and back to grapes. He founded the agriculture department at Santa Rosa Junior College and taught there for years before handing off the torch to his son. It was more entertaining to hear Sonoma history from him than to read about it in such books as the 1880 *History of Sonoma County,* which reads like an advertisement for Sonoma, not a chronicle of events and people. There were "no extremes of heat and cold and nothing like winter," the book's anonymous authors declared. The county had a "beneficent nature" and must have struck the first settlers as "a veritable Paradise." Further on, one reads, "All kinds of vegetables grow in rank luxuriance." Bob Sr. was proud and patriotic, and he spoke in praise of an American political tradition that goes back to Jefferson and Emerson. "We have to be self-reliant," he said. "Everyone should be, and that's what our schools should teach right now." He defends the ideal of the yeoman farmer who made democracy possible. "The man who walks the land and works the land should make all the decisions about the land— not the men in the corporations who don't eat what they grow," he declared.

Bob Sr. has a vision. He speaks eloquently about organic farming and critically about the petrochemical industry and agribusiness. "The most important thing this country could do now would be to persuade people to buy locally and not from corporations controlled by conglomerates," he said. "That would change the world. We can do it. Everyone must spend a dollar a day on locally grown food. That will boost our economy, generate local jobs, and create local butcher shops, bakeries, and groceries. Then we will have the kind of country that Thomas Jefferson envisioned, and we will put the food giants out of business. It will rejuvenate the family, and it will be a peaceful revolution, too."

He may have wanted me to become more self-reliant, but he wasn't furthering that aim when he sent me home with enough fresh food to last a whole family for a week. I was sorry that my father and Bob Cannard had never crossed paths. They would have enjoyed each other's company—and perhaps have gotten into trouble together by speaking out against corporations.

Joseph Imwalle in Santa Rosa provided a bittersweet parable of an older farmer who has lost his passion for farming. But perhaps he never really had one. He struck me as a solitary survivor trying to continue his life and work with quiet dignity while tragedy hovered about him. Santa Rosa wanted his land for development, and cities usually get what they want, by hook or by crook and with the help of lawyers. Imwalle's land was worth at least a million dollars per acre, which made him a multimillionaire. "I'm land rich," he said, though he would not say exactly how rich. A sister of his had just sold twelve acres to the city. Houses would spring up there. Joseph was the last in his family to hold on to a piece of the old farm.

The Imwalles had farmed in Sonoma County since 1886. Joseph took up the reins of the family business when his father died of a heart attack at the age of sixty-three, though more than anything else he had wanted to be a schoolteacher like his mother and sisters and have summers off. "Farming killed my father," he said, and I could hear his grief. "When I was a kid, we had prunes, hops, grapes, twenty acres of vegetables, cows, pigs, and chickens. My father did almost all of it himself, though Mexicans in the Bracero Program helped. Hops were okay for a while. Then the hop kiln burned down, and all the hop growers went broke."

Joseph worked seven stressful twelve-hour days a week, and he didn't see how he could go on working much longer. His children saw how hard he worked and didn't want to continue the farm. "I do it because it's a tradition, but a lot of traditions have gone, and so can this one," he said on a warm evening when we sat at his kitchen table. Later we strolled through ragged fields that ran along Santa Rosa Creek, which were farmed out and no longer fertile. "The soil here has been used again and again and again, and we have to use chemical fertilizers or we wouldn't be able to harvest anything," he said. One field was infected with a virus, and nothing would grow there. Another field had been planted with crane melons again and again, and they weren't doing well at all. "We shouldn't be planting the same crop in the same spot," he said. "We need to rotate and we haven't." Under a dark sky, and in those depleted fields, I thought that I might have been listening to an Old Testament Joseph recounting the agonies of the plague years.

In fact, Joseph Imwalle made a living not by farming on his own land but by selling, wholesale, conventionally grown produce that arrived by truck at 5:30 A.M. every morning from an immense warehouse in Sacramento. Joseph sold it to mom-and-pop restaurants that served Mexican, Laotian, Thai, Himalayan, Vietnamese, and Indian food, and to neighborhood grocery stores. From a culinary perspective, Santa Rosa wasn't what it had been in his father's day, and the business ethic had changed, too. "It's a rat race now, and everyone is more demanding," he said. "Customers used to be nicer." But the big barn his grandfather built in 1919 was still standing, and seven old palm trees towered above the old farmhouse. Joseph liked to remember the past, and I could see why. "When I was a kid, Dad used a horse to cultivate," he said. "Tom was the horse's name, and he lived in the barn. Later, Dad bought a tractor, and I learned to drive it. In the evening, we always sat down at the table together and ate well. Sunday was a day of rest, and we would visit relatives. Now it's the second-busiest day of the week. That's how it goes. And nearly everything from that time is gone."

The last of the old-time farmers I visited was the one geographically closest to me. Richard Crane is the proud owner of the 2,250-square-foot Crane Melon Barn, built when barns were the pride of every community and now a local landmark. Shoppers come from far and wide to soak up the barn's ambience and talk to the Cranes—Richard, his wife, Cynthia, and their daughter, Jennifer. The Cranes raise grapes to sell to the distinguished winemaker David Noyes. At the height of summer, locals can buy the sweet Crane melons developed by a Crane who was Luther Burbank's contemporary. Richard remembered summers when he harvested hay—four tons a day at the peak of the season. "It was hard, but no one died out there," he said as we sat in the sun behind the barn. "Nobody these days works as hard as we did. When Hispanics tell me that we couldn't do without them, I remind them that they're the latest in a long series of cheap laborers. Before they arrived, there were the Portuguese, and before them, the Italians and the Chinese. This country has consumed wave after wave of cheap immigrant labor." That is as unfortunate as it is true. But it can't go on as before. Agriculture in California can't be humane and at the same time continue to consume human beings—using them and disposing of them—just as it can't continue to deplete the land and the water if agriculture is to survive and thrive. Once again, I could see that the hands on the hoes in the fields are connected to the hands on the knives and forks at the dinner table, and that they are also connected to the fish in the streams and the trees in the forests. And I could appreciate all over again why, after Dachau, growing garlic was so life-affirming for Chester Aaron, the paragon of the garlic grower.

12

I AM WHAT I EAT

THE FARM-TO-TABLE MOVEMENT

For much of my life I ate without thinking and without knowing what I was eating. I ate to fill a spiritual emptiness, to assuage my anxieties, not because I was hungry in my belly. That was the truth of the matter, hard as it might have been to admit it to myself and others. I had glimpses of that truth from time to time, but now I knew it. Meeting farmers, working with them, and bringing home organic produce made me more aware of what I fed myself, where it came from, and what it did to my body—my kidneys, liver, skin, and heart. Long ago I had heard the slogan "You are what you eat" and dismissed it. Now I saw the veracity of that pithy remark, which is attributed to the nutritionist Victor Lindlahr, who published *You Are What You Eat: How to Win and Keep Health with Diet* in 1942. Now I noticed what was at the end of my fork and my spoon. I ate more slowly, tasting what I ate, and not shoveling it in unthinkingly.

Going back to the soil—planting, harvesting, weeding, and cultivating—changed what I prepared in my kitchen and how I prepared it. Farming changed my feelings about food and my rituals of eating, whether by myself or with friends. Decades-old habits shifted in a short season, or so it seemed, though I also knew that the revolution in my kitchen and dining room had been a long time in coming. Now I wanted to be healthy from the inside out, and I believed that the quality of my life could be improved, as Lindlahr and others argued, by diet, though not by dieting according to a strict regimen.

The principal lesson I brought home from Oak Hill and other farms was my recognition of the force of individual responsibility. I could not assume or expect anyone else to lead a healthy life for me or to legislate better eating habits. Still, a new farm bill would be nice if it recognized the importance of small, local, organic farms and didn't kowtow to big growers of corn, soybeans, and wheat. I e-mailed my senators my wishes. All through that year of farming, I followed the debates about the proposed farm bill in Congress and read the coverage in newspapers. I saw the eaters of America uniting and demanding nutritious food, and that was cause for celebration. But I also knew that I couldn't and wouldn't wait for Congress to act. No law about farming and food could make me feel better in my gut. I had to eat for myself; no one else could do it for me. I had to make conscious decisions about what to buy, where to buy it, how much of it to prepare, and I also had to know when to stop eating, and not go on simply because there was still food on my plate.

No longer did I have to belong to what my parents had called "the Clean-Plate Club." I was a grown-up and didn't have to eat everything. At sixty-five, I was no longer a growing boy. I didn't need to eat in the riotous way I had eaten at seventeen and eighteen, when I played football and lacrosse and worked at construction in the summers, burning up hundreds of calories in an afternoon. I could give up the food habits I had inherited from my parents, who argued all their lives about meals versus snacks, pizza versus barbecue. I didn't need to eat pizza once a week, or hamburgers on a bun, though my father thought he did. Nor did I have to add sugar and cream to my coffee. I didn't have to go to expensive restaurants and order everything on the menu to prove to others that I was a cultured and intelligent human being.

The farm-to-table movement has been changing the ways families are eating in small towns and in big cities across America. In Sonoma, the chef John McReynolds was at the forefront of that movement. I met McReynolds at an event entitled "Harvesting Our Future," which was billed as "a slow foods feast" at Sonoma Garden Park, a community plot and kind of commons, where citizens grow their own fruits and vegetables. A panel discussion preceded the feast. Ignacio Vella, who makes excellent cheese, argued in favor of sustainability, which he said meant "balance——putting back into the earth what you take out of it, so it's a continuous cycle." Anne Teller touted farmers' markets, gardens in schools, and fresh, nutritious produce. Bob Cannard Jr. argued against tractors, machines, and the war in Iraq. "Those trillions of dollars could have been spent to turn the Sahara and all the deserts of the world into forests with rich soils," he said. Chris Benzinger, from Benzinger Winery, which adheres to biodynamic, organic, and sustainable farming practices, said that his aim was to "create life in the vineyard" instead of spraying everything to death.

After having met him at Sonoma Garden Park, I ran into McReynolds again at the Red Barn, where he was shopping for vegetables. I followed him to his home, which is enlivened by the artwork of his German-born wife, Brigitte. McReynolds is semiretired. He doesn't own a restaurant anymore or work in a kitchen nine to five, but he cooks for people who hire him, and he teaches cooking classes, too. Like me, he was in danger of becoming a diabetic, and, like me, he was on a low-carb diet. His doctor had recently given him the sobering news that he has high blood pressure and high levels of the bad kind of cholesterol. Though he had been cooking for much of his life, and eating all his life, he had never before realized what goes on inside his body chemically and biologically. "I never understood before how refined carbs are turned into sugar and how that leads to the pancreas's creating more insulin," he said. "I can't eat the way I used to eat, or drink the way I used to drink. I have to be conscious of what I'm consuming and keep blood sugar levels down." He also pointed out that a whole generation of baby boomers who had eaten wildly and richly for decades, often without a worry about health, would have to change their eating habits if they wanted to go on eating and drinking—and living.

Born in San Jose, California, in 1950, McReynolds went through what he calls a "fast food phase" when he was a teenager. As a young man he traveled to Europe, Asia, and Latin America and there discovered some of the rich and varied foods of the world. "The draw of travel was food and different cultures," he said. "I was always interested in food as the language of a particular country; I ate all over the world, and that experience shaped the ways I have cooked." In 1980, at the age of thirty, he enrolled at the California Culinary Academy (CCA) and studied with Ken Hom, Carlo Middione, and Ron Batori, one of CCA's founders.

"It was an exciting time to be at CCA," McReynolds said. "It felt like the epicenter of the food revolution. I learned to cook by watching, reading, and doing. I copied established chefs who had a repertoire, and then I began to cook in my own style." What had always been essential to McReynolds's style was going to the source, walking the farm, and shopping for fresh local ingredients in season. "The old way of cooking was to read a recipe and then to go shopping," he said. "The new way is to go shopping and then prepare what you buy—to cook without thinking. Very often I don't know at the time I'm making it what the final outcome will be. The greatest compliment I received was from a food writer who looked at my menu and didn't want to come into the restaurant. He said it didn't look interesting. Then he came in and ate, and said that it was really exciting. That's what I want—for the food to be better than the menu."

When people looked at John McReynolds skeptically and wondered if he really cooked without thinking, he looked them right in the eye and explained exactly what he meant. "It's called improvisational cooking," he said. "You can't think, you don't think, and you don't have to think because you've cooked so many times before that it's an ingrained part of you at the cellular level. It's like sex, and like jazz, when you improvise and don't think about the notes you're playing, or what you're going to play. That's the kind of cooking I do." No one who ate the food he prepared ever came away convinced he ought to stop improvising. One late summer evening, he cooked for eighty people at Oak Hill, using the fresh produce from the farm, and he persuaded one and all to borrow his cooking style.

His first big cooking job was at Skywalker Ranch in Marin for George Lucas, the movie director and producer of *Star Wars*. McReynolds began as sous chef, making commissary food and dishes for the executive dining room; when the executive chef departed, he was promoted. "I didn't have to cook to get the job," he said. "I have never had to cook to get a job." When McReynolds and his business partner, Saul Gropman, opened Café La Haye in Sonoma in 1996, he went on cooking as the whim took him and as suggested by the fresh local ingredients he was buying from Paul Wirtz. When McReynolds went into the kitchen he'd forget about recipes and directions. He used his imagination. If two vegetables—pumpkins and fava beans, say—were in season and on sale at the Red Barn, he cooked with them, knowing they'd taste good together. "When I came up with the menu for the opening of Café La Haye, my partner said, 'Don't we have to cook it first, taste and tweak it?' I said, 'I know exactly what it will taste like.'"

McReynolds has clear views about farming and food in America. "It didn't take long to change the small family farm to agribusiness, and it can change back," he said. "I'd like to see more small farms everywhere all across the country. I'd like it, too, if the government would stop subsidizing the huge farms that operate on the business model of manufacturing." He had recently visited Cuba, and he liked what the Cubans are doing with agriculture. They are reclaiming land from sugarcane production, developing small-scale farming, and rediscovering their food history. "We're an island, too," he said. "If the Cubans can be self-sufficient and not import food, we can do the same thing."

A few weeks later I attended a cooking class taught by McReynolds. I tasted his food and listened to him talk about his favorite subjects. "Chefs like Thomas Keller at the French Laundry are successful not only because of the food they cook but because they take us to that emotional place we went to as kids when we sat down to eat," he said. "They connect us to primal feelings and to earliest memories." McReynolds is modest; he gave such chefs as Keller credit for their work, and he didn't advertise his own talents. He praised small farms and farmers more than he praised restaurants and chefs. "It all starts with the farm," he said. "Being a farmer is going to be the sexy job of this century." Before a small audience, McReynolds made ravioli with Sonoma goat cheese and a sauce of orange and yellow tomatoes from Oak Hill. He made polenta with delicata squash topped with mushrooms in a cream sauce, and a sensational duck salad with persimmons, pomegranates, arugula, and beets. It didn't take me back to my childhood, but it made me feel as though I had eaten food that was healthy and fun to eat. It awakened me to new possibilities and encouraged me to be brave in the kitchen—to combine ingredients like beets, persimmons, and pomegranates that I never would have brought together had it not been for McReynolds.

I went to Café La Haye to try the food from its new chef, Norman Owens, who arrived in the restaurant shortly after 5:30 P.M., just as I sat down at a table with Sheana Davis, a chef, caterer, and fourth-generation Sonoman. The waitress informed us that Owens had returned from last-minute shopping at the Tuesday night farmers' market in the plaza—the last of the year. Owens struck me as a chef who started with a menu, recipes in place, and then went shopping. His menu that Tuesday featured local greens and beets, as well as oysters and blue cheese from nearby Point Reyes, but the trout wasn't local and neither was the Arctic char. The quail, chicken, and steak entrées all included vegetables, but the vegetables didn't play starring roles.

Sheana is the perfect dining companion, and I thought that if M. F. K. Fisher were alive, she'd write about Sheana. Sheana grew up in Sonoma. She likes to eat and to talk about food and Sonomans of all stripes: radicals, conservatives, bohemians, and what she calls the "town's underbelly." Almost all the vegetables Sheana uses in the dishes she makes come from Oak Hill. Since Katrina devastated New Orleans, she has, more than a dozen times, brought the best of Sonoma food and wine to New Orleans, where she teaches at the Savvy Gourmet cooking school. Sheana calls herself "a radical and a rebel," and she isn't afraid to speak critically of her hometown. "It's hard to get through the doors to Sonoma," she admitted when I described the resistance I had met when I arrived in Northern California for the first time. "This place doesn't accept you right away if you're an outsider."

LIFE IS A GARDEN; DIG IT

Now that it was fall, I was spending more time eating in restaurants and less working on farms than over the summer, but when I heard about Sol, a new farm near my old house in Occidental, I drove there to meet the farmers, most of whom, I was told, were in their late twenties and early thirties, and most of them apparently idealistic about farming. I knew the area well. For decades I had walked the land with my dogs Lily and Ida; I knew the ridges and valleys, the cool spots and the hot ones, the precise time of day when the fog blows in and when it retreats back to the coast. I knew the smell of the place—a mix of redwood, bay, and eucalyptus, which changes decidedly with the end of the apple season or when hay and grapes come in.

The town of Occidental had become a new place, full of young, energetic newcomers who are environmentalists, organic farmers, and gourmet chefs. My former student Courtney Meyer bought the old Bohemian Market and turned it into an organic food store, and the town also had a new Cultural Center for the Performing and Visual Arts, and a radio station, too. There was a farmers' market on Fridays, and a new generation had gone back to the land.

Andy, Leo, Brandon, and Amber were renting a four-bedroom house on two acres with a southern exposure, which received sun in the afternoon. "Life is a garden," the sign here read. "Dig it." They didn't call their place a commune, but it seemed like one. They worked together, ate together, sang, danced, and made music together, which is what young people had done in Occidental in the 1960s, when they drifted in from all over the country to become rural hippies.

When I arrived at about 11 A.M., the four new farmers were eating breakfast outdoors with Maggie, a neighbor whom I knew from years past, who had generously allowed Sol's young farmers to use her well when theirs ran dry. That's the kind of place Occidental at its best has always been: neighborly. The skirmishes between hippies and rednecks are now a thing of the past; indeed, these days it is hard to tell one from the other. Sol's owners sold their produce at Occidental's Friday open-air market to Bistro des Copains, a gourmet French restaurant; to their loyal neighbors Maggie, John, and Shirley, whose land touched

theirs; and to their landlord, who allowed them to use his tractor for free.

Brandon had grown up in a farming family in Arkansas and
studied agriculture at the University of California at Santa
Cruz, which trains excellent agriculturalists and agrarians. Leo
helped to found Sol; he was about to leave for upstate New York
to work on a biodynamic orchard and dairy in Columbia
County. "Sol is a good place to learn about business, partnership,
and how to market," he told me. "It's great for beginning farmers because you get to have a dress rehearsal before the big
time." What would he remember most, I asked, when he went
east? "The beauty," he said. "It's so frickin' beautiful, the community is wonderful, and so is the food and the pot."

Andy had moved to Sol from Massachusetts, where he had
worked at Brookfield Farm. "California always sounded great
to me, and now I'm here for the dreamin' and the farmin'," he
said. Young men and women from the East are lured by the
promise of the good life in California, and young men and
women from California are drawn to the mystique of the East.
Even today, a generation of young farmers and wanna-be farmers is moving from region to region, planting and cultivating,
and I admired them for their mobility and freedom. An organization called World Wide Opportunities on Organic Farms
(WWOOF)—and known alternatively as Willing Workers on
Organic Farms—had sprung up to help young farmers who
were moving from place to place and country to country.
Founded in England in the early 1970s, the organization spread
across Europe to New Zealand, Mexico, and Japan. In exchange
for room and board, middle-class migrants with dreams of
someday owning their own farms work in the fields and learn

about crops, soils, and labor. They *wwoof* it from coast to coast, rub shoulders with fellow *wwoofers,* and make *wwoofing* into a lifestyle, in much the same way that Kerouac and the Beats made their transcontinental journeys into a way of life. Sky De-Muro, a young woman from Massachusetts and the daughter of 1960s hippies, *wwoofed* her way to California and showed up at my doorstep. From Florida to New Mexico and Utah, she saw at first hand the renaissance in farming that the young farmers at Sol knew from personal experiences. "There is a resurgence of small, local farming," Andy said. "I have seen it everywhere I have traveled." Leo added, "We want to step outside of the whole crazy fast food agribusiness monster. But this isn't a revolution; it's a return to what was."

From where I stand, the resurgence of the small, local farm is a revolution *and* a return—like so many other upheavals in history that aimed to turn back the clock and undo the harm that had been done by industrialism, commercialism, and the factory system. The Victorian critics John Ruskin, William Morris, and Thomas Carlyle wanted to go back to a less commercial, less mechanized age. Now it's time again to turn back the clock and erase an array of contemporary forces, including global warming, pollution, dependency on foreign oil, agribusiness that poisons land and water, and the fast food industry that pumps out the harmful burgers, fries, chicken, and tacos that have turned America into a land of obesity and heart attacks.

Before I left Sol, Brandon gave me a box of fresh produce—they were especially proud of the broccoli, as well as the lettuce, basil, and cilantro. I was only four-tenths of a mile from my old house, so I thought, why not go there and take a look. I drove slowly down Morelli Lane; the house my parents built was still

Crops are grown year round in the Valley of the Moon, thanks to its Mediterranean climate, and farmworkers pick vegetables even in the middle of winter, when it can feel like the middle of July.

there, and the contours of the land were the same. A whole new generation of oaks had sprung up. I remembered my lush persimmon tree. I stopped the car in the middle of the lane, found an empty cardboard box that I always carried in the trunk for just this kind of purpose, and filled it with persimmons. It felt wonderful to steal fruit from my own tree, and I went home without getting caught, which was even better.

I had passed a year visiting farms, working on farms, and talking to farmers, and now I had come back to the place where I had started, the place where my parents once farmed. I still felt an emotional connection to the land. Seeing it again rekindled memories of my mother and father, and of family feasts at Thanksgiving when we ate together and told stories about life on Long Island and talked about how we'd all come to California to start anew.

To shop for pumpkins and butternut squash for this Thanksgiving I couldn't help but return to Oak Hill and the Red Barn, which did a booming business the day before the holiday— always the busiest day of the whole year. Gael proudly told me she had taken in $4,600. Not bad for a hundred-year-old barn with a wood-burning stove that took away the chill on the cold days of November.

THANKSGIVING REDUX

For my Thanksgiving I went to Occidental to be with Dee and Peter Swanhuyser, who lived in a log house, raised chickens for eggs, and grew their own vegetables. I went to their home for the food and for the feeling of community that I always felt there, whether it was for Thanksgiving, a wedding, or the Super Bowl. The Swanhuysers' huge log house was about as close as one could get in size and feeling to a barn, and it was *the* place I wanted to be this year at Thanksgiving. Peter, who is big and bearded, had built several barns and salvaged at least one old barn that was tumbling down to the ground when he was hired to fix it. He had worked as a builder, contractor, and carpenter for more rock stars, including Janis Joplin and David Crosby, than anyone else I knew. He was also a consummate craftsman, and he paid as much attention to the details in a barn as to those in a house. "A house is a series of closed spaces," Peter said. "A barn is a big open space. I like to build big, and barns lend themselves to bigness. When you're inside a barn, you can see its ribs and its bones. There's something organic about it. I would love to have a barn of my own where I could keep my tools and equipment and where I could sit and entertain guests."

At the Swanhuysers' there was a feast with turkey, gravy, stuffing, potatoes, vegetables, salad, and pies. I was satisfied. But I was also curious about what Moselle Beaty had made for Thanksgiving at Stone Edge, and, when she later showed me her menu, I wished I could have been there, too, to taste all these delicious dishes:

Waldorf salad of celery, honey-crisp apple, fresh grapes,
blue Stilton, toasted walnuts, and honey-lemon dressing
Herb-brined organic turkey
Spinach and Parmesan stuffing with sage, parsley, and thyme
Mashed potatoes with giblet gravy
Yams Texas style with roasted pecans and maple syrup
Creamed pearl onions
Fresh garden peas and carrots
Cranberries grappa gelle
Pumpkin pie

After Thanksgiving, I attended an end-of-the-year meeting at Oak Hill in the Red Barn with Paul, Gael, Jesús, Anne, and Lynn. This last meeting of the year also felt like the next year's first meeting. Everyone talked about what needed to be done in the year ahead, as well as what had been done in the year that was ending. The field that had been sick with a virus and planted with radishes to cure it was still fallow; recuperation would take more time. "The garlic crop came up quickly," Paul said. "It's beautiful, and we can develop a whole range of different kinds of garlic." He added, "The tractor needs work, and we'll have to order parts." Anne said she wanted to grow rose hips and develop a farm-to-school link. Jesús noted that the flowers for spring were almost all planted, but that the tulips had not yet arrived from Holland. Lynn handed out the spreadsheets that showed financial success in black and white—more than twenty thousand dollars in revenue week after week.

A change had come over me at Oak Hill. The more I went *down* to the ground, the further *up* my imagination and my spirit had soared. The earth elevated me even as it held me in its embrace. Brother Toby, a lay Catholic priest who worked the land, told me that that was the way it was supposed to be. "Working in the fields is the best thing you can do for your own spiritual growth," he said. "Going down to the ground is the way to go up to heaven." With my hands and face in the dirt I had been inspired. I was delighted to read the words of the Italian artist and farmer Gianfranco Baruchello, who traced the connections between the natural space on a farm and the personal space in one's head. "Being here," Baruchello said of his farm outside Rome, "means removing all of these things that belong to cities from the landscape of your mind, and it enables you to create a far more radical space for imagination." To that I would add, "If you want to feed your imagination, go to a farm." Farming at Oak Hill helped to liberate me from the fetters I had created for myself. I could imagine more freely now than ever before.

I felt local now, too, a part of the earth, attached to the barn, the contours of the land, the valley and mountains, and these people—Jesús, Paul, Gael, Anne, Candi, Miguel, Patrick. When I went home to my barn, I felt as happy as I had at any time in my life. Feelings of happiness I had learned to distrust over the course of my life. If something was good, it was sure to change for the worse. I had learned that lesson early and well. But this time I trusted the happiness; it felt a part of me— something inside and organic, and I allowed it to surge.

I sensed, too, that if I should happen to lose that happiness, I might find it again by reconnecting to the earth from which I had come and to which I would return. I had found paradise, but I knew I might also lose it. In fact, I did. At Christmas, my landlord informed me that I would have to leave my dear precious barn, my home. The county had condemned the barn; the whole structure was illegal and had to be torn down, I was told. I felt sad but not brokenhearted. I had learned that paradise is a place you cannot lose forever. To be human means to want paradise and search for it everywhere. It exists out there in the world around us—though sometimes it may be invisible and unseen. It also exists, I knew now, in the world inside.

WALLACE STEGNER'S CRANKS

In 1969 Wallace Stegner suggested that humanity might be "on the brink of the greatest period of human history." He added that the people who would usher in this new age might be "the kind of people many would call cranks, who insist on organically grown vegetables and unsprayed fruits." How prescient he was—and how contemporary! I grew up with cranks like the ones Stegner described. They were my parents, the cranks on Long Island at the time it turned from rural to suburban, and in California in the 1970s when organic made a comeback. I had met cranks all that year of my odyssey, from Oak Hill to Sol, Quetzal to Full Belly, Valley End to Tierra. It seemed to me that we were on the brink once again.

The scientists agree. Global warming is upon us. Almost everywhere you turn on the planet you can see the destruction of the environment. At the same time you can see individual human beings acting to save the planet. I saw them in Sonoma Valley. I saw them at Oak Hill and at the farmers' markets. I saw them at small organic farms all over California, as well as at warehouses like Veritable Vegetable and at stores like San Francisco's Other Avenues. They are cooks and chefs such as Mark Malicki, Sheana Davis, John McReynolds, and Craig Stoll, and grape growers and winemakers such as Tony and Phil Coturri and Will Bucklin. Perhaps scientists and historians will look back at the year that was ending—my year of farming and eating and drinking wine—and say that human beings on the fringes, not those at the centers of power and wealth, had taken steps to farm and eat cleanly without polluting the planet or their own bodies.

Did I see the future of farming and food during that year? I thought I could when I was at César Chávez Elementary School in San Francisco just before Christmas, when Russell McCall's third graders—all of them Hispanic—listened to him talk about seeds and then went into the garden to plant sugar peas. In chalk, McCall had written on the blackboard a sentence with blank spaces: "Seeds wait for _____ and _____ to grow." He had invited the children to fill in the blanks, and they had all done so, eagerly shouting out their answers. McCall had spoken the way a seed might speak. "I want to grow, I want to grow, I want to grow," he had said in a little voice, and there had been a chorus of laughter. Outside, he showed the students how to make a small hole in the earth, plant a seed, and cover it with earth. Otto Teller would have said, "Let's plant a seed," and would have meant it literally and figuratively. Otto would have been pleased by the sight of Jasmine, Jesús, Elías, and their classmates planting pea seeds in the ground in December. Jasmine smiled and showed me the palms of her small hands, dirty and cold from digging in the earth. "I like planting seeds," she said. "I want to see the plants grow—and I can't wait to eat the peas."

CODA

New Year's Day stole into the Valley of the Moon, and Oak Hill noted its arrival. Anne Teller recovered from surgery in time to worry about climate change, rainfall, and the environment. Will Bucklin raked leaves and carted them away. Lizanne Pastore sat down at her computer and went online. Jesús relaxed after a long night. Gael and Patrick made art. Candi cooked enough food to feed a small army, and a small army arrived and wolfed it down. Paul drank beer, talked with old friends, and soon afterward did the first planting of 2008: salad greens, parsley, and broccoli rabe. He hired an assistant, put him to work driving the tractor, and felt a weight lift from his shoulders. Miguel and his wife celebrated the New Year in Mexico with their family. The Red Barn was closed, though there were vegetables in storage, and Gael gave me more than enough to take home. Soon afterward, when the tulips came up, I took some home, and for the first time in my life I awakened to the beauty of tulips. I could understand now why tulip mania had taken hold of the Dutch. At night coyotes came down to the farm from the forest, and mountain lions curled up in oak trees and waited for prey. The lakes and the ponds were more than full, and there were predictions of rain and flooding. Real winter, with its nasty weather, was about to begin. It would be the last day to be outdoors for many days to come.

I walked about the fields, sniffed the air that smelled of winter, and looked at the tractors at rest and at Anne's dogs roaming freely. Oak Hill seemed to be suspended in time, and I remembered that Anne said that people would come and go and that the land would be all that remained. She had been— she still was—a good steward of the land, and I wanted her family to carry on her and Otto Teller's tradition, too. Stewardship was good, and so was the land. It provided a place to live for human beings, plants, animals, birds, and bees. There was work to be done here—clean work in the fields that provided food for people to eat, enjoy, and share with friends and family. I was glad that I had been a part of Oak Hill for a brief time in my life.

I watched the sun go down slowly. I felt the chill rise up from the ground. Then the sky turned black. I climbed into my car and drove through the Valley of the Moon and over the top of Sonoma Mountain to my own home.

Early in the New Year, Paige Green returned from her adventures, and it was a delight to see her again. She came to Oak Hill and immediately recognized the beauty of the place that had captivated me. She noticed the special quality of light, which prompted her to take photographs. "It's all about the light," she said on a day of bright sunshine when the creeks were filled with water, Valde and Jesús harvested kale, and Anne Teller walked about the orchard with a clipboard taking stock of her fruit trees. Everything was reborn. Everything had come full circle. It was spring again in the Valley of the Moon, and you could almost hear the crops in the field poking their heads up from the darkness into the light of day.

ACKNOWLEDGMENTS

I feel like the movie producers who film a picture in a real town or city and thank the location and all its citizens in the credits. Let me say here that I appreciate the hospitality and generosity of all the people I met in the town of Sonoma, in Sonoma Valley, and all over Northern California. I especially want to thank Anne Teller for opening Oak Hill Farm to me. I want to thank her children for sharing their lives with me, and I want to extend my appreciation to all the people who live and work at Oak Hill and welcomed me into their personal space and their homes. Andy and Lilla Weinberger provided encouragement very early on, pointed me in the right directions, and offered sound suggestions about whom to talk to. Kathleen Hill talked about her ties to M. F. K. Fisher and helped to make Fisher's personality come alive for me. David Bolling, the editor of *The Sonoma Index-Tribune,* talked about his view of the town and the valley and added to my sense of the place with his perspectives as resident, reporter, and editor. Sandi Hansen dug out old

articles from the paper for me. Judith and Tony Marciante offered delicious food, excellent wine, and nourishing conversation at their home in Sonoma. Dee and Peter Swanhuyser
linked me with people and places, and they, too, opened their
home and gave me a sense of community. Don Emblen looked
through his vast library and found books for me to read on the
subject of farming and nature, including Thoreau's *Wild Fruits*
and *Faith in a Seed*. J. J. Wilson fed me, conferred with me, and
gave me books to read. Gaye LeBaron talked with me about
the history of agriculture in Sonoma County. Dana Biberman
gave me the use of a pied-à-terre in New York and took me to
the Union Square Farmers' Market. And Susan Seifert made
me feel at home in London. Noelle Oxenhandler made wishes
come true; Greg Sarris shared his knowledge of Indians in
Northern California; and Katherine Zsolt took me around the
plaza in the town of Sonoma and up into the hills. Stacey Tuel
shared meals and wines at the best of restaurants. Jean-François
Bourdic and Virginie Girard showed me the insider's Provence.
Robert Friedman did what he has been doing for decades: reading my work and helping to make it better. Chip McAuley was
indispensable as usual. My brothers walked with me in the Valley of the Moon and up to the top of Sonoma Mountain. Bill
Pinkus flew me over the valley in his plane and enabled me to
see it all from up above—the bird's-eye view. Dan Smith gave
me my first glimpse of the farm-to-table-connection at his farm
and his Sebastopol restaurant, the French Garden. Mark
Dierkhising showed me how excellent a neighborhood café
could be. Diane Albracht taught me a lot about food and farming and hospitality at her home in Sebastopol and at her restaurants. Paige Green started the odyssey with me and helped me

to see clearly. Gretchen Giles published my restaurant reviews and articles about food and farming in *The Bohemian*. KQED broadcast my radio commentaries about Northern California as a place on "Perspectives." Professor Steve Norwick, at Sonoma State University, offered a wealth of valuable information about history, geography, and literature. Lynn Thomas came through in a pinch, again and again. George Webber kept me entertained and well-informed. Sarah Baker read the manuscript with a sharp eye, as did Gael, Anne, Paul, Arden, Ted, Candi, Jesús, and Will. I thank them all. My editor, Naomi Schneider, pushed me to tell the truth about farmworkers without glossing over their hardships. Laura Harger was the efficient, sensitive project editor, and Julie Brand the vigilant, scrupulous copy editor. Sandy Drooker designed the spectacular jacket. Michael Slosek came through in the clutch again and again. Uriel Sierra shared his experiences in Mexico, the United States, and the border between the two countries.

MY MOVABLE FEAST: A NOTE ON THE JACKET

The jacket of this book commemorates a dinner I made for eight friends—and myself, too, of course. I wasn't going to be a spectator at my own feast. Paige came with her camera, and Mimi Luebbermann came to serve as the art director and offer her experience. She has worked on books about food with photographers for decades and had excellent suggestions. I decided to make a vegetarian meal, and of course I shopped locally. I bought organic onions, corn, squash, peppers, tomatoes, basil, and salad greens at Oak Hill. For the risotto I also bought Arborio rice and

Parmesan and Gruyère cheeses at Whole Foods Market in Sebastopol. I cooked everything myself and enjoyed every minute of it. Nothing burned, and nothing was overcooked or undercooked.

The plan was to eat outside, under the oak trees behind my kitchen. Mimi and Paige carried my picnic table to the backyard, moving it several times to find the right spot, and someone quipped that it was going to be a movable feast. And indeed it was: we had to move the table again when it was already set, but miraculously nothing fell off. At about 5:30 my guests started to arrive. In addition to Paige and Mimi I had invited Sarah Baker, Timothy Williams, Thora Lares, Bill Pinkus, Katherine Plank, and Michael Frost. I had eaten with all of them individually many times before, and I knew what they liked and didn't like. Bill brought local beers, and Katherine brought local artisan breads. I had several bottles of wine, including a Coturri Zinfandel and Hey Mambo, an inexpensive but tasty California red, and we started right in sipping it.

The first course was a tomato soup that I had made by roasting ripe red tomatoes and basil in olive oil for about an hour in the oven. Everything cooked down, and I put what remained through a food mill. Then I served individual portions of soup, to which I added Gruyère—a touch I had learned from Moselle Beaty, the cook at Stone Edge. Then came the main part of the meal. For the risotto I had begun by sautéing onions in olive oil, then adding the rice and little by little a stock I had made by cooking vegetables. At the end I stirred in grated Parmesan, which made it creamy and added a distinctive flavor. I prepared a green salad and a dressing that combined DaVero olive oil and rice wine vinegar. I cooked corn on the cob and served it with butter from the local Straus Family Creamery. Mimi sliced a dozen or so of the tomatoes I had in my kitchen and brought them to the table as well. An assortment of colorful peppers from Oak Hill that were sautéed in olive oil completed the meal. The small table, which my friend Michael Saaks had made from my own redwood tree, became crowded. We ate and ate and ate and talked and drank wine and told stories and watched the sun go down and the shadows lengthen. Eating outdoors—al fresco—improved the taste of the food. It's something I recommend to one and all.

All the while, nonstop and from every conceivable angle, Paige took photos of the food and every single thing that happened. We could make a whole book of her photos of the meal, which lasted for several hours. Mimi provided assistance every step of the way. Surprisingly, it didn't feel odd to be photographed while we ate.

For dessert I served pears I had picked from Diane Albracht's bountiful old pear tree in Sebastopol. Someone—Thora or Katherine—noticed that the peach tree in my backyard was laden with peaches and that there were dozens of them on the ground. So we all picked peaches, eating them and the pears with Scharffen Berger dark chocolate. I also made a big pot of tea with mint from the San Francisco Herb Company. By the time we finished, it was almost dark. Everyone helped clear up and bring the table back to my deck. It had been a perfect meal. I hadn't stressed about it at all. There were dishes to wash, but I left them for the morning and slept peacefully all night long.

NOTES

2   **"all life seemed to live in harmony"** and later quotations: Rachel Carson, *Silent Spring* (Boston: Houghton Mifflin, 1962).

20   **"Local does not"** and **"understanding the local":** Lucy Lippard, *The Lure of the Local* (New York: New Press, 1997).

44   **"I firmly believe":** Peter Dreyer, *A Gardener Touched with Genius: The Life of Luther Burbank* (Berkeley: University of California Press, 1992).

51   **"change the world"** and later quotations: "Voting with Your Trolley," *The Economist,* December 9, 2006.

53   **"away from the centric super-industrial":** Robert Rodale, *The Basic Book of Organic Gardening* (New York: Ballantine, 1971).

60   **"The Sonoma chapter":** Kevin Starr, *Americans and the California Dream: 1850–1915* (New York: Oxford University Press, 1973).

60   **"The pioneer has done his work"** and later quotations: Jack London, "Navigating Four Horses North of the Bay," *Jack London Reports* (New York: Doubleday, 1970).

61   **"Welcome to Oak Hill":** www.oakhillfarm.net; accessed July 30, 2008.

71 **"live in each season as it passes"** and later quotations: Henry David Thoreau, *Wild Fruits,* ed. Bradley P. Dean (New York: Norton, 2000).

82 **"The history of every nation":** Robert Carrier, *Great Dishes of the World* (London: Sphere, 1967).

84 **"Vegetables attain an unusual size":** Frank Marryat, *Mountains and Molehills* (Philadelphia: J. B. Lippincott, 1962; originally published 1855).

136 **"knew nothing about running the place"** and later quotations: "Family Ties," *Living on Earth,* October 4, 2002; www.loe.org/shows/shows.htm?program1D+02-P13-0004; accessed July 10, 2007.

142 **"I am here because"** and later quotations: M. F. K. Fisher, "Nowhere but Here," *As They Were* (New York: Knopf, 1982).

143 **"I am from California":** M. F. K. Fisher, *Two Towns in Provence* (New York: Vintage, 1983).

154 **"sex is as important":** www.brainyquote.com/quotes/quotes/marquisdes155362.html.

160 **"We come and go":** Willa Cather, *O Pioneers!* (New York: Vintage, 1992; originally published 1913).

167 **"In nature, and actually throughout the universe"** and later quotations: Rudolf Steiner, *Spiritual Foundations for the Renewal of Agriculture,* trans. Catherine Creeger and Malcolm Gardner, ed. Malcolm Gardner (Kimberton, PA: Bio-Dynamic Farming and Gardening Association, 1993; originally published 1924).

170 **"I may be a link to the past":** Tom Whitmore, *Robert H. Cannard: Sonoma's Last Pioneer* (Sonoma, CA: Sonoma Valley Historical Society, 2005).

195 **"the rise of farm fascism":** chapter 14 in Carey McWilliams, *Factories in the Field: The Story of Migratory Farm Labor in California* (Berkeley: University of California Press, 2000; originally published 1939).

195 **"The businessmen had the farms"** and later quotations: John Steinbeck, *The Grapes of Wrath* (New York: Viking, 1939).

219 **"supermarket pastoral"** and later quotations: Michael Pollan, *The Omnivore's Dilemma: A Natural History of Four Meals* (New York: Penguin, 2006).

252 **"The more civilization advances":** Friedrich Engels, *The Origin of the Family: Private Property and the State* (New York: International Publishers, n.d.; originally published 1884).

253 **"like England a hundred years ago"** and later quotations: Robert Louis Stevenson, *The Silverado Squatters,* originally published 1883; http://sunsite.berkeley.edu/Literature/Stevenson/Silverado Squatters/1silver3.html.

266 **"no extremes of hot and cold"** and later quotations: *A History of Sonoma County* (San Francisco: Alley, Bowen & Co., 1880).

285 **"Being here":** Gianfranco Baruchello and Henry Martin, *How to Imagine: A Narrative on Art and Agriculture* (New Paltz, NY: McPherson, 1984).

286 **"on the brink"** and **"the kind of people":** Wallace Stegner, "Conservation Equals Survival," *American Heritage Magazine,* December 1969.

BIBLIOGRAPHY

The following books and articles have been helpful to me in the process of researching and writing *Field Days:*

Aaron, Chester. *Garlic Is Life: A Memoir with Recipes.* Berkeley: Ten Speed Press, 1996.

Ableman, Michael. *Fields of Plenty: A Farmer's Journey in Search of Real Food and the People Who Grow It.* San Francisco: Chronicle, 2005.

Barich, Bill. *Big Dreams: Into the Heart of California.* New York: Pantheon, 1994.

Baruchello, Gianfranco, and Henry Martin. *How to Imagine: A Narrative on Art and Agriculture.* New Paltz, NY: McPherson, 1984.

Brown, Edward Espe. *The Tassajara Bread Book.* Boston: Shambhala, 1970.

Carson, Rachel. *Silent Spring.* Boston: Houghton Mifflin, 1962.

Crouch, Dora P., Daniel J. Garr, and Axel I. Mundigo. *Spanish City Planning in North America.* Cambridge, MA: MIT Press, 1982.

Fisher, M. F. K. *As They Were.* New York: Knopf, 1982.

———. *Two Towns in Provence.* New York: Vintage, 1983.

Guthman, Julie. *Agrarian Dreams: The Paradox of Organic Farming in California.* Berkeley: University of California Press, 2004.

Hanson, Victor Davis. *Fields without Dreams: Defending the Agrarian Idea*. New York: Free Press, 1996.

Haslam, Gerald. *Coming of Age in California: Personal Essays*. Walnut Creek, CA: Devil Mountain Books, 2000.

Henderson, Elizabeth, and Robyn Van En. *Sharing the Harvest: A Guide to Community-Supported Agriculture*. White River Junction, VT: Chelsea Green, 2007.

Hill, Kathleen, and Gerald Hill. *Sonoma Valley: The Secret Wine Country*. Guilford, CT: Globe Pequot Press, 2005.

Ikerd, John. *Small Farms Are Real Farms: Sustaining People through Agriculture*. Austin, TX: Acres, 2008.

Ketcham, Christopher. "The Hundred Mile Diet." *The Nation,* September 10, 2007.

Kingsolver, Barbara, with Steven L. Hopp and Camille Kingsolver. *Animal, Vegetable, Miracle: A Year of Food Life*. New York: Harper-Collins, 2007.

Klinkenborg, Verlyn. "A Farming Revolution: Sustainable Agriculture." *National Geographic,* December 1995.

Lippard, Lucy R. *The Lure of the Local: Senses of Place in a Multicentered Society*. New York: New Press, 1997.

Lopez, Ann Aurelia. *The Farmworkers' Journey*. Berkeley: University of California Press, 2007.

Maiser, Jennifer. "10 Steps to Becoming a Locavore." www.pbs.org/now/slows/344/locavores,html.

Marryat, Frank. *Mountains and Molehill*. New York: Lippincott, 1962. Originally published 1855.

McNamee, Thomas. *Alice Waters and Chez Panisse: The Romantic, Impractical, Often Eccentric, Ultimately Brilliant Making of a Food Revolution*. Foreword by R. W. Apple Jr. New York: Penguin, 2007.

McWilliams, Carey. *California: The Great Exception*. Santa Barbara, CA: Peregrine Smith, 1979. Originally published 1949.

———. *Factories in the Field: The Story of Migratory Farm Labor in California*. Reprint, with foreword by Douglas C. Sackman. Berkeley: University of California Press, 2000. Originally published 1939.

Nabhan, Gary Paul. *Coming Home to Eat: The Pleasures and Politics of Local Foods.* New York: Norton, 2001.

Petrini, Carlo. *Slow Food Nation: Why Our Food Should Be Good, Clean and Fair.* Trans. Clara Furlan and Jonathan Hunt. New York: Rizzoli, 2007.

Pollan, Michael. *The Omnivore's Dilemma: A Natural History of Four Meals.* New York: Penguin, 2006.

Rodale, Robert. *The Basic Book of Organic Gardening.* New York: Ballantine, 1971.

Scheuring, Ann Foley. *Tillers: An Oral History of Family Farms in California.* New York: Praeger, 1983.

Severson, Kim. "Why Roots Matter More." *New York Times,* November 15, 2006.

Shapin, Steven. "Paradise Sold: What Are You Buying When You Buy Organic?" *New Yorker,* May 15, 2006.

Smith, Alisa, and J. B. Mackinnon. *Plenty: One Man, One Woman and a Raucous Year of Eating Locally.* New York: Harmony, 2007.

Stegner, Wallace. "Conservation Equals Survival." *American Heritage Magazine,* December 1969.

Steinbeck, John. *The Grapes of Wrath.* New York: Viking, 1976. Originally published 1939.

Steiner, Rudolf. *Spiritual Foundations for the Renewal of Agriculture.* Ed. Malcolm Gardner. Trans. Catherine Creeger and Malcolm Gardner. Kimberton, PA: Bio-Dynamic Farming and Gardening Association, 1993. Originally published 1924.

Thoreau, Henry David. *Faith in a Seed.* Ed. Bradley P. Dean. Washington, DC: Island Press, 1993.

———. *Wild Fruits.* Ed. Bradley P. Dean. New York: Norton, 2000.

Trubek, Amy B. *The Taste of Place: A Cultural Journey into Terroir.* Berkeley: University of California Press, 2008.

Whitworth, Tom. *Robert H. Cannard: Sonoma's Last Pioneer.* Sonoma, CA: Sonoma Valley Historical Society, 2005.

Young, Allen. *Make Hay While the Sun Shines: Farms, Forests & the People of the North Quabbin.* New York: iUniverse, 2007.

INDEX

Page references in italics refer to illustrations.

TEXT: 11/15 GRANJON

DISPLAY: CASLON ANTIQUA, COPPERPLATE

COMPOSITOR: BINGHAMTON VALLEY COMPOSITION, LLC

PRINTER AND BINDER: MAPLE-VAIL BOOK MANUFACTURING GROUP